Foreign Enterprises in China (Volume 1)

Chief Editors: Pei Changhong, Feng Lei

Translators: Chen Ling, Zhao Wenxuan

Polisher: Virginia L. Conn

Paths International Ltd

社会科学文献出版社
SOCIAL SCIENCES ACADEMIC PRESS (CHINA)

The Institute of Finance and Trade Economics, Chinese Academy of Social Sciences "Operational Status of Chinese Enterprises with Foreign Investment" Research Group

Project Leader

Pei Changhong, Director of the Institute of Finance and Trade Economics, Chinese Academy of Social Sciences, Researcher

Members of the Project Group

Feng Lei, Institute of Finance and Trade Economics, Chinese Academy of Social Sciences, Researcher
Xia Xianliang, Institute of Finance and Trade Economics, Chinese Academy of Social Sciences, Research Associate
Peng Lei, Institute of Finance and Trade Economics, Chinese Academy of Social Sciences, Research Associate
Li Feng, Institute of Finance and Trade Economics, Chinese Academy of Social Sciences
Dong Minjie, Institute of Finance and Trade Economics, Chinese Academy of Social Sciences

Author by Chapter

Chapter 1	Feng Lei
Chapter 2	Li Feng
Chapter 3	Peng Lei
Chapter 4	Peng Lei
Chapter 5	Feng Lei
Chapter 6	Xia Xianliang
Chapter 7	Dong Minjie
Chapter 8	Pei Changhong Pei

Contents

contributions still accounted for more than 50% of total foreign investment).

Chapter 6 analyzes the operational and profitable tax status of foreign-invested enterprises. While foreign-invested enterprises in China have developed rapidly, their unbalanced industrial structure is indicative of regional characteristics. For example, the decline of the contribution and growth rate of imports and exports by foreign-invested enterprises, compared to the expanding role of domestic consumption, reflects the fact that the advantages provided by the Chinese market have gradually become one of the main characteristics attracting foreign investment to the country.

Although the business assets of foreign investment have grown steadily, the majority of foreign investment has been invested in the services industry—contrary to the predominant trend of a lack of worldwide FDI in the services industry. Foreign-invested enterprises in China, however, have increased their asset turnover rate along with their annual profit margins, which is also contrary to international trends.

What's more, from the perspective of the growth rate of assets, efficiency of asset utilization, and the growth rate of profits, foreign investment in China is increasingly indicating a clear trend towards being wholly proprietary, signifying that other types of investment models may be less efficient. What's more, foreign-invested enterprises in China are under a relatively light tax burden. As such, both the profits and losses of foreign-invested enterprises in China have increased annually, with the rapid growth of profits meeting average international levels, insofar as the margin on total assets has increased along with that of the industrial capital margin. Ultimately, this chapter aims to show that the return on the capital of foreign-invested enterprise has increased overall while simultaneously demonstrating regional variations.

Chapter7 analyzes the scale of employment and labor remuneration of those enterprises with foreign investment. From 2003 to 2007, the number of employees employed by foreign-invested enterprises expanded from 8.631 million to 15.83 million, for an average annual growth rate of 16.4%. As a result of the global financial crisis, employment in foreign-invested enterprises only increased by 2.5% in 2008, reaching 16.22 million. Although the growth of employment by foreign-invested enterprises slowed, however, the overall proportion of employment by these enterprises to employment as a whole has increased. From 2003 to 2008, employment by foreign-invested enterprises increased from 1.2% to 2.1% of all employment in the country, increasing by 0.9%. Urban employment by foreign-invested enterprises increased from 2.9% to 5.4%, a 2.5% increase.

During this time, the average return on employment in foreign-invested enterprises was consistently higher than the average salary of urban employment overall. In 2008, the average salary of those employed by foreign-invested companies was 3081 RMB, a full 1933.1 RMB higher than the average urban salary. From 2003 to 2008, the annual growth rate of the average return on employment by foreign-invested enterprises was lower than the overall urban salary annual growth rate—12.4% compared to 15.3%—but, in 2008, the growth rate shot up to 21.5% for foreign-invested enterprises, as opposed to only 15.9% for urban employment remuneration overall. This chapter looks into these differences in salary between different industries and regions as regards foreign-invested enterprises.

Chapter 8 concludes the book. The chapter begins by summarizing the most important characteristics of foreign investment in China since the 21st century, especially the periods at the end of the tenth "Five Year Plan" and eleventh "Five Year Plan." These characteristics include the fact that the proportion of foreign investment in the tertiary industry grew while foreign investment in China's secondary industries declined; wholly foreign-owned companies are becoming the preferred business model; free ports have become a major source of foreign investment; and that China's proportion of foreign capital has declined on a global scaleTo explain these features, Chapter 8 offers the following explanations: the "two-gap theory" cannot adequately explain the continuing need for China to attract foreign investment, but only through the ongoing use of foreign capital in the country can China enter the "global value chain" production system. Once involved in such a system, China has the opportunity to take advantage of international benefits and strengthen their own competitiveness, which, in turn, will enhance the country's ranking in the "global value chain."

In recent years, the service industry—especially the financial services industry—has been the beneficiary of an increase in foreign capital investment that is closely linked to an appreciation of the Renminbi. Regardless of financial and real estate investments or the systematic risk of assets that goes along with portfolio investment, a high degree of capital mobility is required, which is more likely to be invested in financial capital, rather than industrial capital. Free ports are often a paradise of financial capital due to its comparatively lax financial regulations, making it an important source of investment in China as a result of its ensuing high degree of liquidity and efficiency.

The increasing tendency towards wholly foreign-owned enterprises can be explained by the theory of internalization, which reveals the fact that technological investments and knowledge in China's multinational companies are increasing, necessitating improved market development and intellectual property protection technology on the part of the country itself. An incorrect or one-sided understanding of national economic security has influenced the motivation behind attracting foreign investment, and is an important factor behind the slow growth of foreign direct investment in recent years. Chapter8 goes on to discuss new directions for the growth of foreign investment in China in the future, and points out that export-oriented and import-substitution manufacturing still have the potential to attract foreign investment. What's more, in the secondary industry, urban infrastructure is an attractive point of growth for foreign investment, while in the services industry, financial and real estate sectors may be the largest beneficiaries. To this end, the author concludes that China should continue to focus on the efficient use of foreign investment and continue to improve its institutional and policy environment.

Chapter 1 An Analysis of Foreign Investment Utilization Policies and the Total Amount of Foreign-Invested Enterprises

The utilization of foreign direct investment (FDI) is of great significance for China's period of economic reform and opening-up. At the same time, challenges have also been encountered at the macro level. Sustained and stable Foreign Investment Utilization Policies provide an institutional guarantee for a virtuous cycle and for the development of FDI, and play a positive and effective role in promoting the development of China's national economy. In recent years, the number of foreign-invested enterprises and the size of foreign capital inflow into China have continued to expand. Foreign-invested enterprises of different scales have made corresponding contributions to the efficiency of utilizing the domestic capital.

1.1 Foreign Investment Utilization Policies in China

The utilization of foreign capital is an important part of China's economic restructuring and opening-up. From the macroscopic view, the development of FDI inflow in China contributes to the advancement of the developing process of reform and opening-up. The planned economic system has been subjected to intense bombardment from different angles, and higher productivity was released in the market-oriented reform. FDI has also posed a challenge to the economic system of the socialist market. FDI is an important internalized external force to promote the process of China's economic restructuring and opening-up.

1.1.1. Utilization of Foreign Capital and Economic Restructuring and Opening-up

(1) The positive role of Foreign Direct Investment (FDI) in China's economic restructuring and opening-up

Firstly, the variables of foreign capital have changed from external factors to internal ones. The development of special economic zones, which is a breakthrough change in China's planned economy, is inseparable from the participation of FDI. Foreign capital itself represents this external to internal change. The economic boom in developed countries in the late 1970s stands in glaring contrast to the collapsing economic situation after the catastrophe of the "Cultural Revolution." If the political movement is still to remain the focus, the rigid model of the planned economy continues unchanged, and the closed-door policy remains to be adopted, the national economy is bound to be eliminated. The Third Plenary Session of the Eleventh Central Committee of the Party operated from a strategically advantageous position by complying with the aspirations of the people, and made the strategic decision to implement economic restructuring and opening-up. A Special Economic Zone was made to be one of the critical elements of the breakthrough to change the planned economic system. Economic development and the economic management model, which are different from the planned economy, have decided to be implemented in the Special Economic Zones like Shenzhen and Zhuhai. The introduction of FDI and the absorption of the key factors in promoting economic development in developed countries are therefore becoming the internal motivating factors for the restructuring and development of the national economy.

Secondly, absorption of foreign investment is made to be one of the promoting factors in China's economic restructuring and opening-up. With the guide of “manufacturing materials, designs or samples supplied by foreign tradesmen (“Sanlai” trade pattern)” which was gradually extended to the "Chinese-foreign joint ventures, Chinese-foreign cooperatives, wholly foreign-owned enterprises pattern (“Sanzi” trade pattern), international capital is absorbed in order to participate in China’s economic development. As an input factor in the production process, foreign investment contributes to China's economic restructuring and opening-up, initially based on the so-called "three-plus-one" trading mix: assembling with supplied parts, processing with supplied materials and samples, and eventually developing into a large-scale processing trade. From the perspective of developing businesses in Chinese-foreign cooperatives, Chinese-foreign joint ventures and wholly foreign-owned enterprises constitute the basic types of foreign-invested enterprises, which are collectively known as the three kinds of investment enterprises. The phrases “manufacturing materials, designs or samples supplied by foreign tradesmen (“Sanlai” trade pattern)” and "three kinds of investment enterprises" fully reflect the progressive path of China's economic restructuring and opening-up. The gradual penetration of foreign investment contributes to China's economic development gradually. Through co-exist and the exchange of two economic models inside and outside the so-called system, external demonstration and pressure are provided to promote economic restructuring and opening-up, while demonstrations are also provided in the construction of market-oriented systems.

Thirdly, the introduction of Special Economic Zones in the form of FDI provides a space for economic support. The institutional environment for the introduction of FDI is created in the form of Special Economic Zones, development zones, and bonded areas. As a result, FDI is concentrated in a certain geographical area, where special economic policies are given. It is also a feasible way to enhance the institutional demonstration effect, but brings with it questions of feasibility. In the beginning of the reform and opening-up period, Shenzhen, Zhuhai, Shantou, and Xiamen were chosen to be the main trial areas of special export zones. Special economic zones were then quickly converted to the forerunners of implementing the market economic model, which is different from the planned economy. Followed by the establishment of the 14 open coastal cities, the border along the river was opened and Hainan Island's Special Economic Zone was established. At the same time, multiple high-tech Development Zones sprang up like mushrooms, which promoted local economic development and introduced advanced technology and venture investments both at home and abroad. By the end of 2007, 15 bonded areas in China were playing an irreplaceable role in trade and investment promotion. From the functional point of view, the bonded area, which is characterized by a free trade zone, has greater institutional space in the utilization of foreign investment. It also promoted Chinese economic integration with the world economy.

Fourthly, FDI has played an important role in the regional economic development of China. Particularly, the development of China's southeast coastal areas benefited from the entry of foreign-invested enterprises to a great extent. This internal development has brought with it high dynamic capital, advanced production technology and equipment, advanced management experience, and international business channels for China's economic development. The cost of

China's national economy entering the international market was greatly reduced as a result, and the efficiency of many industries and sectors in China's national economy, which are in direct contact with the international economy, were enhanced. This stimulated and promoted the germination and rapid development of private enterprises within the region. Additionally, the private economy accounted for half of the whole economy, providing a new model for economic development and enterprise operation. This model is highly imitative and vital, and quickly became the most important component of China's socialist market economy. With Foreign-invested enterprises gathering to form an international market-oriented industrial chain, and the aggregation of private enterprises taking the lead within the region, the rapid development of the regional economy along the southeast coast of China was greatly promoted. This became an excellent example of China's economic restructuring and opening up.

Fifthly, globally competitive productivity was rapidly transformed by FDI. FDI—combined with the advantage factor of labor in China—can be very competitive worldwide. FDI enterprises and the private enterprises being driven by them have changed the employment system of China's planned economy. The labor supply of China's special economic zones is drawn largely from inland regions, such as the migrant workers from Sichuan and other provinces. Regional economic management under the planned economic system, which was based on provinces being the basic administrative regions, was changed, and a profound reform of the labor-management policies began underway. The overall size of the direct employment scale of foreign-invested enterprises has been maintained at around 30 million. Although China's proportion of the overall labor market is not large, these reforms had a tremendous impact on the entrenched employment model that existed under the planned economy. Sixthly, FDI capital serves as an exemplary model of efficiency. The capital efficiency of foreign-invested enterprises provided a model for the reform of China's investment management system by providing a reasonable incentive to improve the operational efficiency in utilizing domestic capital. The fundamental reason for the capital efficiency of foreign-invested enterprises being higher than the domestic operational efficiency of domestic capital lies in the clarity of investment decision-making system and the relations of property rights. Capital operation mode is based on the modern enterprise system and its capital efficiency, providing a new impetus to the factors affecting the GNP-based development of the national economy and the efficiency comparison between capital stock and the continuous, incremental improvement of the overall quality and efficiency of capital. The investment management of the planned economy has created a so-called "investment hunger" phenomenon, which results in invalid investments, irresponsible investment, repeated investment, and duplicate introductions that have caused great waste of the entire national wealth.

Seventhly, FDI is an exemplary model of the allocation of production. New ideas of the diversified allocation system in China's socialist market economy were provided by the allocation model of foreign-invested enterprises. In the process of breaking with the practice of having everyone "eat from the same big pot," ideas of allocation underwent improvement, and in the ongoing process of reform and opening up, new practices are emerging continuously, while the balance between fairness and efficiency continues to undergo reasonable adjustments. The establishment of the elements allocation model broke the limitations of traditional economic theory. In accordance with those principles conducive to the development of the productive forces of socialism, equilibrium represents advanced productive forces through the balance of productive forces and production relations. The innovation of the allocation mechanism greatly mobilized enthusiasm for domestic production in all walks of life, and national, corporate, and personal interests have been taken into account throughout the process of social reproduction.

Eighthly, FDI is foundational to Chinese products entering the international market. The output of foreign-invested enterprises has grown to become an important force for our products to enter the international market. In the 1990s, under the guidance of those Foreign Investment Utilization Policies firmly advocated by the central government, FDI increased rapidly, with China subsequently becoming a leader in the utilization of foreign investment in developing countries. The import and export activities of foreign-invested enterprises have gradually grown into an important part of China's foreign trade, making up more than 50 percent of trade overall. In terms of the exportation of high-tech products, foreign-invested enterprises are closer to 70 to 80 percent. In a certain sense, the so-called advantages of "Made in China" products lie in the products manufactured by the investment of foreign-invested enterprises in China. A boat borrowed from another may sail to the mutual benefit of both. So, the use of the products and international marketing channels of foreign-invested enterprises can improve the reputation of Chinese-made products in the international market, which is one of the important effects of China's foreign policy.

Ninthly, the spillover effect of FDI has promoted the development of China's technology and management inputs. The spillover effects of foreign-invested enterprises has promoted the development of the Chinese national economy in many aspects, including technology, management, and competition. The technology spillover of FDI presents an important contribution to China's economic development. The generalized technology spillover covers multiple levels of the involvement of foreign-invested and domestic enterprises in the use of advanced products, the technical equipment trade, and the level of industrial technology, while also promoting the reform and improvement of China's technology imports and technological innovation system. For Chinese entrepreneurs who were limited to the planned economy, management overflow is of great significance. As early as the mid-1980s, developed Western countries have generally believed that management *is* productivity, and as such, the management consulting firm has become a key factor in the development of many industries internationally. Under the new rules of the market economy, useful references and practical experience were provided by management overflow for the development of enterprises, along with the emergence and upgrading of professional management. Productivity overflow directly increased the competitiveness of the domestic industry. Through advanced products, foreign-invested enterprises occupied the market at home and abroad. Due to the effect of market mechanisms, the survival and development of domestic enterprises has faced a serious threat. In the 30 years since China's period of reform and opening up, domestic enterprises have constantly been facing market competition squeeze. Domestic enterprises should focus on “self-establishments” and implement refocusing strategies so that a virtuous circle mechanism can be established, which is the construction and improvement of economic reform and the opening-up process, as well as the foundation for a socialist market economic system and for the improvement of the social efficiency of resource allocation.

Tenthly, the agglomeration of FDI has consolidated China's position in the division of labor in international industry. The effects of agglomeration and the international industrial transfer of foreign-invested enterprises consolidated China's position in the international division of labor. In the late 20th century, with the advancement of economic globalization, multinational corporations instigated a new round of worldwide industrial measures. A systematic platform was established through China's reform and opening up for domestic industries to participate in the integration of the international division of labor. The in-depth development of Foreign Investment Utilization Policies and the simultaneous constant improvement under the guidance of foreign investment industries has promoted foreign investment to reach a higher level.

The industrial structure of investment has become more rational, and, to some extent, regional structures have also been improved after overcoming a series of obstacles such as an unproductive institutional environment, infrastructure, and transportation costs. Belts of industrial accumulation have formed one after another throughout the country, domestic enterprises have started from auxiliary products, to then consolidate and enhance their positions within the international industry supply chain and to improve the level of international competitiveness. In several important industry fields, some of the domestic enterprises have already become well-known as internationally-renowned multinational corporations.

(2) The Challenges Encountered by Foreign Investment Utilization Policies at the Macro Level

Firstly, the diversification of foreign investment is a challenge to China's macro-economic management model. After joining the WTO, China's foreign investment policy has undergone a major adjustment, and foreign-invested enterprises have only gradually generated diversification objectives after entering Chinese market.

The provisions for foreign-invested enterprises, such as the proportion of exports, local content, foreign exchange balancing, and other requirements, have been gradually phased out, which provided a suitable system for the diversification of foreign investment to enter the Chinese market. The path of China's integration into the world economy shifted from being focused on supplying labor to the supply of both a labor advantage and domestic market potential. The former created a position for China as a significant manufacturing country, and the latter created a consumerist country. Foreign investment strategy started with the establishment of manufacturing plants and a production base that can function as a global supplier, and then focused on the huge potential of China's domestic market, as well as efficient utilization of China's high-tech talent and industry. Global transfer and the new layout of R & D institutions highlighted the high opinion of China's economic development and domestic market potential. Diversified foreign investment remains a great challenge to China's macroeconomic policies and management models.

Secondly, preferential policies for foreign-invested enterprises have destroyed the environment of competition within the domestic market. Initially, the policies of using foreign capital provided a wide range of preferential treatment for foreign-invested enterprises, among which a specific arrangement of the corporate income tax—the so-called "two exemptions and three reductions" policy—is most criticized by the industry that has made domestic enterprises in an unfavorable market a competitive position. Early foreign investment utilization policies restricted the sale behavior of foreign-invested enterprises in the domestic market, and the domestic enterprises therefore faced competition with both domestic and foreign-invested enterprises of similar products in the international market. After accession to the WTO, the restriction on foreign-invested enterprises' sales behavior was canceled, and the competition between the two sides transferred to the domestic market. Six years after, the merger of the corporate income tax was finally implemented on January 1, 2008. However, for certain industries, the basic pattern of the status of market competition has been fixed, and domestic enterprises need to pay excess costs to eliminate the backward position that still exists in the current state of market competition.

Thirdly, China has become the country of destination for the international transfer of industries with high energy consumption and high pollution. Along with many international transfers of the manufacturing sector, developed industries with high energy consumption and high pollution have moved to developing countries, with China foremost among them. How to grasp a policy balance between making full use of foreign capital and controlling industries with high energy consumption and high pollution, and whether to maintain a consistent foreign policy or to maintain sustainable development of the national economy have become one of the core issues of China's macro-economic strategy, which is also one of the key issues to be resolved for harmonious and scientific development.

Fourthly, the employment practices of foreign-invested enterprises have posed a challenge to China's labor and employment system. Notably, foreign-invested enterprises employed workers from the labor market according to the needs of production and operation. Meanwhile, workers were also injected into the labor market, and the employment system remains highly market-oriented. With the gradual deepening of the reform and opening up policy, China's dual economic structure has transferred from an agricultural labor force transferred as the primary industry to a mainly manufacturing-based labor market. Labor forces from agriculture poured into foreign-invested enterprises in southeast coastal areas, where the labor supply is almost unlimited. Because of the newly added laborers, the price of the labor market has remained very low, with the scale of production maintained by simple reproduction and without adequate protections for working conditions. The labor party has always been in an unfavorable position in labor disputes, and the legitimate rights and interests of workers were often subjected to various forms of infringement. In addition, in the mode of China's planned economy, labor and social security dealt with the employees of state-owned and collective enterprises, so migrant workers were not included in China's labor system. The new labor contract of 2008 has caused a lot of controversy, thus detailed rules for the implementation needed to be formulated. For foreign-invested enterprises which are market-oriented, the protection of the workers' rights has become a problem to be carefully examined.

Fifthly, foreign-invested enterprise has a crowding-out effect = on domestic industries or enterprises. The development of foreign-invested enterprises formed a hugely competitive market pressure on the domestic enterprises of the same industries. The economic strengths of domestic enterprises are far less than that of foreign-invested enterprises. Multinational corporations possess advantages in capital, technology, management, resources, and available channels, compared with those of the domestic enterprises. The markets of domestic enterprises were therefore squeezed by foreign-invested enterprises. In the field of foreign trade, processing trade has formed a relatively closed loop. For example: orders are made from overseas, after which, foreign-invested enterprises in China buy Chinese-made products, which are then, in turn, sold overseas after processing. Domestic enterprises, guided by the government's policy, became more competitive in the processing trade as a result, and then became a member of the global supply. Through improvements in technology and management skills, domestic enterprises can obtain a competitive advantage and merge into the international division system.

1.1.2. The Guiding Principle and Effect of the Implementation of Foreign Investment Utilization Policies

Guiding ideologies and the effects of their implementation, on the one hand, came from the positioning of macroeconomic policy with the functional positioning of foreign investment utilization policies, and on the other hand, from the ongoing adjustment of foreign investment utilization policies based on the actual situation of China's economic development and opening up. The innovative spirit of "keeping pace with the times" has been fully reflected in the practice of China's investment utilization policies.

(1) The Guiding Principle of Foreign Investment Utilization Policies

In the last thirty years of reform and opening up, the system of foreign investment utilization policies has developed and continuously improved, and has played a positive role in the development of the Chinese national economy and reform.

Firstly, a clear policy of foreign investment plays an important, positive role in the development of the national economy. From a strategic point, the guiding principle of China's foreign investment utilization policies can be generally expressed as adhering to the basic state policy of opening to the outside world, along with further expansion of the breadth and depth of opening up and the development of an open economy. Following this idea, the goal of foreign investment utilization policies has always been centered on the needs of China's economic reform and opening up. Great achievements have been achieved in the 30 years' experience of using FDI, and the positive role of FDI was effectively utilized. Utilization of foreign capital has also made positive contribution to the development of the national economy and to China's economic reform and opening up.

The utilization of foreign capital is an important component of China's opening up, the same as the basic national policy of opening up, which has also gone through a tortuous process of being understood and has encountered interference from a variety of factors both at home and abroad. Opening up to the outside world means learning from the developed countries of the world, to bring in their experience and those favorable factors which are conducive to the development of China's national economy and which can serve to promote China's socialist modernizations. However, there are different views on the relationship between the utilization of foreign capital and the development of national enterprises. Some commentators note that a common development cannot be accomplished, and that furthermore, the development of national enterprises might even be prevented. Under the interactive mode of resources and the market at home and abroad, the influence of processing trade into general trade was, to some extent, exaggerated. This interference mainly derived from some international countries and interest groups with ulterior motives, who feared that China's development posed a threat to the world or to some specific countries. Those rumors were an imputation against China's economic development and revival from a security and political point of view, and China's utilization of foreign capital has been disturbed as a result.

Secondly, the clear objectives of foreign investment utilization policies have been of strategic significance to the utilization of foreign capital. China's policy of utilizing FDI was targeted, and under the new economic situation, utilizing foreign capital was adapted to the economic development at home and abroad with the principal of turning it to the country's own advantage. Foreign investment, an innovative way of using foreign capital and optimizing the structure of foreign investment should be encouraged. The active role of promoting independent innovation, industrial upgrading and coordinated regional development should be promoted in the use of foreign capital.

The objective transition of foreign investment utilization policies in different stages is determined by the status of China's economic development relative to the world economy. At the beginning of reform and opening up, China, as a long-closed economy, needed to open the windows for a better understanding of the world and to introduce mechanisms for structural reform through system effects brought about by the use of FDI.

In the 1990s, 10 consecutive years of stable economic growth made China realize the transformative value of using foreign capital on a massive scale, which meant the quality of foreign capital became a central focus, and the selective requirements of foreign capital became the basic requirements for the development of China's manufacturing competitiveness in the international market. The upgrade and optimization of investment objectives must be taken seriously after the occupation of the leading position among the developing countries to attract foreign investment.

Thirdly, the continuity, stability and adaptability of foreign investment utilization policies. The continuity, stability and adaptability of foreign investment utilization policies is two complementary features of a policy. Since the consistency of these two features is where the vitality of a policy lies, the core is how to understand the function of the two features in different aspects of foreign investment utilization policies. China's foreign investment utilization policies gone through more than thirty years of history, persisted in reform and opening up, adhered to the fundamental guiding principle of the utilization of foreign capital while remaining unchanged, expanded the depth and breadth of opening up, and unfalteringly improved China's open economy. At the strategic level, the two "constants" can ensure the continuity and stability of China's foreign investment utilization policies. But at the operating level, given the constant adjustment of new pattern of reform and opening up to adapt to the needs of foreign investment, the development of the national economy and the construction of a comprehensive well-off society still depends on adapting to the needs of China's reform and opening up.

Adjustment at the operational level has been the main cause of concerns about foreign investment utilization policies. With China's accession to the WTO, adjustments towards China's foreign investment utilization policies have been made, such as the abolition of export requirements, the self-seeking of foreign exchange balance requirements, and local content requirements, so that the interests of FDI development in China can be increased. Abolishing preferential treatment in corporate income tax was also based on the reality of China's economic development and international practice, as well as the inherent requirements of the basic norms of the WTO. A competitive market environment, which is more in line with international standards, was created for domestic-funded enterprises. Moreover, a fair competitive market environment was also provided for the structural adjustment of foreign market competition. After the transitional period following China's inclusion in the WTO, China's economic development entered a new period, which included the development of foreign investment utilization policies with new content. The introduction of the full statistical caliber of foreign investment was as far-reaching as Guangzhou Export Commodities Fair's rebranding as the Guangzhou Import and Export Commodities Fair. The landmark breakthrough in the field of finance and insurance is the entrance of productive service industry by foreign investment.

The demand for the productive service industry has increased with the establishment of the status of China's manufacturing power in the world. The expansion of foreign investment in the field of R & D means that China's position in the global supply has been enhanced. A large number of multinational companies have located their R & D institutions in China, of which their core technologies were blockaded as high commercial secrets. However, from the perspective of the levels of technology development and integrated technological development of production capacity and technical support, China has obtained spillover effects regarding the industry's core technology, which promote the speed at which China's industrial technology is able to advance and upgrade.

Foreign investment in research and development and its expansion in the service sector are also important factors. The focus of foreign investment utilization policies by the Industrial Guidance Catalogue pointedly focused on China's industrial restructuring, which lead to the upgrading of China's economic structure and followed up on the forefront of the international development. This upgrade phase has only just begun, and is far from over. From a strategic point of view, foreign investment in research and development will be accompanied by the whole process of building a moderately prosperous society and the rejuvenation of the Chinese nation. From the stage level point of view, it will be accompanied by China's post-industrial process, which is to transform from a large nation to a powerful nation in manufacture and trade. From the technical point of view, it will be accompanied by a basic balance of China's import and export trade, which also means a great improvement in the competitiveness of China's participation in the international division of labor, as well as further enhancement in the country's position in the global supply chain. A strong competitive advantage can be found through the introduction of technology and technological innovation based on the country's comparative advantage in labor. The problems faced by the practice of the utilization of foreign capital included the challenge of neighboring countries to China's comparative advantage in labor, especially those which can function as new options for international investment. India's rapid economic development and opening up, to some extent, formed a competitive relationship with China in attracting foreign investment. Deepening China's own reform and opening up, and continuing to implement a proactive foreign investment policy, are still the country's long-term strategic plans. But their focus will inevitably shift with the progress of the nation. The pre-formed pattern of FDI has faced structural adjustment. In order to meet this requirement, one of the most important considerations in the utilization of foreign investment in the coming period is how to make reasonable arrangements to safeguard the smooth operation of the domestic economy.

China's foreign investment utilization policies are currently maturing. With the "Law of the PRC on Enterprise Income Tax," implemented on January 1, 2008, the domestic and foreign-invested enterprises shall be subject to the corporate income tax rate of 25%, the previous preferential treatments are canceled. As such, pre-tax deductions for foreign-funded enterprises alone enjoy tax rebates for reinvestment in productive enterprises and preferential arrangements for the time at which a liability to tax arises. Beginning January 1, 2007, super-national treatment for foreign-invested enterprises using urban land has been terminated, so they are required to pay the same urban land use tax as domestic enterprises. The Catalogue for the Guidance of Foreign Investment Industries, which has been promulgated by the State Development Planning Commission and the Ministry of Commerce, came into force as of December 1st, 2007. The content of the catalogue includes a total of 478 articles, which includes 351 encouragements, 87 restrictions, and 40 prohibitions, among which the encouraged articles accounted for 73 percent of the whole. The focus of this new category was to encourage foreign investors to invest more in high-tech industries, the modern service industry, the high-end manufacturing sector, modern agriculture and infrastructure, and, for the first time, outsourcing of international services. With the selective expansion of foreign capital and foreign sources, it has become imperative to adjust foreign policy.

According to the actual situation at this stage, work requirements for the use of foreign capital in the future have been proposed by the departments concerned, which is to adhere to the principal of utilizing foreign investment positively and effectively, to ensure the continuity and stability of the policy, to push forward income tax adjustment actively and steadily, to implement "tax combinations," to optimize the utilization of foreign investment and promote industrial restructuring and upgrading, to encourage foreign investors to focus on investment in high-tech industries, advanced manufacturing, the modern service industry, modern agriculture, and environmental protection industries, to improve foreign investment utilization policies, to further improve the quality of the utilization of foreign capital, to improve the regional distribution of foreign investment, to promote the coordinated development of a regional economy, to carry out various forms of cooperation, to maximize foreign technology spillovers, to explore new ways of utilizing foreign investments, to further improve the environment of investment, and to actively strengthen the sense of social responsibility of foreign invested enterprises.

(2) The Implementation Effect of Foreign Investment Utilization Policies

Firstly, FDI injected new impetus into the progress of fixed capital formation. China has consistently led developing countries in direct foreign investment, with the inflow increasing from USD 37.5 billion in 1995 to USD 74.7 billion in 2007. The total fixed assets of the same period increased from 13.7239 trillion yuan to 2.03 trillion yuan, and the proportion of actual use of foreign capital in total fixed assets was affected by strong domestic investment and depreciation of the dollar, which decreased from 15% to 4%. However, as an international capital with high dynamic, FDI has long retained a steady rise year by year, and the overall efficiency of the fixed capital has been effectively promoted through various spillover effects.

Secondly, the structure of FDI becomes more reasonable year by year. At the beginning of the investment field, FDI was based on industry, which accounted for 56% of total investment. FDI mainly came from Hong Kong, Taiwan, the United States, Japan, Macau and Singapore, among which the number and the amount of foreign-invested enterprises in Hong Kong, Macao, and Taiwan accounted for more than 80 percent. The distribution area of investment mainly lay along the eastern coastal areas, including Guangdong, Fujian, Jiangsu, Shanghai and Shandong, where the amount of investment accounted for 67 % of the total. By contrast, in the east and west, the number of investment projects, the protocol investment amount, and the actual investment amount lagged far behind. Foreign mergers and acquisitions were still prohibited by the policy at that time, so more than 90% of the investment was made up of new investments. This investment was mainly in the form of joint ventures, accounting for 55%, so that the proportions of wholly foreign-owned enterprises were relatively low. The structure of foreign investment changed in the 21st century; the secondary industry, which accounted for 67%, still occupied the first place, but the tertiary industry experienced rapid growth, which reached a proportion of 32 %. The focus of the source of investment shifted to the United States, Japan, and the European Union. Additionally, the M & A and wholly foreign-owned enterprises experienced rapid progress. The intensity of the country's industrial technology improved greatly through the advances in machinery, metallurgy, petroleum, electronics, telecommunications, chemicals, textiles, light industry, food, agriculture, medicine, environmental protection, finance and insurance, and other pillar industries of the national economy. The adjustment of the industrial structure of the investment reflected the guidance of Industrial Guidance Catalogue and regional economic development investment policy. Western investment began to increase, and the investment objective shifted from industry to agriculture, environmental protection, and then to the services sector, which reflected the commitment to progressive development demonstrated by China's accession to the WTO.

Thirdly, the regional distribution of FDI reflected the reasonable interaction of policy guidance and market-inducement. The unbalanced regional distribution of foreign investment has been consistent with the imbalance of regional economic development in China. In general, the basic norms of foreign capital market behavior are to seek a favorable target for investment, yet the regional imbalance of distribution of foreign investment remained obvious when considered from the local point of view. The Catalogue of Priority Industries for Foreign Investment in Central and Western China (2008 Revision), which has been promulgated by the State Development Planning Commission and the Ministry of Commerce and approved by the State Council, has been promulgated and came into force as of December 1st, 2007. The principle of comparative advantages was reflected in the revised catalogue, which highlighted the specific resources, characteristics, and dominant industries in the central and western regions, and improved the quality of foreign investment, focusing on the convergence of the "Catalogue for the Guidance of Foreign Investment Industries," and preventing projects with high consumption of energy, heavy pollution and low technology, and backward technology and equipment transfer to the Midwest. All the above certainly contribute to the reasonable distribution of foreign investment.

Fourth, the service industry has become the new focus for attracting FDI. The attraction of the service trade for investment constituted a small proportion in paid-in foreign investment, which demonstrated the imbalance of the pattern of foreign capital utilization. The small proportion made up by the service trade was normal because of its relatively recent origin. In addition, the opening of the service industry was a complex issue, and the development of China's tertiary industry lagged behind the primary and secondary industries, and was significantly lower than the international competitiveness. There were many controversial issues for the WTO on trade-in services, and also the rules remained unclear. As a developing country, the development in the field of service trade was significantly behind that of developed countries, and opening up the services trade prematurely and excessively was not conducive to the healthy development of the domestic industry. Viewed from the current state of development, the opening up of the circulation industry with a high degree of market share has become the first to attract foreign investments, and the well-known retailers in the world have entered the Chinese market. As the current focus, the financial and insurance industries played a important role in the national economic security. With the participation of the international capital, other productive areas such as logistics and similar industries should be opened as soon as possible, and quickly reach the requirements of the development of China's manufacturing industry.

Fifthly, FDI directly drives the development of China's foreign trade. FDI has played an important role in the progress of China's import and export trade. There are two diametrically opposite views of the relations between international direct investment and international trade. On one hand, international direct investment will promote the development of international trade; on the other hand, international direct investment poses an alternative to the development of international trade. During the early stage of China's reform and opening-up, FDI greatly promoted the development of China's foreign trade, and, since the 21st century, more than half of China's foreign trade volume was obtained by foreign-invested enterprises. The processing trade, as a pioneering attempt of China's reform and opening up, was commendable. On the one hand, starting from the simple concept of foreign order to processing trade as the main method of a large number of three-capital enterprises, the foreign investment policies were introduced in an orderly fashion and advanced reasonably. On the other hand, the strategic objectives to participating in the international economic cycle with large-scale exports to be built on the basis of large quantities of import and promote of the national economic development were achieved. While promoting the development of China's export trade, processing trade has also led to a corresponding growth in China's imports.

In the 30 years of China's reform and opening up, the spillover effects of FDI in the promotion of China's foreign trade have promoted the development of other sectors of the national economy, and the rapid growth of production efficiency, trade, and output. In 2007, China's foreign trade was ranked third among world trade, the total growth of the national economy leaped to second in the world, and China become an international manufacturing and trading power.

Certainly, the achievement of this objective was conditional on the choice of public policy. The objectives of foreign investment could be diversified, and trade substitution of FDI was beginning to work when China's socialist market economy provided the environment with stronger market features for FDI enterprises. The huge potential of the domestic market in China has become the major incentive for FDI. With the cancellation of the non-market economic requirements for FDI enterprises, a growing number of products of FDI enterprises sold in the domestic market in China and the crowding-out effect to the domestic sectors began to emerge.

1.1.3. The Foreign Investment Utilization Policies on the Micro-Level

The successful implementation of foreign investment utilization policies on the micro-level has provided a solid foundation for the development of the economy and FDI inflow into China. Technology spillover and the diversified goals of FDI inflow has become an innovation of utilization of foreign investment. External effects of the FDI should be paying attention the new situation and new problems.

The Establishment and Operation of FDI Enterprises

Firstly, with Chinese-foreign joint ventures, Chinese-foreign cooperatives and wholly foreign-owned enterprises have formed a cascade model of development in the utilization of foreign investment. This cascade model of development made it possible for the enterprises to choose the right investment mode according to the actual situation. The first is that other resources from enterprises, as well as capital, can be combined with the perspective of cooperation input. The second is, the operation models could be Chinese-foreign jointly-owned as well as foreign-owned, from the perspective of an investment mode with capital combinations. The third is that the equity ratio of joint venture partners could be diversified in the investment model of joint ventures. Through multi-level institutional arrangements, the utilization of FDI inflow in China exhibits great developing potential, and has also promoted the establishment of FDI enterprises. In particular, under the institutional arrangement of joint ventures, the equity ratio of a given foreign party had been restricted at the beginning of reform and opening up. The restriction effectively turned the foreign investment into an endogenous variable in economic operating mechanism, which made the foreign investment a characteristic of a market economy.

Secondly, at the beginning of the period of foreign investment promotion, the provision of export, local content, and foreign exchange balancing has eliminated the negative effects on the economic system in China. On the purpose of protecting domestic industries and markets, the provisions of export, local content, and foreign exchange balancing were put on the table before FDI enterprises when the policies of making use of foreign investment were initially implemented.

These provisions became necessary auxiliary conditions of China's opening up and its implementation of foreign investment policy promotion, and also reflected the basic features of the progressive mode of China's reform and opening up. Although it is contrary to the principle of a market economy, these provisions—as a transitional arrangement—started the process of China's opening up, ensured the planned economic system transit to market economic system smoothly, and made the domestic market withstand the shock of opening up. These institutional arrangements effectively eliminated the negative impact on the host country by FDI inflow, especially in developing countries and transition economies like China. Thus, the advantages of high capital efficiency, marketable products, advanced production technology, and management innovation can be developed. Through various spillovers, liberalization of the FDI had a positive effect on the economic system of China, which made a great contribution to promoting the reform of planned economic system and the process of opening up.

Thirdly, due to the socialist market economy, the market in which foreign-invested enterprises participated could be predicted. During the early 1990s, China established the strategic objectives of constructing a socialist market economy, and correspondingly provided a predictable market environment for foreign-invested enterprises. The proposal of a socialist market economy opened the door for restoration of the multilateral trading system, and then established and improved the socialist market economy in China regarding the negotiations of rejoining the GATT and WTO accession. Since then, the establishment and operating of FDI enterprises has become more international. Through a series of industrial operations, including the choice of production and business sites, the procurement of materials and equipment, the recruitments of labors, the marketing of products, additional investments, and the exportation of profits, FDI enterprises gradually became a part of the domestic market, which was geared towards imitational conventions. After the transitional period, the Chinese government fulfilled the promise of opening the domestic market: the extent of opening-up of industries and regions reached an unprecedented level and the central and local governments provided multifaceted services for FDI such as institutions, infrastructure, information, communication, and legal protection, which effectively improved the convenience for FDI.

Technology Spillover and the Diversification of Foreign Investment Objectives

Firstly, technology spillover became a significant objective for the implementation of foreign investment utilization policies. The utilization of foreign-investment policy mainly concentrated on promoting labor productivity by importing advanced technology and equipment, offering a reference to modern corporate systems for the reform of the management system in state-owned and collective enterprises by introducing advanced management modes, providing external pressure for domestic enterprises to participate in market competition by introducing market-oriented mode of operation. Technology spillover was one of the basic goals and the driving forces behind China's foreign investment utilization policies.

The technology spillover covers a wide range. It can refer to either a simple diffusion of advanced production technology by FDI enterprises—including the marketing of the advanced products and the sharing and transferring of the technology—or to various changes within the domestic economic sector caused by the presence of FDI. Periodic features of foreign investment utilization policies have changed from simply promoting foreign investment to utilizing the direct or indirect impact on national economy caused by FDI. That is to say, foreign investments affect transitional economies through a wide range of technology spillover.

Secondly, the diversification of FDI objectives is both released and retained. The prerequisite for multinational corporations' (MNCs) global strategic layout and the basic driving force behind foreign investment in China was the diversification of investment objectives. Early investment in China aimed at seeking cheap labor. Capital from Hong Kong, Macao, and Taiwan mostly concentrated on labor-intensive industries such as the toy and garment industry. Competitive products were provided to world markets through the "Three Plus One (三来一补)" trading mix of custom manufacturing and compensation. The objective of single investments was mainly affected by the constraints of specific implementation details on the early export requirements of the foreign investment utilization policies. The deepening of reform and opening up and the accession of China to the WTO diversified the objectives of foreign investment in China.

These investment objectives have diversified from trading to investment, and the investment motivation has extended from seeking competitive labor to going directly into the target market by bypassing trade barriers, which led to industry transfer. Outsourcing has become an important form of MNCs' investments in China, reallocating their worldwide resources, including industry and services. A growing number of product designs which were adapted to China's domestic market have been sold within the Chinese market itself. This has meant that FDI began to flow into China's domestic market and meanwhile, because of the policy advantage, the domestic-targeted FDI was promoted effectively. The Chinese market has become an important structural support within a multinational global strategic layout.

The External Effects of the Business Operations of FDI Enterprises

The operation of FDI enterprises increased the scope of Chinese enterprises' participation in the whole production chain, and resulted in the agglomeration of the similar enterprises forming a highly dense distribution. Buying Chinese promoted the development of Chinese enterprises.

Firstly, we must consider the industry-leading effect. Along with the operation of FDI enterprises, there are two certain phenomena that have demanded our attention: one is that complementary enterprises overseas followed the leading industry to invest in China because of their operation drifting, which resulted in an international transfer of the industrial chain. A foreign-leading enterprise has the potential to bring the entire industrial chain to China, including the complementary enterprises, as well as producer services enterprises. The other is that the localization of operations has led to the development of the domestic industrial chain. Refocusing the strategy of MNCs and their supporting outsourcing became an important worldwide trend at the turn of the century, which was an important manifestation of economic globalization. The effect on the economy of the host country by the localization of enterprises operation increased. This phenomenon has been particularly obvious in China. The sufficient supply of an adequate labor force of all levels has become an important basis for MNCs to invest in China in advanced industries, especially the IT industry.

Secondly, the effect of industrial agglomeration. Industrial agglomeration is one of the important driving forces for regional economic development. FDI inflow in China formed an industrial agglomeration by gathering in certain regions. Industrial agglomeration formed with a competitive advantage in scale, and promoted highly specialized resources from both the supply and demand sectors. The member of certain groups have the ability to obtain resources like highly specialized components, raw materials, machinery and equipment, business services, human resources, and more, with the result being that they would be able to reduce their transaction costs. From a logistics point of view, this industrial agglomeration serves as the basis for the development and optimization of the logistics industry. Industrial agglomeration also promoted the advancement and diffusion of technology, which is to say that competition between manufacturers as well as clusters directly led to the spillover of technology and improvement of productivity. Whether driven by industry or industrial agglomeration, the operating activities of foreign-invested enterprises have largely contributed to the development of China's national economy and provided a powerful demonstration of the external economies of scale. Only the former is often linked to a larger concept, while the latter tends to be highly concentrated in certain regions. The best example of the former is that the enterprises from both inside and outside the New and High-Tech Development Zones are all in line, and the IT industry with hi-tech and high-density agglomeration of Kunshan Taiwanese[1] is the best interpretation of the latter.

Thirdly, the effect of buying Chinese. An important part of localization is buying locally-extracted raw materials and locally-produced intermediate products. In China, policies have been put in place to encourage foreign enterprises to favor domestic suppliers of production input, which benefits Chinese enterprises by increasing the scope of their participation in the whole production chain. Meanwhile, some of the multinational corporations that operate in China have also begun to favor Chinese suppliers as an integral part of their global business strategy. The best example of this is Wal-Mart. The US-based Corporation chose to set up its center for global procurement in China, thereby opening a new channel through which Chinese-made products can enter foreign markets. For any Chinese company, being a supplier for Wal-Mart means its products can go directly from factory floor to the shelves of Wal-Mart stores worldwide. However, Wal-Mart has also used its superior bargaining power to reduce the profit margins of their suppliers to an absolute minimum. This has led some commentators to note that great bargaining power disparity exists between Wal-Mart, on one hand, and its mid- and small-sized suppliers on the other, causing damage to the interests of many of the latter. Perhaps paradoxically, their strong bargaining powers and the ability to shape the market are the very reasons why procurement policies of multinational corporations can be so consequential. It is thanks to the high quality standards to which they hold the products they sell and the strict rules of commercial transactions to which they adhere that the companies that supply them have been able to acquire a competitive edge in the international market by learning how to play by the rules.

1.2 The number of Foreign-funded Enterprises and the Size of Foreign Capital Inflow in China

Since the advent of the policies of reform and opening-up three decades ago, FDI inflow in China has been growing at an annual rate of over 20 percent. Since 1992, China has, for 17 consecutive years, led developing countries in FDI inflow.

1.2.1. Foreign Capital Inflow in China through FDI

The Rapid Growth of Foreign Investment Used Effectively

In 2008, China's effective use of foreign investment reached USD852.610 billion, an increase of 90.4% compared with USD 447.97 billion in 2002. The annual growth rates were between 10%

[1] Kunshan Taiwanese: a group of Taiwan businessmen invested in manufacturing in Kunshan, Jiangsu province, China, which quickly became one of the most densely populated areas of Taiwan-funded enterprises in mainland China.

and 12% in the meantime. The growth rates remained very stable. These indicate the stability of FDI policy and the willingness of foreign companies to invest in China, on a platform of a relatively stable international economic situation and China's rapid economic growth (See Table 1-1).

Table 1-1 The Effective Use of Foreign Investment in China (1979-2008)

Year	Amount (USD 100 million)	Change Rate	Accumulated Amount (USD 100 million)	Change Rate
1979-1984	41.04	-	41.04	-
1985	19.56	-	60.6	-
1986	22.44	15	83.0	37
1987	23.14	3	106.2	28
1988	31.94	38	138.1	30
1989	33.92	6	172.0	25
1990	34.87	3	206.9	20
1991	43.66	25	250.6	21
1992	110.08	152	360.7	44
1993	275.15	150	635.8	76
1994	337.67	23	973.5	53
1995	375.21	11	1348.7	39
1996	417.26	11	1765.9	31
1997	452.57	8	2218.5	26
1998	454.63	0	2673.1	20
1999	403.19	-11	3076.3	15
2000	407.15	1	3483.5	13
2001	468.78	15	3952.3	13
2002	527.43	13	4479.7	13
2003	535.05	1	5014.7	12
2004	606.3	13	5621.0	12
2005	603.25	-1	6224.3	11
2006	630.21	4	6854.5	10
2007	747.68	19	7602.2	11
2008	923.95	24	8526.1	12

Source: China Statistical Yearbook 2009

Since the advent, three decades ago, of the policies of reform and opening-up, China's effective use of foreign investment has maintained a positive growth except for the years 1999 and 2005. In accordance with the scale of the effective use of foreign investment, this development can be divided into four stages: during the first stage (from 1979 to 1991), the effective use of foreign investment annual level was maintained at less than USD 5 billion, with a steady and modest growth year by year; during the second stage (from 1997 to 1992), for the initial consecutive years of 1992 and 1993, China's effective use of foreign investment jumped up to a growth of 150%, which meant an increase from USD 4.366 billion in 1991 to USD 27.515 billion in 1993. This reflected the soft landing of China's national economy and the establishment a socialist market economy, which led to a new phase of reform and opening up, both domestic and international. Since then, the amount of effective use of foreign investment slightly increased to USD 40 billion. During the third stage (from 1998 to 2001), the amount was generally maintained at USD 40 billion, during which time there was a slight decline as a consequence of the Asian financial crisis. During the fourth stage (from 2002 to 2008), in the first year after China's accession to WTO, the amount of effective use of foreign investment broke through the USD 50 billion mark, ushering in a new round of growth, up to a record high in 2008. The amount reached USD 92.395 billion in 2008, and stepped onto a new growth level of 24% based on 19% in 2007, which was an exception to all the declining trends in the global financial crisis (see figure 1-1).

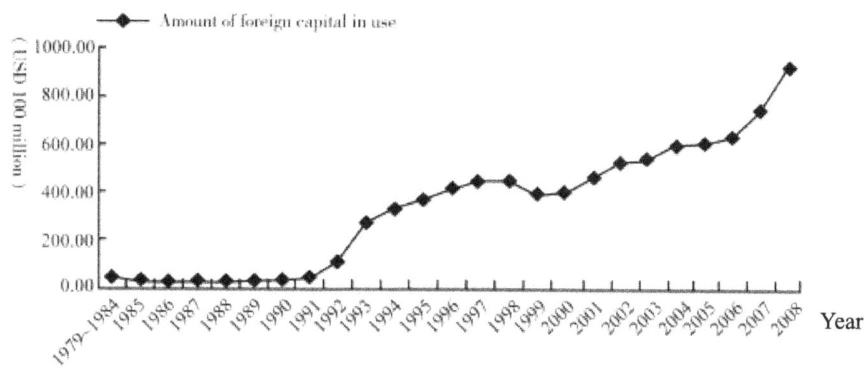

Figure 1-1 Amount of foreign capital in use: 1985-2008

China has spent 17 years making total effective use of a foreign investment of more than one hundred billion U.S. dollars, and reached USD 134.87 billion in 1995, only to exceed USD 200 billion in two years, USD 300 billion in three years, USD 400 billion in one year, USD 500 billion and USD 600 billion, respectively, in two years, and USD 700 billion and USD 800 billion, respectively, in one year.

The cumulative effective use of foreign investment, in accordance with the estimated USD 80 billion in 2009, will reach USD 930 billion. The development of cumulative actual use of foreign capital can also be divided into two stages in accordance with the terms of the changes of the growth rate of the total effective use of foreign capital. The first stage: before 1999, annual growth was more than 20%, while in 1993, there was a jump, and the annual growth achieved 76%. The second stage: after 1999, with the expansion of the absolute scale, annual growth rate fell to under 20% and gradually stabilized at between 10% and 12%.

1.2.2. The Number of Foreign-Invested Enterprises Continuously Increased

The number of foreign-invested enterprises continuously increased from 2003-2008. In 2003, the number was 226,373, and 242,284 in 2004, 260,000 in 2005, 274,863 in 2006, and 286,232 in 2007. With this expansion, the increase slowed down year by year, from the annual growth rate 8.8% in 2004 down to 4.1% in 2007 (See Table 1-2).

Table 1-2 The Number of Foreign-Invested Enterprises in China (2002-2008)

Year	The Number of Foreign-Invested Enterprises	Change Rate	Total Enterprises in China	Change Rate
2003	226373	8.8	5214144	-
2004	242284	7.0	5168302	-0.9
2005	260000	7.3	5647489	9.3
2006	274863	5.7	6068364	7.5
2007	286232	4.1	6494350	7
2008	434937	-	-	-

Annotation: The number of foreign-invested enterprises in 2008 is the sum of the enterprises and their branches, thus the change in proportion is not calculated, because of the dramatic expansion and the incomparability of the number.

Sources: China Statistical Yearbook of the Tertiary Industry (2006, 2007, 2008), China Statistics Press, 2007, 2008, 2009; survey data of "Operation Status of Chinese Foreign-invested Enterprises" Research Group, Institute of Finance and Trade Economics and Chinese Academy of Social Sciences.

According to data available in the China Statistical Yearbook of the Tertiary Industry, the number of domestic bodies incorporating the primary, secondary and tertiary industries in China has largely maintained a sustained growth trend from 2003-2007. Compared to 2003, there was a slight decline of -0.9% in 2004. In 2005, 2006, and 2007, the number increased by 9.3%, 7.5%, and 7.0%, respectively, compared to the previous year. The growth rate also shows signs of a slowdown, while the direction and growth rate of the quantitative development of the foreign-invested enterprises and domestic enterprises of the primary, secondary and tertiary industries shows a rather consistent regularity. That is, in the years 2003-2007, foreign-invested enterprises maintained a yearly-increasing trend; however, the growth rate was basically in a declining channel, except for a slight increase in 2005.

Chapter 2 The Investment Models and the Capital Structure of Enterprises with Foreign Investment

With the continuing development of China's economic society and foreign investment policy, enterprises with foreign investments have been adjusting their investment models and capital structures. In the long run, these measures are beneficial to the competitiveness and development of enterprises with foreign investment.

From the perspective of foreign investment, the number of wholly foreign-owned enterprises is increasing rapidly. Running foreign-owned businesses as wholly foreign-owned enterprises has become a favorite with foreign investors. Meanwhile, the real foreign funds of foreign-owned enterprises have accounted for the rise in the proportion of total real foreign funds. Wholly foreign-owned enterprises have become the dominant enterprises actually using foreign funds in China. With the maturation of the foreign investment system in China, the trend of enterprises with foreign investment becoming foreign-owned enterprises continues to expand. From the perspective of capital structure, the percentage of foreign registered capital among the total registered capital enterprises with foreign investment continues to increase. The majority of enterprises with foreign investment are under absolute control by foreign parties.

2.1 The Overall Patterns of Investments and Capital Structures

2.1.1. The investment methods of foreign-invested enterprises are moving from diversification to centralization

The direct foreign investment methods includes: Chinese-foreign joint ventures, Chinese-foreign cooperatives, wholly foreign-owned enterprises, and joint stock enterprises with foreign investment.

In recent years, the investment models of foreign-invested enterprises have further concentrated on wholly owned foreign enterprises. This new trend can be seen from the absolute and relative change in the number of enterprises with foreign investment.

Looking at the situation from the absolute number of enterprises with foreign investment from 2004 to 2008, it's obvious that despite the number of newly-established enterprises with foreign investment decreasing, the decrease in speed of the number of the new established wholly foreign-owned enterprises is actually slower than average, while the number of newly-established Chinese-foreign joint ventures and Chinese-foreign cooperatives are also decreasing rapidly. In 2008, there were 27,514 new enterprises with foreign investment in China, a decrease of 36.99% from 2004. Among these, 22,396 wholly foreign-owned enterprises were newly established, a decrease of 27.07% from 2004; 4,612 Chinese-foreign joint ventures, decreased by 60.14% from 2004; 468 Chinese-foreign cooperatives, decreased by 65.15%; and 38 stock companies with foreign investment, decreased by 11.63% from 2004.(see Figure 2-1)

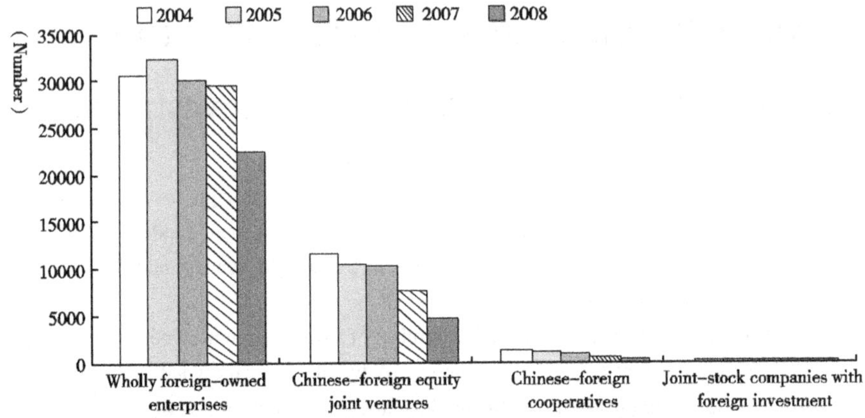

Figure 2-1: Number of newly-established foreign capital companies of different types, 2004-2008

Source: China Statistical Yearbook 2005, 2006,2007,2008,2009

From the perspective of the relative number of foreign-invested enterprises, the proportion of wholly foreign-owned enterprises has continuously increased amongst the newly-established foreign-invested enterprises, while the proportion of Chinese-foreign joint ventures and Chinese-foreign cooperatives has obviously decreased. In 2004, there were 43,664 foreign-invested enterprises newly-established in China. Among these, the number of wholly foreign-owned enterprises accounted for 81.40% of the total number of foreign-invested enterprises, an increase of 11.07% compared to last year; the number of Chinese-foreign joint ventures accounted for 16.76%, a decrease of 9.76%; the number of Chinese-foreign cooperatives accounted for 1.70%, which was decreased by 1.38%; and the number of stock companies with foreign investment accounted for 0.14%, an increase of 0.04%.(see Figure 2-2)

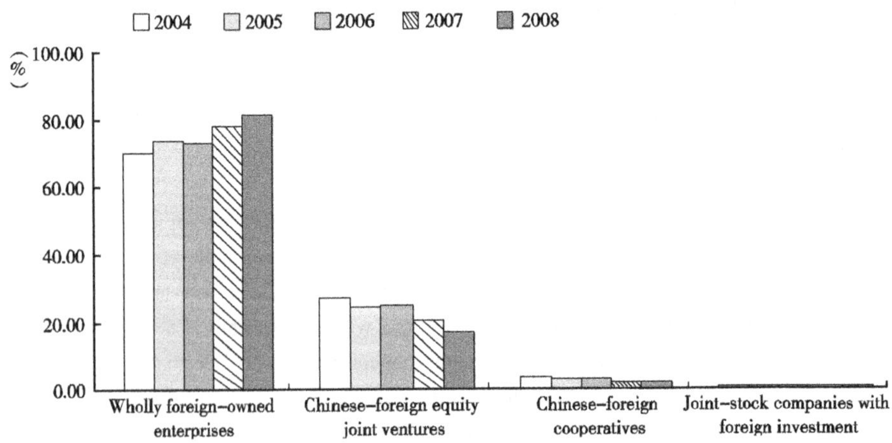

Figure 2-2: Relative shares of different types of newly established foreign capital enterprises, 2004-2008

Source: China Statistical Yearbook 2005, 2006, 2007, 2008, 2009

Generally speaking, it can be seen from comparing the data from different investment companies set up in China between 2004-2008 that foreign-invested enterprises have become the most important means of FDI in China, and this trend is still expanding. （see Table2-1）

Table 2-1: the number of newly-established foreign-invested companies with different investment models from 2004-2008.

Year	Foreign-owned	Chinese-foreign joint	Chinese-foreign cooperative	Stock companies	total
2004	30708	11570	1343	43	43664
2005	32308	10480	1166	47	44001
2006	30164	10223	1036	50	41473
2007	29543	7649	641	38	37871
2008	22396	4612	468	38	27514

Source: China Statistical Yearbook 2005, 2006,2007,2008,2009

2.1.2. There are large differences among foreign-invested enterprises with different investment models.

When considering the absolute amount of FDI influx from foreign-invested enterprises with differing models of investment, the gap in the inflow of FDI between wholly foreign-owned enterprises and Chinese-foreign joint ventures has been expanding since 2000. In 2008, the actual FDI inflows utilized by wholly foreign-owned enterprises reached USD72.315 billion, an increase of 79.79% compared to 2004; the actual FDI inflows used by Chinese-foreign joint ventures reached USD17.318 billion, an increase of 5.69% compared to 2004; the actual FDI inflows used by Chinese-foreign cooperatives reached USD1.903 billion, a decrease of 38.85% compared to 2004; and the actual FDI inflows used by stock companies with foreign investments reached USD0.859 billion, an increase of 10.55% compared to 2004. From the growth rate of the actual use of FDI inflows by foreign-invested enterprises with different investment models, the expanding share of FDI inflows by wholly foreign-owned enterprises can be seen. (see Figure 2-3)

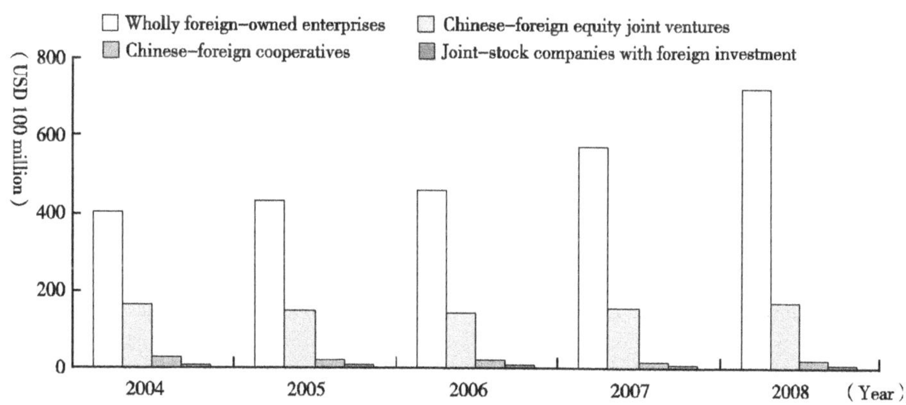

Figure 2-3: Amount of foreign capital in use by different types of foreign capital enterprises, 2004-2008

Source: China Statistical Yearbook 2005, 2006, 2007, 2008, 2009

From the perspective of the relative amount of the actual use of FDI by foreign-invested enterprises with differing models of investment, the proportion of wholly foreign-owned enterprises in foreign-invested enterprises has been increasing. In 2008, the amount of actual FDI inflows by wholly foreign-owned enterprises was USD72.315 billion, accounting for 78.27% of the total amount of the actual use of FDI inflows by foreign-invested enterprises, an increase of 11.93% compared to 2004; the amount of FDI inflows used by Chinese-foreign joint ventures was USD17.318 billion, accounting for 18.74% of the total amount of the actual use of FDI inflows by foreign-invested enterprises, a decrease of 8.28% compared to 2004; the amount of FDI inflows used by Chinese-foreign cooperatives was USD1.903 billion, accounting for 2.06% of the total amount of the actual use of FDI inflows by foreign-invested enterprises, a decrease of 3.07% compared to 2004; and the amount of FDI inflows used by stock companies with foreign investment was USD0.859 billion, accounting for 0.93% of the total amount of the actual use of FDI inflows by foreign-invested enterprises, a decrease of 0.35% compared to 2004. (See Figure 2-4)

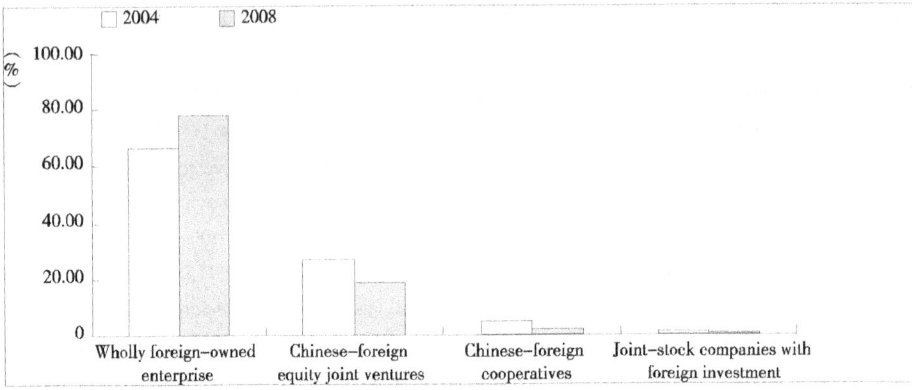

Figure 2-4: Relative shares of foreign capital in use by different types of foreign capital enterprises, 2004 and 2008

Source: China Statistical Yearbook 2005, 2006, 2007, 2008, 2009

2.1.3. There are significant differences between the average amounts of the FDI inflows actually used by foreign-invested enterprises with differing models of investment

From the perspective of the average amount of FDI utilization, stock companies with foreign investment have the largest average amount, significantly larger than other types of enterprises. From 2004 to 2008, the average amount of FDI utilization of wholly foreign-owned enterprises, Chinese-foreign joint ventures, Chinese-foreign cooperatives and stock companies with foreign investment was USD 1.868 million, USD 2.002 million, USD 2.407 million and USD16.31 million. The amount of the actual use of FDI inflows by wholly foreign-owned enterprises, joint ventures, and Chinese-foreign cooperatives were at the same level, while the stock companies with foreign investment had a larger scale of FDI utilization, but also large fluctuations. (see Figure 2-5)

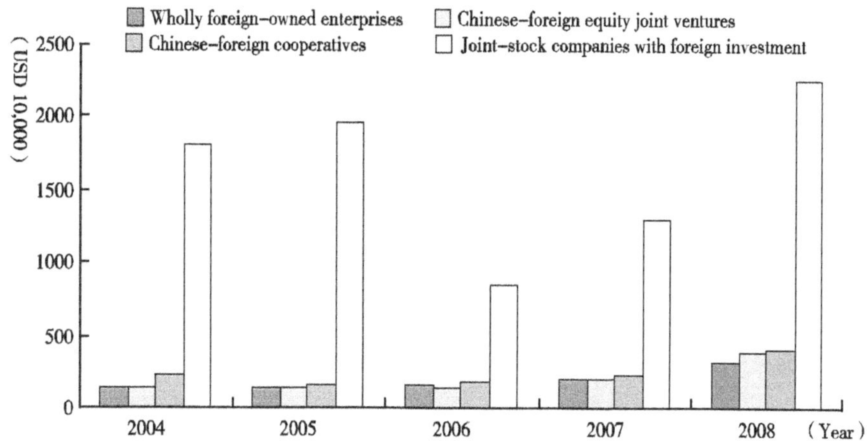

Figure 2-5: Average amount of foreign capital in use by different types of foreign capital enterprises, 2004 - 2008

Source: China Statistical Yearbook 2005, 2006, 2007, 2008, 2009

2.1.4. The proportion of registered foreign capital in foreign-invested enterprises has been increasing

The foreign-invested enterprises registered across regions at the end of the year show that, in recent years, the proportion of foreign-registered capital in foreign-invested enterprises has continuously increased. By the end of 2004, the registered capital of foreign-invested enterprises was USD728.5 billion, of which foreign-registered capital was USD558 billion, accounting for 76.60% of the total registered capital. By the end of 2005, the registered capital of foreign-invested enterprises was USD812 billion, of which foreign-registered capital was USD 631.9 billion, accounting for 77.82% of the total registered capital, increased by 1.22 percentages. By the end of 2006, the registered capital of foreign-invested enterprises was USD946.5 billion, of which foreign-registered capital was USD740.6 billion, accounting for 78.25% of the total registered capital, an increase of 0.43 percent. By the end of 2007, the registered capital of foreign-invested enterprises was USD1.1554 trillion, of which foreign-registered capital was USD921.1 billion, accounting for 79.72% of the total registered capital, an increase of 0.47 percent. By the end of 2008, the registered capital of foreign-invested enterprises was USD1.3006 trillion, of which foreign-registered capital was USD1.0389 trillion, accounting for 79.88% of the total registered capital, an increase of 0.16 percent. (See Figure 2-6)

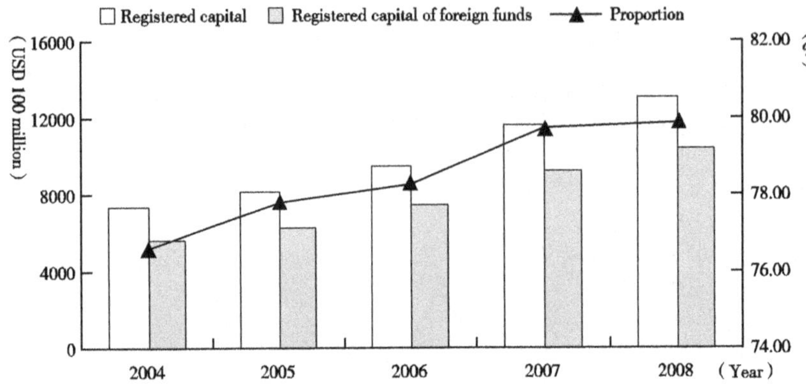

Figure 2-6 Registered capital of foreign capital enterprises, 2004-2008

Source: China Statistical Yearbook 2005, 2006, 2007, 2008, 2009

2.2 Wholly foreign-owned enterprises

2.2.1. Wholly foreign-owned enterprises have become the main model of FDI in China

In 2004, 30,708 wholly foreign-owned enterprises had been set up in China, accounting for 70.33% of the total foreign-invested enterprises. In 2005, 32,308 wholly foreign-owned enterprises were set up in China, a rise of 73.43% in the total number of foreign-invested enterprises. In 2006, 30,164 wholly foreign-owned enterprises had been set up in China, which accounted for 72.73% of the total foreign-invested enterprises. In 2007, 29,543 wholly owned foreign enterprises were set up in China, which accounted for 78.01% of the total foreign-invested enterprises. In 2008, 22,396 wholly foreign-owned enterprises had set up in China, which accounted for 71.40% of the total number of foreign-invested enterprises, and accounted for more than four-fifths of the total number of foreign-invested enterprises.

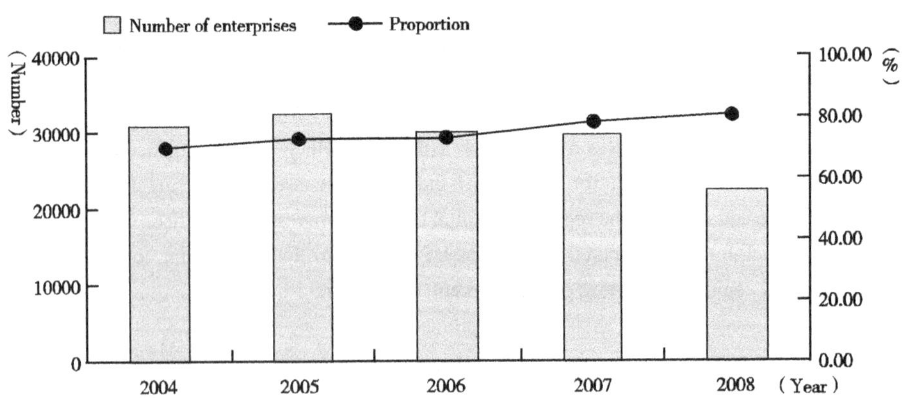

Figure 2-7: Number of newly-approved wholly foreign-owned enterprises and its share in all foreign capital enterprises, 2004-2008

Source: China Statistical Yearbook 2005, 2006, 2007, 2008, 2009

2.2.2. The proportion of the foreign capital used by wholly foreign-owned enterprises continues to rise

In 2004, the actual use of foreign capital by wholly foreign-owned enterprises was USD40.222 billion, which accounted for 66.34% of the total amount of foreign capital actually used by foreign investment enterprises overall. In 2005, the actual use of foreign capital by wholly owned foreign enterprises was USD42.961 billion, which accounted for 71.22% of the total amount of foreign capital actually used by foreign investment enterprises overall. In 2006, the actual use of foreign capital by wholly foreign-owned enterprises was USD46.281 billion, which accounted for 73.44% of the total amount of foreign capital actually used by foreign investment enterprises overall. In 2007, the actual use of foreign capital by wholly foreign-owned enterprises was USD57.264 billion, which accounted for 76.59% of the total amount of foreign capital actually used by foreign investment enterprises. In 2008, the actual use of foreign capital by wholly foreign-owned enterprises was USD72.315 billion, which accounted for 78.27% of the total amount of foreign capital actually used by foreign investment enterprises. (See Figure 2-8)

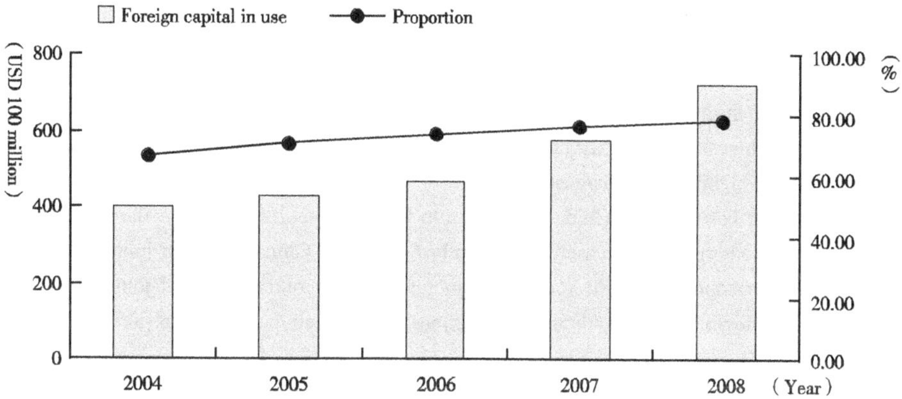

Figure 2-8: Amount of foreign capital in use by wholly foreign-owned enterprises and its share in all foreign capital in use, 2004-2008

Source: China Statistical Yearbook 2005, 2006, 2007, 2008, 2009

2.2.3. The average size of the actual use of foreign investment by wholly foreign-owned enterprises continues to rise

In 2004, the average size of foreign investments actually used by wholly foreign-owned enterprises was USD1,309,800, which grew 5.71% over the previous year. In 2005, the average size of the actual use of foreign investments by wholly owned foreign enterprises was USD1,329,700, which grew 1.52% over the previous year. In 2006, the average size of the actual use of foreign investments by wholly foreign-owned enterprises was USD1,534,300, which grew 15.39% over the previous year. In 2007, the average size of foreign investment actually used by wholly foreign-owned enterprises was USD1,938,300, which grew 26.33% over the previous year. In 2008, the average size of the actual use of foreign investments by wholly foreign-owned enterprises was USD3,228,900, which grew 66.58% over the previous year. Overall, the average size of foreign investment actually being used by wholly foreign-owned enterprises experienced an accelerated upward trend over nearly five years. (See Figure 2-9)

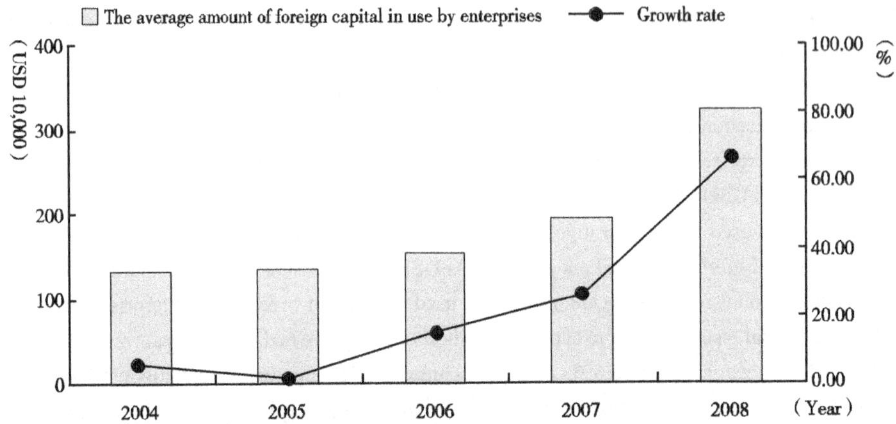

Figure 2-9: The average amount and growth rate of foreign capital in use by wholly foreign-owned enterprises: 2004-2008

Source: China Statistical Yearbook 2005, 2006, 2007, 2008, 2009

2.2.4. The trend toward a larger share of wholly foreign-owned enterprises will continue.

The fact that, in the beginning, joint ventures or cooperatives were necessary for foreign capital to enter the Chinese market has changed. The willingness to establish wholly foreign-owned enterprises has significantly increased because of the lowering of tariffs and reducing or even abolishing trade barriers after China's accession to WTO. From 2003 to 2007, the rate of wholly foreign-owned enterprises increased significantly faster than Chinese-foreign joint ventures and Chinese-foreign cooperatives. Moreover, the increase in the total number of joint ventures has been slowing down, while the number of Chinese-foreign cooperatives has already begun to decline.

First, the main reason that foreign-owned enterprise has gained a foothold in China is that the country's foreign investment regime has been maturing. At the beginning of reform and opening up (改革开放), foreign investors usually preferred Chinese-foreign joint ventures and cooperatives because they combine the advantages of local companies' domestic marketing channels and close relationships with the local government with their own technologies, capital, and quality products and are less risky than other types of enterprises. At present, the utilization of FDI policy in China is continuously improving.

In 2001, the Bureau for the Registration of Foreign-Invested Enterprises and State Administration For Industry & Commerce of the People's Republic of China was founded; on April 1st, 2002, the “Catalogue for the Guidance of Foreign Investment by Industries” was implemented in order to relax the restrictions on the proportions of foreign investment and expand the scope of market access; in 2006, the “Implementation Opinions on the Applicability of the Law of Registration Approval for Foreign-Invested Companies” was implemented to offer specific guidance on law issues for foreign-invested companies in the approval, registration, and management processes, and to make foreign companies and domestic companies equal regarding the administrative regulations of registration and management level, and—by coordinating with the Corporate Law and Administration of Company Registration and other laws on foreign investment—effectively protect the continuity of China's utilization of foreign investment laws and policies, and create transparent legal conditions for foreign investment. As the domestic investment environment in China is geared towards international standards, more transparent investment policies, laws and regulations, and the rules of the market are brought into line with international practice. As such, the external advantages of joint ventures and cooperatives are gradually being weakened. Foreign companies are becoming more familiar with the domestic situation, and foreign companies are now not only able to control their own business, plan business operations according to their own strategies in China, and expand their business scope and area, but marketing and sales are also becoming possible, so a foreign-owned enterprise is a rational choice for foreign investment.

Secondly, wholly foreign-owned enterprises are preferred in foreign investment because of the low transaction costs. As joint ventures and cooperatives demonstrate some differences between their enterprise system, management, cultural, political and moral aspects, they are prone to contradictions in the process of operations. Whether the impact of opportunism and moral hazards arises from hiding actions after they have taken place or through concealing information beforehand by contract parties, it nevertheless will have transaction costs. In wholly foreign-owned enterprises, as the special assets and control improve, much uncertainty can be avoided and various frictions between the joint venture partners and internal management costs can be reduced. Therefore, the original joint ventures are now becoming more inclined to sole and absolute control of management.

Thirdly, the willingness of Chinese companies to establish joint ventures with foreign companies continues to decline. At present, more and more Chinese companies are approaching leadership with firm resolve, so they have little demand for economic cooperation.

Finally, the increase in China's IPR protection awareness provides a guarantee for the establishment of wholly foreign-owned enterprises. Currently, the competitiveness of global enterprises is not only reflected in the labor, resources, and optimization of the allocation of capital, but also in technological and management innovations. The latter has strong external economic influences, which can lead to an increased awareness of self-developed intellectual property protection. Wholly foreign-owned enterprises have high production and management autonomy and control systems, which can improve production efficiency while protecting patents, technology, and other intellectual property rights, so that the number of wholly foreign-owned enterprises is steadily increasing.

2.3 Other types of investment for foreign investment enterprises

2.3.1. Chinese-foreign joint ventures

In 2004, 11,570 foreign joint ventures were set up in China, which accounted for 26.50% of the total foreign-invested enterprises. In 2005, 10,480 foreign joint ventures set up in China, which accounted for 23.82% of the total foreign-invested enterprises. In 2006, 10,223 foreign joint ventures set up in China, which accounted for 24.65% of the total foreign-invested enterprises.

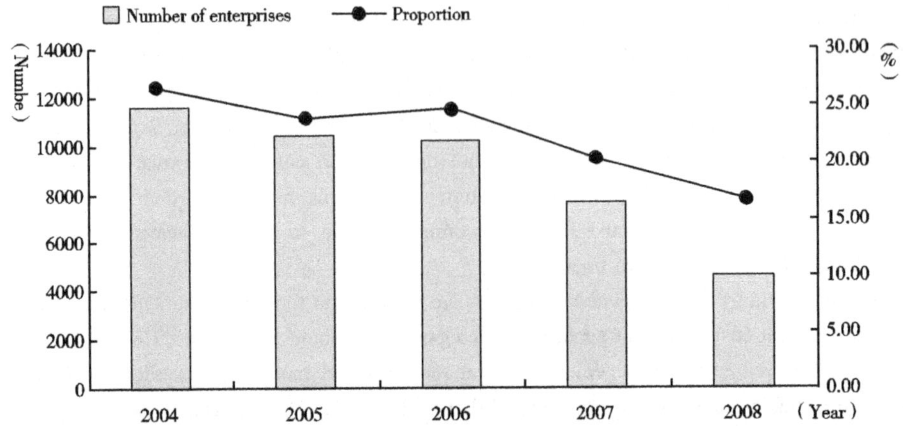

Figure 2-10: Number of newly-approved Chinese-foreign equity joint ventures

Source: China Statistical Yearbook 2005, 2006, 2007, 2008, 2009

In 2007, 7,649 foreign joint ventures set up in China, which accounted for 20.20% of the total foreign-invested enterprises. In 2008, 4,612 foreign joint ventures set up in China, which accounted for 16.17% of the total foreign-invested enterprises, but less than a fifth of enterprises overall.

In 2004, the actual use of foreign capital by foreign joint ventures was USD16,386 billion, which accounted for 27.03% of the total amount of foreign capital actually used by foreign investment enterprises. In 2005, 2006, and 2007, the actual use of foreign capital by foreign joint ventures was USD14,614, USD14.378, and USD15.596 billion, respectively, which accounted for 24.23%, 22.81% and 20.86% of the total amount of foreign capital actually used by foreign investment enterprises. In 2008, the actual use of foreign capital by foreign joint ventures was USD17,318 billion, which accounted for 18.74% of the total amount of foreign capital actually used by foreign investment enterprises. (See Figure 2-11)

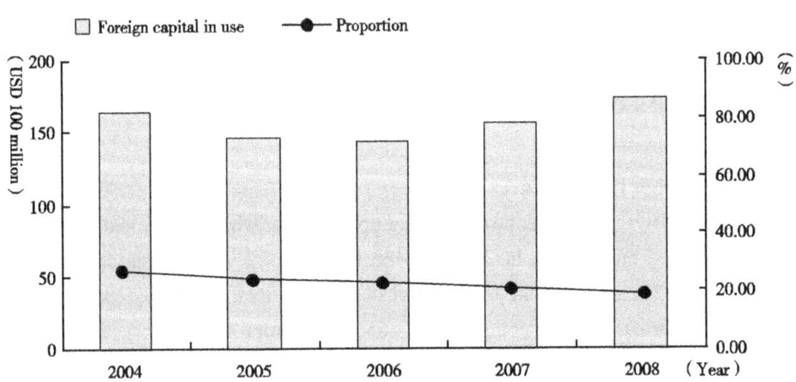

Figure 2-11: Amount of foreign capital in use by Chinese-foreign equity joint ventures and its share in total foreign investment, 2004-2008

Source: China Statistical Yearbook 2005, 2006, 2007, 2008, 2009

In 2004, the average size of foreign investment actually used by foreign equity joint ventures was USD1,416,200, which grew 15.21% over the previous year. In 2005, the average size of foreign investment actually used by foreign equity joint ventures was USD1,394,500, which decreased 1.54% from the previous year. In 2006, the average size of the actual use of foreign investment by foreign equity joint ventures was USD1,406,400, growing 0.86% over the previous year. In 2007, the average size of foreign investment actually used by foreign equity joint ventures was USD2,039,000, an increase of 44.97% over the previous year. In 2008, the average size of the actual use of foreign investment by foreign equity joint ventures was USD3,755,000, growing 84.16% over the previous year. Overall, the average size of the actual use of foreign investment by Chinese-foreign joint ventures experienced an accelerated upward trend over nearly five years. (See Figure 2-12)

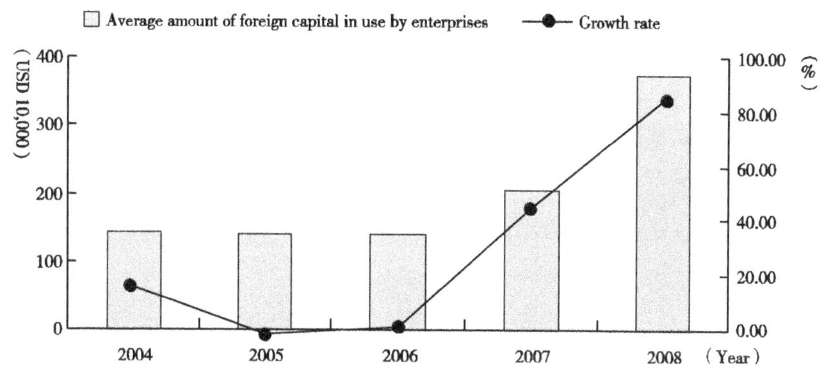

Figure 2-12 The average amount and growth rate of foreign capital in use by Chinese-foreign equity joint ventures, 2004-2008

Source: China Statistical Yearbook 2005, 2006, 2007, 2008, 2009

2.3.2. Chinese-foreign co-operative enterprises

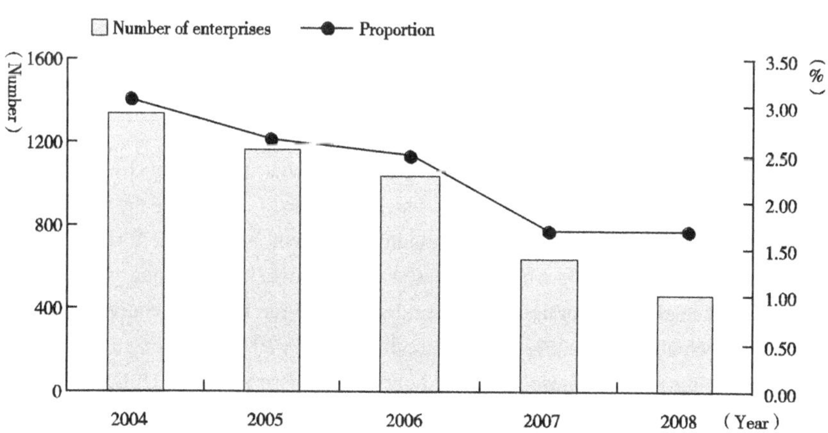

Figure 2-13: Number of newly-approved Chinese-foreign cooperatives and their share in all enterprises with foreign investment, 2004-2008

Source: China Statistical Yearbook 2005, 2006, 2007, 2008, 2009

By the end of 2004, 1,343 Chinese-foreign co-operative enterprises have been set up in China, accounting for 3.08% of the total foreign-invested enterprises. In 2005, 1,166 Chinese-foreign co-operative enterprises set up in China, which accounted for 2.65% of the total foreign-invested enterprises. In 2006, 1,036 Chinese-foreign co-operative enterprises set up in China, which accounted for 2.50% of the total foreign-invested enterprises. In 2007, 641 Chinese-foreign co-operative enterprises set up in China, which accounted for 1.69% of the total foreign-invested enterprises. By the end of 2008, 468 Chinese-foreign co-operative enterprises had been set up in China, which accounted for 1.70% of the total foreign-invested enterprises. (See Figure 2-13)

In 2004, the actual use of foreign capital by Chinese-foreign co-operative enterprises was USD3.112 billion, which accounted for 5.13% of the total amount of foreign capital actually used by foreign investment enterprises. In 2005, 2006, and 2007, the actual use of foreign capital by Chinese-foreign co-operative enterprises was USD1.831, USD1.940, and USD1.416 billion respectively, which accounted for 3.04%, 3.08%, and 1.89%, respectively, of the total amount of foreign capital actually used by foreign investment enterprises. In 2008, the actual use of foreign capital by Chinese-foreign co-operative enterprises was USD1.903 billion, which accounted for 2.06% of the total amount of foreign capital actually used by Chinese-foreign co-operative enterprises. (See Figure 2-14)

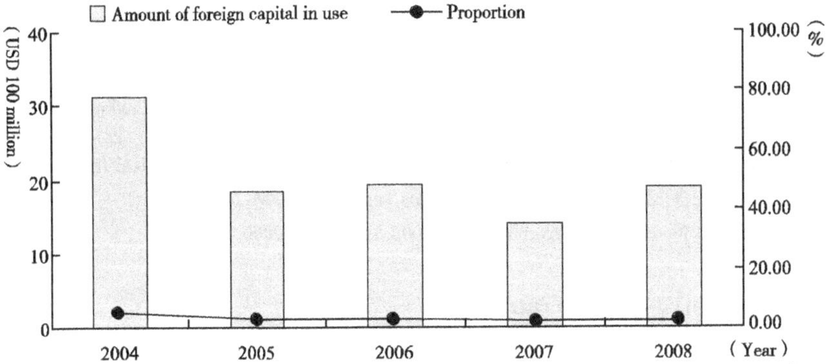

Figure 2-14. Amount of foreign capital in use by Chinese-foreign cooperatives and is share in the total, 2004-2008

Source: China Statistical Yearbook 2005, 2006, 2007, 2008, 2009

In 2004, the average size of the actual use of foreign investment by Chinese-foreign co-operative enterprises was USD2,317,200, which decreased 6.55% over the previous year. In 2005, the average size of actual use of foreign investment by Chinese-foreign co-operative enterprises was USD1,570,300, which decreased 32.23% over the previous year. In 2006, the average size of actual use of foreign investment by Chinese-foreign co-operative enterprises was USD1,872,600, which grew 19.25% over the previous year. In 2007, the average size of actual use of foreign investment by Chinese-foreign co-operative enterprises was USD2,209,000, which grew 17.97% over the previous year. In 2008, the average size of actual use of foreign investment by Chinese-foreign co-operative enterprises was USD4,066,200, which grew 84.07% over the previous year. Overall, the average size of the actual use of foreign investment by Chinese-foreign co-operative enterprises experienced an accelerated upward trend over nearly five years. (See Figure 2-15)

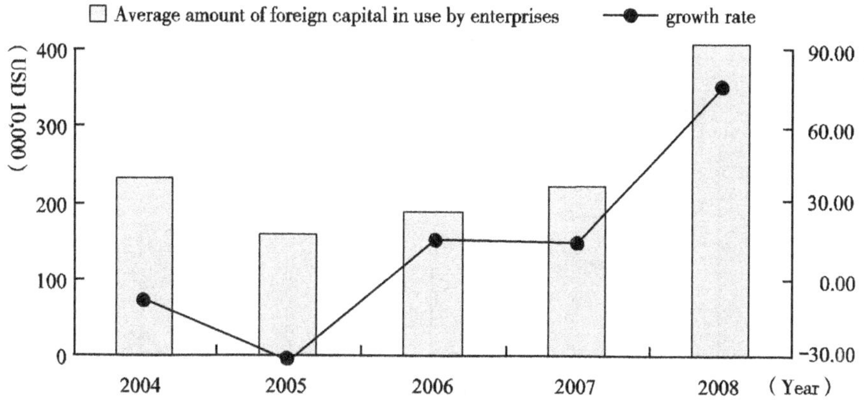

Figure 2-15: Average amount and growth rate of foreign capital in use by Chinese-foreign cooperatives, 2004-2008

Source: China Statistical Yearbook 2005, 2006, 2007, 2008, 2009

2.3.3. Foreign-invested joint-stock companies

In 2004, 41 foreign-invested joint-stock companies have set up in China, which accounted for 0.10% of the total foreign-invested enterprises. In 2005, 2006, and 2007, 47, 50, and 38 foreign-invested joint-stock companies set up in China, which accounted for 0.11%, 0.12%, and 0.10% of the total foreign-invested enterprises, respectively. By the end of 2008, 38 foreign-invested joint-stock companies had set up in China, which accounted for 0.14% of the total foreign-invested enterprises. (See Figure 2-16)

In 2004, the actual use of foreign capital by foreign-invested joint-stock companies was USD777 million, which accounted for 1.28% of the total amount of foreign capital used by foreign investment enterprises. In 2005, 2006, and 2007, the actual use of foreign capital by foreign-invested joint-stock companies was USD 918, USD422, and USD492 million, respectively, which accounted for 1.52%, 0.67%, and 0.66% of the total amount of foreign capital available to foreign investment enterprises. In 2008, the actual use of foreign capital by foreign-invested joint-stock companies was USD859 billion, which accounted for 0.93% of the total amount of foreign capital actually used by foreign investment enterprises. (See Figure 2-17)

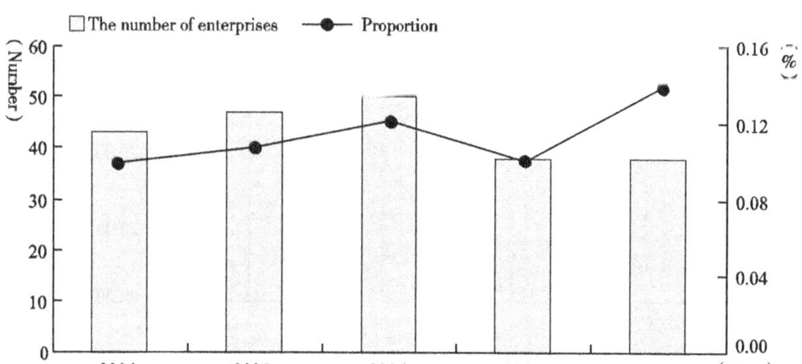

Figure 2-16 Number of newly-approved joint-stock companies with foreign investment and their share in all enterprises with foreign investment, 2004-2008

Source: China Statistical Yearbook 2005, 2006, 2007, 2008, 2009

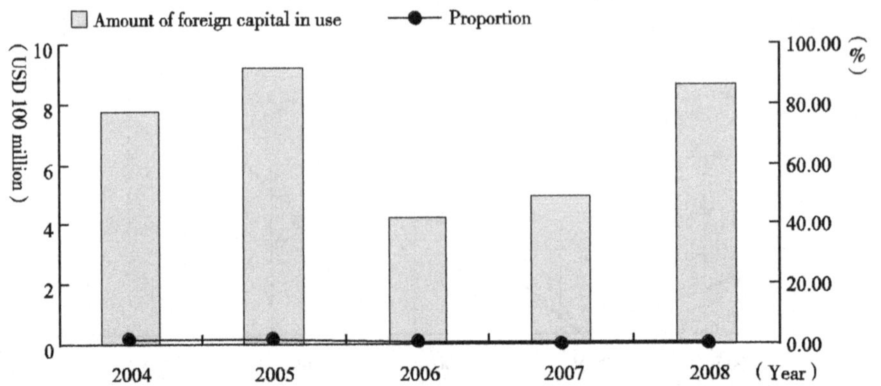

Figure 2-17 Amount of foreign capital in use by joint-stock companies with foreign investment and its share in total foreign capital in use, 2004-2008

Source: China Statistical Yearbook 2005, 2006, 2007, 2008, 2009

In 2004, the average size of the actual use of foreign investment by foreign-invested joint-stock companies was USD18,069,800, which grew 103.84% over the previous year. In 2005, the average size of the actual use of foreign investment by foreign-invested joint-stock companies was USD19,531,900, which grew 8.09% over the previous year. In 2006, the average size of the actual use of foreign investment by foreign-invested joint-stock companies was USD8,440,000, which decreased 56.79% from the previous year. In 2007, the average size of the actual use of foreign investment by foreign-invested joint-stock companies was USD12,947,400, which grew 53.40% over the previous year. In 2008, the average size of the actual use of foreign investment by foreign-invested joint-stock companies was USD22,605,300, which grew 74.59% from the previous year. Overall, the average size of the actual use of foreign investment by foreign-invested joint-stock companies was large, but also experienced large fluctuations over five years. (See Figure 2-18)

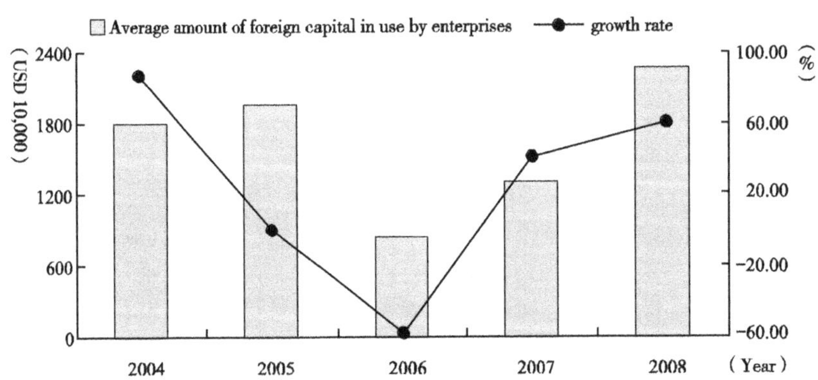

Figure 2-18: Average amount and growth rate of foreign capital in use by joint-stock companies with foreign investment, 2004-2008

Source: China Statistical Yearbook 2005, 2006, 2007, 2008, 2009

2.3.4: Foreign holding enterprises with foreign investment increasingly have an impact on China's economic development

In the process of reform of state-owned enterprises, more and more companies have been opting for the method of joint restructuring. This model of equity cooperation has begun to change in recent years, and the number of foreign-invested enterprises constantly seeking to achieve absolute control or whole foreign ownershipthrough increasing capital and shares has risen correspondingly. If this trend continues to develop without being curbed, it may lead to the loss of part of the absolute controlling position of China's state-owned enterprises in the foreseeable future.

Among foreign-invested enterprises, the increase of foreign-controlled enterprises can benefit foreign-invested enterprises by adjusting business strategies in accordance with domestic economic situation changes and by increasing the use of advanced technology and competitiveness of enterprises, thus promoting the development of China's economy. However, this concurrently changing mechanism and vigor will also bring a series of changes to China's economic development.

Firstly, China's economic control is being challenged. In the modern market economy, fundamental control is established through the implementation of equity control over enterprise under absolute control by the holding party. If a considerable part of state-owned enterprises have been under absolute control by foreigners, then state influence on these enterprises will necessarily be reduced, so will the state's ability to regulate the economy through enterprises.

Secondly, China's capacity for independent innovation is weakened. Once the foreign-funded enterprises have accounted for their absolutely controlling position, they will squeeze out similar Chinese enterprises through advantages in technology, capital, scale, and brand, and will then seize market shares, squeeze their market space, and then dominant the Chinese market. Moreover, in the process of foreign investments gradually becoming dominant, many foreign holding enterprises with foreign investment have asked China to give up their own brands. They will devour a large number of state-owned brands, resulting in a huge loss for state-owned enterprises, and then the market, freed up, will quickly be flooded by foreign brands. Even if individual enterprises achieve technological innovations, their innovations, without exception, belong completely to the controlling party. As such, the capacity for independent innovation by Chinese enterprises has been seriously weakened.

Thirdly, the long-term development and optimization of industrial structures is restricted. Foreign holding enterprises with foreign investments often have a variety of intentions, some focused on business purposes and some on strategic needs, which brings a variety of uncertainty to foreign invested enterprises that are under absolute control by foreigners, so much so that they may even come to gradual end. Similarly, foreign holding enterprises with foreign investment have also had an impact on China's industrial structure, because absolute control strengthens the abnormal development of industry and adversely affects the adjustment and improvement of China's industrial structure.

2.4 Main Conclusions and Policy Suggestions

2.4.1. Main Conclusions

In recent years, setting up wholly foreign-owned enterprises has increasingly become the preferred model for foreign investors. Among the newly established foreign-funded enterprises, the proportion of wholly foreign-owned enterprises has increased while the proportion of Chinese-foreign equity joint venture enterprises and cooperative businesses has remarkably decreased. In 2008, wholly foreign-owned enterprises established by foreign investors occupied 81.40% of the total foreign-funded enterprises, a growth of 11.07 percent compared to 2004.

The actual foreign investment utilized by wholly owned foreign enterprises surpassed that of Chinese-foreign equity joint venture enterprises for the first time in 2000, and the investment for the former has only increased. From the perspective of the absolute amount of foreign investment actually used in different investment models, in 2008, the foreign investment utilized by wholly foreign-owned enterprises reached 72.315 billion dollars, a growth of 79.79% compared to 2004, which experienced the most rapid increase. That of Chinese-foreign equity joint venture enterprises only increased by 5.69%, that of Chinese-foreign cooperatives decreased by 38.85%, and that of foreign-founded stock enterprises increased by 10.55%. From the perspective of the relative amount of foreign investment actually utilized by different investment models, the proportion used by wholly foreign-owned enterprises has gradually increased. In 2008, the actual utilized foreign investment of wholly foreign-owned enterprises reached 72.315 billion dollars, occupying 78.27% of the total, a growth of 11.93 percent compared to 2004, while the proportions of the actual utilized foreign investment for Chinese-foreign equity joint venture enterprises, Chinese-foreign cooperatives, and foreign-founded stock enterprises decreased.

The number of registrations of foreign-invested enterprises in each region shows that, in recent years, the proportion of the registered capital of foreign-invested enterprises is increasing. By the end of 2008, the registered capital of foreign-invested enterprises reached 1300.6 billion dollars, among which, foreign registered capital accounted for 1038.9 billion dollars, occupying 79.88% of the total registered capital (a growth of 3.28 percent compared to 2004).

First, the main reason for foreign investors to establish wholly owned foreign enterprises is that the Chinese system for utilizing foreign investments is becoming more mature. Second, exclusively foreign-owned investments can lower transaction costs. Third, Chinese enterprises are becoming less willing to establish cooperatives with foreign investors. Last, rising awareness of Chinese intellectual property protections offers protection for those exclusively foreign-owned investments.

2.4.2. Policy suggestions

Wholly-owned enterprises and joint ventures are essentially a kind of corporate act, which is determined based on the global tactical goals of foreign-invested enterprises and Chinese markets at different times. As more and more foreign-invested enterprises choose to establish wholly-owned enterprises, domestic enterprises should make choices based on the current situation, change their traditional cooperative models, and choose to establish real strategic partnerships with foreign investors to establish tactical alliances. Such alliances are important for Chinese enterprises in achieving their tactical goals, improving competitiveness, expanding markets, seeking economy of scale, promoting R&D, and reducing operating risk. Domestic enterprises must pay attention to international enterprises, try to seek opportunities to cooperate with multinational enterprises, grasp at opportunities to establish tactical alliances with foreign-invested enterprises, strengthen themselves through cooperation, and study to achieve the goals of turning a unidirectional adoption of technologies and investments to a bidirectional and multidirectional flow of knowledge while turning the imbalance of operational capacity and resources to a balance based on tactical alliances.

The goal of certain multinational enterprises that invest in China is to gain more control over the Chinese market by lowering costs and creating a monopoly. This type of external market penetration has negative effects on the long-term development of the Chinese economy. As the number of foreign-invested enterprises with foreign investors assuming the majority of shareholding increases, the possibility of creating a monopoly by multinational enterprises is also increasing. Therefore, China needs to break the monopoly held by multinational enterprises over the Chinese market through various means, and to reduce or get rid of the country's dependence on multinational technologies by innovating and introducing technologies, speeding up the development of independent brands, and mastering industry initiatives. China should introduce and intensify economic competition and encourage the conglomeration and merger of domestic enterprises in order to form domestic enterprises that can compete with multinational enterprises. China should supervise enterprises that have a monopoly on the Chinese market through antimonopoly laws and the regulation of monopolized activities that affect fair competition. China should make full use of the differences in multinational enterprises' investment motivations, as well as the competition between multinational enterprises, by deepening the divisions between them. China should also seek out various means of introducing investments that are advantageous when introducing investment technologies that undermine the monopoly of multinational enterprises.

In recent years, the proportion of intellectual property rights investments by foreign-invested enterprises has rapidly increased, which is favorable toward expanding the technological spillover effect of foreign-invested enterprises and promoting independent innovation by domestic enterprises. China should further strengthen the management and protection of intellectual property rights, promptly revise intellectual property rights protection laws—including patent, trademark, and copyright—and manage the execution of such laws. China should accelerate the speed at which it revises laws and rules governing the violation of intellectual property rights, and strengthen judicial protections and administrative law enforcement. China should properly define what constitutes intellectual property rights, prevent the violation of intellectual property rights, and protect people's legitimate interests. China should also conduct a variety of educational programs, encourage innovation, carry forward the spirit of sincerity, and criticize plagiarism, copyright pirates, and counterfeiting acts. China should support and encourage enterprises to apply for domestic and international patents for both absorbed and innovative technologies, actively provide patent information and legal services regarding intellectual property rights for enterprises, guide enterprises to use methods of patent retrieval and patent application, consciously protect intellectual property rights, and improve the ability to use the system of intellectual property rights. Based on the above criteria, China should further encourage multinational enterprises to establish R&D institutions in China, to industrialize the technological achievement of foreign-invested R&D institutions in Chinese market, and to transfer technologies to domestic and private Chinese enterprises.

Chapter 3 The Industrial Distribution of Foreign-Invested Companies

China's entry to the WTO has witnessed the rapid increase of foreign-invested companies, which reflects different characteristics of industrial distribution: the increased rate of foreign investment in primary industries is stable; the manufacturing industry attracts the most significant foreign investment, but the rate of increase has slowed; the service industry has become a new area of attraction for foreign investment with a correspondingly rapid growth rate; and certain particular areas, such as real estate, are beginning to play a significant role in attracting foreign investment. From an investment perspective, we can see that more foreign-funded companies have been established at a rapid pace; but though the proportion of joint ventures and Chinese-foreign cooperative companies have increased, their rate of growth has obviously slowed down. Additionally, with the improvement of laws and regulations on foreign mergers and acquisitions, attracting foreign investment through shareholding is expected to expand and develop into the future's most active method of attraction.

3.1 The General Situation of Industrial Distribution

In 2008, there were a total of 27,537 projects with foreign direct investment in China, with an actual use of foreign investment reaching USD 108.312 billion. The primary industry attracted 917 projects, accounting for 3.33% of the total; their actual use of foreign investment reached USD 1.191 billion, accounting for 1.10% of the total. Secondary industries attracted 12,299 projects, accounting for 44.66% of the total; their actual use of foreign investment reached USD '53.256 billion, accounting for 49.17% of the total. Tertiary industries attracted 14,321 projects, accounting for 52.01% of the total; their actual use of foreign investment reached USD 53.865 billion, accounting for 49.73% of the total. Statistics of specific industries show that the industry of agriculture, forestry, animal husbandry, and fishery attracted 917 projects, accounting for 3.33% of the total; their actual use of foreign investment reached USD 1.191 billion, accounting for 1.10% of the total. The mining industry attracted 149 projects, accounting for 0.54% of the total; its actual use of foreign investment reached USD 0.573 billion, accounting for 0.53% of the total. The manufacturing industry attracted 11,568 projects, accounting for 42.01% of the total; its actual use of foreign investment reached USD 49.895 billion, accounting for 46.04% of the total. The industry of producing and supplying electricity, gas, and water attracted 320 projects, accounting for 1.16% of the total; its actual use of foreign investment reached USD1.696 billion, accounting for 1.57% of the total. The construction industry attracted 262 projects, accounting for 0.95% of the total; its actual use of foreign investment reached USD1.093 billion, accounting for 1.01% of the total. The industry of transportation, storing, and mailing attracted 523 projects, accounting for 1.90% of the total; its actual use of foreign investment reached USD 2.851 billion, accounting for 2.63% of the total. The industry of information transmission, computer services, and software attracted 1,286 projects, accounting for 4.67% of the total; its actual use of foreign investment reached USD 2.775 billion, accounting for 2.56% of the total. The wholesale and retail industry attracted 5854 projects, accounting for 21.26% of the total; its actual use of foreign investment reached USD 4.433 billion, accounting for 4.09% of the total. The industry of accommodation and catering attracted 633 projects, accounting for 2.03% of the total; its actual use of foreign investment reached USD 0.939 billion, accounting for 0.87% of the total. The financing industry attracted 48 projects, accounting for 0.17% of the total; the actual use of foreign investment within this industry reached USD 16.490 billion, accounting for 15.22% of the total. The real estate industry attracted 452 projects, accounting for 1.64% of the total; its actual use of foreign investment reached USD 18.59 billion, accounting for 17.15% of the total. Leasing and business services attracted 3138 projects, accounting for 11.4% of the total; their actual use of foreign investment reached USD 5.059 billion, accounting for 4.67% of the total. The industry of scientific research, technology services, and geological investigation attracted 1839 projects, accounting for 6.68% of the total; the actual use of foreign investment within these fields reached USD 1.506 billion, accounting for 1.39% of the total. The industry of water conservation, the environment, and public facility management attracted 138 projects, accounting for 0.5% of the total; its actual use of foreign investment reached USD 0.34 billion, accounting for 0.31% of the total. The industry of residential and other services attracted 205 projects, accounting for 0.74% of the total; its actual use of foreign investment reached USD 0.57 billion, accounting for 0.53% of the total. The education industry attracted 24 projects, accounting for 0.09% of the total; its actual use of foreign investment reached USD 0.036 billion, accounting for 0.03% of the total. The industry of health care, social security, and social warfare attracted 10 projects, accounting for 0.04% of the total; the actual use of foreign investment between these fields reached USD0.019 billion, accounting for 0.02% of the total. The industry of culture, sports, and entertainment attracted 170 projects, accounting for 0.62% of the total; its actual use of foreign investment reached USD 0.258 billion, accounting for 0.24% of the total. The industrial make-up of foreign direct investment shows that there were not distinct changes. The manufacturing industry has made up the largest part of foreign investment, followed by tertiary industries and the primary industry.[2]

3.1.1. Two Changes in the Industrial Distribution of FDI Enterprises in Recent Years

In recent years, China has enjoyed an ever-increasing influx of foreign direct investments in the fields of trade and services, yet the overall level of FDI in these fields is still very low. When compared with manufacturing, they hold a subordinate position, yet investments in the service industry have been increasing annually at a relatively rapid rate. Among all segments of the service industry, foreign investors have historically preferred sectors with lower risks and smaller investments at the initial stage, but recently segments with higher risks and more required up-front investments have been attracting investments at a rate appreciably higher than that of other segments of the service industry. The low percentage of utilized foreign investments in the service industry, accounting for 22% of total investments, is closely related to the low percentage held by the service industry in China's Gross National Product as a whole. The attraction of the service industry to foreign investments is another opportunity for China's economic leapfrogging transition, and the best starting point is by diverting international investment towards services. Differentiated incentives for foreign investments are created according to the different characteristics of trade in services and outsourcing industries, as well as their contributions to

[2]Data quoted above were from research materials from a seminar on the operation of foreign-invested companies in the Finance and Trade Institute under the Chinese Academy of Social Sciences.

China's economy, in order to give them free reign in China's new round of growth. Viewed from its overall structure, FDI worldwide is observably directed towards the service industry, and its dominant strategy has changed from passive to active.

The service industry developed multinational operations following those of the manufacturing industry before the 1980s. After the 1990s, however, the service industry gradually shook off its traditional role as a provider of purely intermediate products, and actively expanded to other fields of service across other segments of the industry. Internally, FDI is mainly concentrated on trade and finance, with significant improvements in the status of other industries such as power generation and distribution, telecommunication, the storage and carrying trade, and enterprise services. Entering the WTO represents a watershed in China's service industry's attracting of foreign investments. Within the country's borders, commercially, over 100 segments of trading services have been opened to foreign investments. These segments have gained momentum in attracting foreign investments, and the total volume as well as their structure has changed significantly. In China, foreign investments in the service industry enjoy the fastest growth rate among all comparable fields of investment. As the service industry is now becoming more knowledge-intensive worldwide, only the countries and regions that develop a knowledge-intensive service industry can profit from already-available FDI and attract further FDI. Taking into consideration the low structural level of China's service industry—traditionally labor-intensive and resource-intensive service industries like catering, commercial retailing, and transportation are still dominant, and modern ones like telecommunication, IT, modern logistics, and finance count for only a very small proportion—it's necessary to vigorously develop modern service industries, transform and improve traditional ones, constantly optimize existing structures, and improve the overall quality along with international competitiveness, both for the sake of China's restructuring of its industries and for attracting more FDI.

Two starting points by which to optimize the industrial structure and its ability to undertake foreign investments are: firstly, to prioritize the development of productive service industries such as information services, modern finance, modern logistics, and e-commerce, and to vigorously develop intermediary service industries like consultancy, law services, and scientific and technological services, as well as to actively develop industries with huge potential demands such as tourism, culture, and sports. These are all knowledge- or technology-intensive service industries, the full development of which is indispensable to a high-level modern service-industrial system with a sound structure. Secondly, it is necessary to take full advantage of all forms of international industrial shifts within service industries. Generally speaking, the international industrial shift has three tiers: project outsourcing, business outsourcing, and foreign direct investments. The specific forms include new investments, mergers and acquisitions, venture capital, etc. The international industrial shift of the service industry is no exception. A favorable political climate should be created to support Chinese enterprises in undertaking international project outsourcing. Relevant departments should provide necessary information and consultancy services for enterprises in China and guide them to play an active role in the international project outsourcing market, undertake outsourced projects, and cooperate effectively with foreign service enterprises. Investors shall be permitted and encouraged to invest through mergers and acquisitions (M&A), and an institutional climate beneficial to attracting M&A investments should be created to provide advantageous conditions for service-providing multinational enterprises participating in enterprises' reorganization and transformation.

In 2008, among China's FDI-attracting models, joint ventures' FDI projects numbered 4,612 and accounted for 16.57% of the total projects with foreign direct investment; of the actual utilized foreign investment, 17.318 billion dollars accounted for 15.99%; Chinese-foreign cooperatives' FDI projects numbered 468 and accounted for 1.70%; their actual utilized foreign investment, USD 1.903 billion, accounted for 1.76%. Foreign businesses' FDI projects, numbering 22,396, accounted for 81.33% of all FDI-attracting models; their actual utilized foreign investment, USD 72.315 billion, accounted for 66.77% of the total. Foreign-invested joint-stock companies' FDI projects, numbering 38, accounted for 0.08%; their actual utilized foreign investment, USD 15.917 billion, accounted for 14.70% of all foreign investment. The trend of a decreasing percentage of joint ventures and cooperative businesses and an increasing number of exclusively wholly foreign-owned enterprises shows a significant change in the investment strategies of foreign traders in China.

Thirty years after China's reform and opening up (改革开放) policies were implemented, the foreign investment environment in China and foreign traders' adaptability to such an environment are becoming more mature. Multinational companies, conforming to the reorganization of foreign investments and a whole new round of strategic layouts are adopting an exclusive investment model to maintain their unique advantages in their respective playing fields. This change reflects the deepening influence of capital and technological progress on foreign investments, and also demonstrates its steady qualitative improvements. In order to conform with this new trend and improve the quality of foreign capital mergers and acquisitions, since 2002, a series of policies have gradually been implemented and relevant regulations issued since. On November 4th, 2002, China issued the Notice of Transferring State-owned Shares and Corporate Shares of Listed Companies to Foreign Traders, opening the door for foreign traders to buy listed companies' non-tradable shares. Interim Provisions for Foreign Investors' Merging and Acquiring Enterprises in China, a symbolic regulation and a breakthrough concerning foreign capital M&A, went into effect on April 12th, 2003. In August 2006, Provisions for Foreign Investors' Merging and Acquiring Enterprises in China was issued. This new provision is an amendment to the Interim Provision of 2003. On one hand, it intensified the approval process of anti-monopoly review; on the other hand, it has more detailed prescriptions for operational procedures of foreign capital M&A, especially for technical details such as the establishment of SPV (Special Purpose Ventures) and transnational share exchanges.

3.1.2. Changes in the Industrial Structure of Foreign Investments and the Transformation of China's Economic Growth Pattern

After 30 years of reform and opening up, China's economic environment has undergone a dramatic change. The average annual income of Chinese people reached 3,000 dollars in 2008, and residents' consumption and production structures have begun fundamentally changing as a result. Accordingly, the demand for foreign investments has changed from focusing on quantity to paying equal attention to both quantity and quality, along with the circulation of capital, including expenditures as the more important of a two-way pattern (expenditures versus income), the absorption of foreign investment, setting up and investing in new enterprises, new businesses, and M&A. Prior to this, attracting foreign investment was primarily quantity-oriented to make up for shortages in capital, but in the future, it shall be structure-oriented—that is, attention will paid to structural factors such as rational industrial flow, regional distribution, and the coordination of foreign investments. As a result, China still needs to vigorously attract foreign investments, yet its change in strategy for introducing foreign capital shall be in accordance with the needs of economic construction, with free choice and rational utilization.

Practices of transnational investments show that developed countries with abundant capital absorb 2/3 of all total transnational investments. The pattern of international capital flow cannot be explained solely by whether or not a country is short of capital supply. Capital flow, as an important indicator of the flow and distribution of all other factors of production, increases the specialization of global value chains along with the international division of labor as more and more factors depends on such a capital flow. Developed countries cannot possibly possess every advantage in all products and value chain processes, which holds doubly true for developing countries. Therefore, the acquisition of all competition factors such as technology, knowledge, management, talented persons and brands, etc., relies on international capital flow.

With a view towards future trends, the utilization of foreign capital still vigorously contributes to China's economic development. But with the change of direction and restructuring of international investments, along with that of the contraction of the domestic economy, other effects and functions of utilizing foreign investment will become more central to development. China's demands for utilizing foreign investments will also change gradually; to be specific, they will change in order to realize the transformation of the economic growth pattern, to improve resource utilization efficiency to ease the constraints on resources, and to reduce pollution and rationally readjust the economic structure. Viewed from the standpoint of the economic development of developed countries and of some developing countries, the rational utilization of foreign capital absolutely contributes to the transformation of economic growth patterns and the restructuring of the economy. When viewed from the experiences of developing economies in Asia, however, simple labor-intensive production and processing that gradually develops towards substitutes for capital-intensive, technology-intensive, and knowledge-intensive ones, is the general rule of industrial growth, and China will resemble this model to a certain degree. During this process, the first important step of utilizing foreign capital is whether this utilization can be well combined with the new task of transforming China's economic growth pattern. Meanwhile, the second most important step at this new stage is whether the country can seize new opportunities, enlarge the utilization of foreign investments within service industry, and quicken the pace of restructuring China's economy along the trend of international investment in service industries.

Addressing these new tasks of China's economic construction in the future, the strategic goals of utilizing foreign investments follow two specific directions: firstly, that of promoting the development of new industrialization; secondly, rapidly developing the service industry and increasing its overall percentage of the economy. These are the strategic goals of utilizing foreign investments and also the direction in which foreign-funded economies develop. New industrialization is a new type of economy with less resource consumption, less pollution and higher factor utilization efficiency. Taking a new road to industrialization is an important way which transforms economic growth patterns and attracts more FDI. As China can now be said to be at the middle and late stages of industrialization, its FDI is mainly in industrial fields, which are unlikely to change in the short term. Foreign funded economies shall serve as a leading role on the new road to industrialization, and a role model for the modernization of industry. Later on, the emphasis of the management of foreign investments shall, on the one hand, combine the characteristics of China's economic system and specific conditions of companies to complete and formulate feasible policies and provisions concerning foreign traders investing through M&A, while also encouraging multinational companies to participate in the reorganization and transformation of state-owned enterprises by different means (such as buying shares and buying asset ownership). Meanwhile, multinational companies can transfer advanced technologies and management experiences to state-owned companies with the goal of promoting their reorganization and transformation. Relevant provisions for foreign-invested and joint-stock companies shall be further amended, provisions for promoting BOT (Build-Operate-Transfer), investment through the transfer of concessions, and foreign-invested companies being listed and issuing shares within or outside borders. Additionally, a comprehensive and multi-tiered utilization of foreign investments shall be performed, with FDI and foreign indirect investments creatively combined together. On the other hand, foreign-invested companies' management models shall be changed and an evaluation indicator system should be established with an emphasis on enhancing supervision in order to improve the quality of foreign investment utilization.

Among all the evaluation indicators, the most important ones are indicators for resource consumption and environment pollution. Considering China's resource shortage, the practice of land-for-investment should be changed, foreign investment projects with economized land utilization should be promoted and encouraged, investments in land units should be increased, foreign traders should be encouraged to increase their investments or stakes in existing companies, and merging and acquiring domestic-funded enterprises should be promoted. Technical documents covering the consumption of water, energy, and rare raw materials used by enterprises should be filed, with measures for rewarding and punishing adopted accordingly in order to guide those foreign-funded enterprises towards taking the lead technologically, while simultaneously pushing all kinds of enterprises—including domestic-funded ones—to keep up. An environmental pollution indicator shall cooperate with existing environmental protection departments, to have further-detailed common indicators, based on established technical testing indicators such as water, gas, etc. and to have specific characteristic indicators for different types of industrial production. Departments of commerce and environmental protection, as well as those of reform and development, shall enhance their cooperation and collective sharing of information in order to reform and perfect the market entry system, perfect the motivating and constraint systems, bring all departments and the society's supervision into full play, and make foreign-invested enterprises the leaders in environmentally-friendly economic growth patterns.

3.2 Distribution and Development Trends of Key Industries

3.2.1. The Distribution of Foreign-Invested Enterprises among Textile and Garment Manufacturing

There is an upstream and downstream correlation among the manufacturing of synthetic textile products, knitwear, woven fabric, and related textile and garment manufacturing. In the years 2005, 2006, and 2007, the numbers of foreign-invested synthetic textile manufacturers numbered 3,858, 3,985, and 3,959, respectively; their registered capital increased from USD 8.501 billion in 2005 to USD 9.901 billion in 2007, an increase of 16.46%; the paid-in foreign capital increased by 30.31% from USD 6.167 billion to 8.036 billion. The number of foreign-invested enterprises of woven fabric were 2,118, 2,210, and 2,166, respectively, in these three years; their registered foreign capital increased by 14.62% from USD 3.391 billion in 2005 to USD 3.886 billion in 2007; disbursed foreign capital, increased by 24.71% from USD 2.578 billion to USD 3.215 billion. The number of textile and garment manufacturing foreign-invested enterprises numbered 15,061, 15,886, and 15,748 across these three years; their registered foreign capital increased by 20.93% from USD 17.080 billion in 2005 to USD 20.652 billion; the paid-in foreign capital increased by 34.04% from USD 12.334 billion to USD 16.532 billion. Viewed statistically, although the number of foreign-invested enterprises was smaller, the volume of foreign capital was increasing by a large margin during this period, showing that the traditional labor-intensive textile industry is still very competitive internationally. It also demonstrates that it has a large margin for profit growth during the process of enterprises' M&A and reorganization, the optimization of regional distribution, and the improvement of product quality. It's still a hot investing field for foreign traders. As the textile industry and manufacturing of textiles and garments, along with shoes and hats, attracted more than 10% of the total foreign investment within the manufacturing industry and provided the majority of employment opportunities, its dominant status within the national economy has not changed. Therefore, it allows for no delay in utilizing foreign investment to upgrade and reform the technology of the historically advantageous textile industry and for enhancing independent brand building and getting rid of outdated production methods.

The readjustment of the textile industry's absorption of foreign investments should conform to the overall requirements of the national readjustment plan for the development and rejuvenation of the textile industry, combining incremental transformation with the readjustment of stock and optimizing the structure of foreign investment in the textile industry. To this end, the *Contents of Outmoded Products and Techniques* was formulated and provisions for foreign investment-absorbing in the textile industry were further detailed according to the *Foreign Investment Guidance Contents*. Industry fields with inefficient production techniques and equipment, such as cotton spinning, woolen spinning, and dyeing, are to be reduced, and the entry of foreign traders, forbidden. Those advanced product manufacturing methods such as the high-tech fiber industry and industrial fabrics shall be included in the encouraged category of foreign investment. For foreign investments in the stock textile industry, the combined governing of "closing, upgrading, and transferring" shall be performed. For industries with heavy pollution and large energy and water consumption, such as viscose and dyeing industries, high standards for entry shall be set, enterprises shall be required to update their technology and clean production, and enterprises that cannot meet such standards shall be closed. Additionally, enterprises shall be encouraged to shift inter-regionally during the process of upgrading their products and technical innovations. China should establish base locations for the production of quality cotton yarn and cotton textiles in its central and western regions and actively encourage those textile services and processing industries to shift their location there.

The trade pattern of having a large import and export volume of foreign raw materials and exported products within the foreign-invested textile industry should be changed, and these processing and trade enterprises shall be stimulated to take root domestically. The brand-name recognition of foreign-invested enterprises should be promoted and the value of textiles increased. Additionally, the export tax rebate policies shall be differentiated from general trade and processing trade exports, with the export of independently-owned brands enjoying preferential tax rebate rates. What's more, in order to accelerate the transformation of foreign-invested enterprises in the textile industry, an increase in the percentage of domestic sales by independently-owned brands and relevant tax reform should be facilitated.

3.2.2. The Distribution of Foreign-Invested Enterprises across the Major Equipment Manufacturing Industry

In general, the equipment manufacturing industry includes many segments, such as the manufacturing of universal equipment, specialized equipment, transport equipment, universal instruments, specialized instruments, etc. This paper selects and analyzes important industries within the broader field of major equipment manufacturing. Among those selected processes are included both the manufacturing of universal equipment using general technologies, and that of the specialized equipment which requires high-tech and intensive capital. By analyzing these fields, we find that foreign investment in equipment industries is mainly concentrated in fields like metal working machinery, specialized equipment for mining, metallurgy, and construction, specialized equipment for the chemical industry, timber and the nonmetal processing industry, the manufacturing of auto mobiles, power transmission and distribution, control equipment, and wires, cables, optical cables, and electrical equipment. Although there is an impressive increase in both the quantity of foreign-invested enterprises and in the volume of capital in high-tech equipment fields like the manufacturing of lifting and transport equipment, medical equipment and appliances, railway transportation equipment, aerospace vehicles, universal and specialized instruments, and the specialized equipment manufacturing of electronic and electrical machinery and for that of environmental protection, its percentage of the total foreign investment across the manufacturing industry is still very low.

The reasons for this foreign investment pattern are numerous. In the late 1990s, against the backdrop of the international industrial shift of equipment manufacturing, system reform, and transformation of China's state-owned companies, foreign investments began a huge round of joint-venture activity. This activity concerned the backbone of China's equipment manufacturing in the form of restructuring and reorganizing state-owned enterprises, which divested quality assets of the state-owned equipment manufacturing industry and gradually resulted in control over shareholding. In addition, as China was blocked out from high-tech fields by developed countries, multinational enterprises tended not to invest in equipment industries with high concision and high-tech out of consideration for technical protections, hence the current foreign investment pattern in China's equipment industry. In recent years, however, along with the easing of the international economic environment and increased foreign investment in China's equipment manufacturing industry, there is a new wave of the merging and acquisition of these enterprises, which tends to display control over shareholding, whole foreign ownership, and high-tech, all of which shall draw the attention of this study.

The *Guidance Contents of Foreign Investment Industries* (amended in 2007) went into effect on December 1st, 2007. Under these regulations, for those domestic enterprises with internationally-advanced technical levels and strong competitiveness, foreign investments are not encouraged. But for foreign investments in high-end equipment manufacturing fields like infrastructure, high-tech industry, and high-end manufacturing processes, for example, foreign investments are encouraged in the form of cooperative and joint ventures in the fields of crawler cranes, the large-set equipment of coal and chemical industries, rail transportation equipment, critical equipment for nuclear power plants of 1 million kilowatts or more, photovoltaic power generation, geothermal power generation, tide power generation, methane power generation, and wind-generating abilities of 1.5 megawatts or more. China shall have a majority share hold in the important fields of designing, manufacturing, and maintaining civil aircraft, designing and manufacturing civil carrier rockets and civil satellites; for the manufacturing of telecommunications equipment, computers, and other electronic devices, such as the ground receiving equipment and critical parts of satellite TV broadcasting, the manufacturing of fiscal cash registers—in short, the industries concerning national economy security—foreign investments are restricted. While developing China's equipment manufacturing industry, foreign traders still play an important role; as a useful supplement to readjusting and rejuvenating the industry, the policies of introducing foreign investments should stress important sectors.

Considering that China's equipment manufacturing industry is highly dependent on the import of key spare parts, which account for 30% of total costs, the industry should focus on promoting manufacturers with spare parts production technologies. China should develop the field of key spare parts and the technical contents that cover common technologies within the manufacturing industry and classify them, such as the structural manufacturing technologies of large-scale casting, forging, and welding, technologies of digital design and manufacturing, smart sensors, precise prototyping and manufacturing, and ultra-precise processing and manufacturing, the application of advanced materials in major projects, and the design and manufacturing of key basic parts and key spare parts. For those purchases of key spare parts and supporting manufacturers' basic parts created domestically, the larger the purchase level, the more favorable the preferential policies.

Apart from the restricted equipment industries in the *Guidance Contents of Foreign Investment Industries*, foreign equipment manufacturers participating in the restructuring and technical reform of China's state-owned equipment manufacturers in the various forms of M&A, asset replacement, equity transaction, and franchised operation are allowed. Differential treatments shall be given to the construction of significant national projects, and bidding enterprises with cooperative or joint-venture backgrounds shall be considered most qualified. Equipment manufacturers investing in China shall be encouraged to make both supporting investments and follow-up investments. With longer industrial chains and more preferential measures, a notable improvement in the basic parts industry will be result.

The enforcement of intellectual property rights protection shall be enhanced, foreign investors' legitimate rights and interests will be protected, and the outsourcing of technical and service-based domestic equipment manufacturers will be encouraged. The integrated innovation of foreign-invested enterprises with organizations such as domestic institutions, universities, and science and technology agents shall be encouraged to improve the ability of systematic technical integration and technical equipment development. Enterprises that develop and manufacture equipment shall be given appropriate compensation for their risks.

3.2.3. The Distribution of the Foreign-Invested Manufacturers of Telecommunication Equipment, Computers, and Other Electronic Devices

Among the manufacturing industries of telecommunication equipment, computers, and other electronic devices, foreign investments are mainly in the manufacturing of telecommunication equipment, TV broadcasting equipment, electronic computers, and electron devices. Viewed statistically, as the domestic enterprises' competitiveness increases day by day in the manufacturing of telecommunication transmission equipment and telecommunication switching equipment, there is a decrease in the volume of foreign investment or paid-in capital. For the manufacturing of entire sets of computers, ancillary computer equipment, electronic vacuum devices, and discrete semi-conductor devices, the number of foreign-invested enterprises is decreasing, yet the actual paid-in capital is increasing. This indicates that small and less competitive foreign-invested enterprises might be washed out from the market with the increasing competitiveness of domestic enterprises and increasingly fierce competition; as for the production of TV broadcasting programs and the manufacturing of transmission equipment, receiving equipment, applied TV equipment, and other TV broadcasting equipment, as they are sensitive products with restrictive policies, foreign investments are also decreasing. For basic parts manufacturing which is high end, with the trend of industrial development and considering that the domestic enterprises lack competitiveness, foreign investments are being shown to have a larger and larger volume of the market, such as in the manufacturing of mobile telecommunication, optoelectronic devices, and other electron devices. This pattern also demonstrates that there is a positive interaction between foreign-invested enterprises and domestic IT manufacturers, and the goal of introducing foreign capital to strengthen China's manufacturing industry of telecommunication and computers has been essentially realized. To reach the goal of pushing forward the development of the electronic information industry through foreign investments, the method for attracting foreign investment should emphasize as follows:

As the three 3G plates of China are compatible with the three internationally popular technologies respectively, and the country's self-acquired TD technology has just begun, the process of attracting investment shall focus on the production of common 3G technologies in order to improve and perfect the industrial chains, whose core product is TD technology, reduce the risk of 3G network development, and encourage and support foreign investments in TD technology and mobile content services.

The construction of a third generation network based on optical fiber communication is becoming the internet's newest growth sector, and the competition within China's network equipment manufacturing industry is becoming increasingly fierce. The production of relevant third generation internet products characterized by high-speed transmission and switching becomes the navigation mark by which to lead the future electronic information manufacturing industry. Therefore, to vigorously attract foreign investments in supporting the manufacture of third generation network equipment for internet communication is the next step for emphasizing foreign investment.

The core of the electronic information industry is still that of key spare parts, so no efforts shall be spared to develop and introduce foreign investments in the manufacturing of integrated circuits, optoelectronic devices, and other electronic devices. Foreign traders' establishing research and development centers and integrators and suppliers of large electron devices investing in China are encouraged, to promote key equipment manufacturing innovation as well as integrated innovation.

3.2.4. Optimizing the Investment Environment and Promoting the Sound Structure, Distribution, and Coordinated Interregional Development of the Manufacturing Industry

China has issued and implemented a series of policies restructuring and redirecting foreign investments since 2007. Among these, three policies stand out, and show a transition in China's foreign investment policies. Firstly, the *Guidance Contents of Foreign Investment Industries* (amended in 2007), which went into effect on December 1st, 2007, clearly guides foreign traders to invest more in the fields of infrastructure, modern agriculture, high-tech industry, high-end manufacturing processes, and the modern service industry by readjusting "encouraged" and “restricted” foreign investment categories. Secondly, the new *Enterprise Income Tax Law,* implemented on January 1st, 2008, unified the tax system for all enterprises, resulting in unified tax law and tax rate, deduction before tax, and tax incentives between domestic-funded enterprises and foreign-funded ones. Additionally, as a component of the implementation of structural tax reductions, value-added tax transition and reform is to be implemented nationwide, allowing enterprises to include their expenses for purchasing the current period’s fixed assets at the taxation base and to permit deductions as an incentive for enterprises’ investments in fixed assets.

Among these measures, the second one is bad news for foreign-invested enterprises, while the third one is beneficial. Yet, both the theories and practices indicate that, when transnational investments enter a certain economy and accumulate to a certain amount and degree, investment motivation will be driven by factors like infrastructure, scientific and technological support, labor quality, industry-supporting capacity, financing conditions, and social stability, and that preferential taxation is no longer the most important factor. Especially for large multinational companies, the most concerning factors during the process of integrated expansion are those of infrastructure, the condition of existing foreign investments, and the degree of industrialization and market capacity. Practices show that preferential taxation may affect medium and small investors, as their operation is mainly within traditional manufacturing industries, with poor technological equipment and a small industrial average profit margin —they are mainly the objects of the industrial shift of developed countries according to international labor divisions. As such, they are sensitive to the preferential taxation of their host countries. The decrease in this type of foreign investment, however, will optimize the structure of the absorption of foreign investments and improve the overall level of introducing foreign investment in the first place.

Before the reform of being able to combine two taxes in accordance with the *Enterprise Income Tax Law*, domestic and foreign-funded enterprises experience an imbalanced income tax rate with preferential policies and tax bases, which, on the one hand, resulted in less competitiveness for domestic enterprises because of the long-term burden, but on the other hand, caused foreign-funded enterprises to lack the motivation to improve and develop their technologies. Viewed from the perspective of the income tax rate, as there are different standards of preferential taxation, deductions before tax, and preferential tax rebates, the actual comprehensive tax rate of foreign-funded enterprises remains around 11%, while that of the domestic ones is anywhere between 20%-24%. With a view towards preferential taxation, foreign-funded enterprises are privileged. For example, foreign-funded enterprises investing in productive fields, energy and infrastructure facilities, and high-tech fields, can enjoy preferential income tax policies that either entail tax exemption for two years and halved tax rates for the next three years, or tax exemption for five years and halved taxes for the next five years, starting from the year they start to profit. For those export-oriented foreign-funded enterprises exporting more than 70% of their output value, their income tax shall be further halved, and there are other preferential policies such as tax rebates for reinvestment by foreign funded enterprises.

Viewed from the tax base, the standard reduction before taxes is also more beneficial to foreign-funded enterprises, and causes an insufficient costs and expenses compensation for domestic ones. For example, the fixed-asset depreciation rate of domestic enterprises is obviously too low, salaries cannot be fully deducted, and the deduction percentage of business entertainment fees, donation expenses, etc. is far less than that of foreign-funded enterprises. In addition, as the preferential income tax policies are applicable to all kinds of foreign-funded enterprises, large amount of foreign investments flow to secondary industries according to the rules of international industrial shift, while the primary industries, which need prompt development—especially infrastructure construction projects with long cycles of return—and the flourishing tertiary industries cannot obtain adequate foreign investment. The final results promises to be that China cannot form a complete industrial chain, being only an international workshop. This developmental model is not good for the transformation and improvement of an economic growth model.

The *Enterprise Income Tax Law* promotes fair competition between domestic and foreign-funded enterprises through the unification of the following four aspects: the unified *Enterprise Income Tax Law* is to be applicable to both types of enterprises; a unified and moderately lowered income tax rate; unified and specialized methods and standards of deduction before tax; and unified preferential taxation policies with a new system of "industrial preferential rules being the main part, and regional preferential rules as supplemental."

(1) The unified enterprise income tax rate is 25%, and there is a five-year transition for those foreign-funded enterprises which previously enjoyed preferential tax policies. Four preferential policy plans were put forward: "preservation, expansion, replacement, and reduction." Preservation is for those enterprises in the fields of agriculture, livestock and fishery, ports, railways, docks, power stations, and water conservation, which can continue to enjoy the tax exemption policy as before. Expansion is for the input of enterprises' research and development; 20% can be allowed to be included in the costs. Replacement is for the halving policy which was only applicable to enterprises within certain high-tech zones; it can be applied everywhere according to the specific industry. Reduction refers to the tax credit of foreign-funded enterprises in the fields of specialized equipment manufacturing related to environmental protection, energy conservation, and safe production.

(2) Former regional preferential policies shall be changed and industrial preferential policy begun. For qualified small enterprises with low profit, the taxation rate shall be reduced by 20%, and for high-tech enterprises supported by the state, reduced by 15%. The preferential taxation for enterprises investing in the fields of environmental protection, energy and water conservation, and safe production is to be expanded. Contents such as enterprises' "incomes from undertaking projects of environmental protection and energy and water conservation" can enjoy tax exemption or reduction. The tax rate levied on the service industry will be reduced from 33% to 25%.

(3) As for regional preferential policies, the two preferential areas—special economic zones and western regions—are preserved, taking into consideration foreign investors' special interests in Hong Kong and Macao and the actual situation of an incomplete investment environment in western regions. Therefore, the combination of two tax rates shows that China's attitude towards foreign investments has changed to emphasize quality. That is, foreign investments are encouraged to flow to high-tech industry, advanced manufacturing, the service industry, and agriculture and environmental protection industries, while entry to projects with heavy pollution and large energy consumption is forbidden. Along with the implementation of the new tax law, the policy of "industrial preferential rules being the main part, and regional preferential rules as supplemental" will absolutely promote a reasonable distribution of quality foreign investments and affect the restructuring of foreign investments— less competitive processing and foreign-funded export enterprises with outmoded technologies and profits, which are earned only through their dependence on preferential tax rates, will have to change their strategies or move elsewhere, or

reposition to enter China's mainland. This will be beneficial to promoting coordinated trans-regional economic development and industrial upgrading. Later on, the perfection of foreign investment policies shall stress following aspects:

For the formulation and implementation of preferential taxation policies, the former preference after tax which only emphasized results shall be changed, and equal attention shall be paid to both results and the process. Preferential practices before and after taxes shall be combined, with indirect preferential policies taking precedence over and being combined with direct methods such as tax reduction and exemptions. Therefore, the preferential taxation process of income tax shall focus on indirect preferential practices of accelerated depreciation, investment tax credit, reinvesting tax exemption, tax deduction, scientific research fees listed as expenses, and withdrawal of technology development funds to stimulate enterprises' initiative of technological reform, development, and innovation, and to promote industrial upgrading and structural optimization. In addition, to encourage foreign-invested enterprises' participating in the capital market and investing through M&A, related stipulations shall be made regarding the tax treatment of capital assets. For example, concerning gains and losses of capital transactions, as foreign-funded enterprises increasingly participate in M&A, the reorganization of state-owned enterprises, and the restructuring of enterprise property rights, capital transactions become enterprises' daily activity. For the consideration of encouraging investments and preventing speculation, the net income acquired from capital transactions of the current period should be included with taxable income and taxed according to the official rate; the losses during capital transactions can only offset gains from capital transactions but not the normal operating profits. If there is a deficit after offsetting with the current gains, the remaining losses can then be offset by the gains made through annual capital transactions.

The current *Provisions for Foreign Investors' Merging and Acquiring Enterprises in China*, as the main legislation and regulation ruling the M&A actions of foreign-invested enterprises, lacks clear operational specifications for many issues deriving from M&A, for example, the M&A objects, the mode of transactions, the settlement of employees, and the handling of debts. It lags behind the operational practices of foreign-invested enterprises' M&A of China's enterprise assets. Therefore, operational methods shall be further specialized and detailed in their legal aspects in order to regulate increasing M&A practices. It is worth considering that foreign investors be endowed with an equal legal status as domestic citizens and legal persons, and thus obtain permission to buy domestic enterprise assets directly. Of course, foreign investors' M&A is unique, and requires the provisions of specialized clauses for its particular issues.

M&A investment practices show that the preferred objects are mainly industries restricted by the *Guidance Contents of Foreign-invested Industries*, especially those industries with great market potential and huge profit margin, and in which foreign investors possess absolute technical advantages, such as automobile, medical, and communication equipment manufacturing. The next most important area of investment in China is the service industry, which is lagging behind those of developed countries in operational theories, management levels, and/or the degree of marketization, such as telecommunication services, wholesale and retailing, finance, insurance, logistics, port and transportation industry etc. When selecting specific target enterprises, those being chosen are usually the quality ones with large domestic market shares, huge development potential, and which serve as a backbone to their respective industries, usually leading listed companies. Consequently, supervision and guidance of foreign investors' M&A should be enhanced to ensure China's control over important strategic industries. Strict review and control mechanisms shall be established for large-scale M&A of these industries to ensure the industrial safety. The determining mechanism of M&A price shall be completed, and foreign investors' M&A through market capital shall be encouraged, as this can ensure a large degree of transparency and fairness, with the price-funding function and the fluidity of listed companies' assets in the capital market. Common international evaluation methods shall be adopted in capital ratings for M&A through a property rights transaction market, with the practice of diverting capital abroad in a disguised form by transferring shares or selling assets at prices obviously lower than the evaluation results to be prohibited.

Exploration for the reform of a value-added tax system shall be furthered according to the development of the economic situation as it continues to change. The current reform is not about the sheer value-added tax of consumption, because it allows only for the deduction of investment in fixed assets such as machinery and equipment. Viewed from the development trend of value-added tax, it's an inevitable choice to include fixed assets investments such as housing and buildings as deductibles, and to permit the deduction of all fixed asset investments. In addition, as the service economy develops, the decision makers shall see the needs of enlarging the coverage of value-added tax. Including service industries such as transportation, wholesaling, retailing, catering and lodging, etc. in the taxation fields of value-added tax is beneficial for enlarging the absorption of foreign investment into service industries and to raising the level of China's service industries.

3.3 The Trends of Distribution and Development within Key Service Industries

With a view towards its overall structure, FDI worldwide is obviously diverted into the service industry, and its dominant strategy has changed from being passive to active. Before the 1980s, the service industry had developed multinational operations following the manufacturing industry. After the 1990s, however, the service industry gradually shook off its traditional role as a provider of purely intermediate production inputs and actively expanded to other service fields across other segments of the industry. FDI in the service industry accounts for more than 50% of global direct investments. Internally, FDI mainly concentrates on trade and finance, with a significantly improved status across other industries such as power generation and distribution, telecommunications, the storage and portage trade, and enterprise services. The M&A of multinational companies in the service industry is increasingly active with the intent of gaining diversified operation advantages. For example, multinational banks not only provide capital for multinational companies in the manufacturing industry, but also provide advisory opinions regarding capital turnover and settlement, foreign exchange market conditions, production, and operations within the system. Apart from auditing, accounting firms combine the services of management consultancy, market research, and market PR.

Foreign investments in the service industry account for a small part of the total investment. Especially when compared with manufacturing, FDI in the service industry holds a subordinate position, yet investments in the service industry have been increasing annually at a rather rapid rate. Among all segments of the service industry, foreign investors preferred segments with lower risks and less investment at the initial stage, but segments with higher risks and more investments have increasingly been attracting investments at a higher rate than that of other segments of the service industry. Entering the WTO is a watershed in China's service industry's attracting of foreign investments. The total volume, as well as the structure, of the economy has changed significantly; in China, foreign investments in the service industry enjoy the fastest growth among all fields of investment, and may eventually replace the manufacturing industry and become the main field attracting foreign investments. However, with the change of directions and structure of international investments, as well as that of the principal contraction of the domestic economy, other effects and functions apart from foreign investment's role in forcefully promoting economic development will increasingly be seen. China's demands for the utilization of foreign investments will also change gradually, such that the percentage of the service industry's attracting of foreign investments will continue to increase.

3.3.1. The Distribution of Major Productive Service Industries and the Real Estate Industry

Viewed from the internal structure of the service industry's utilization of foreign investments, and as the service industry and manufacturing industry' demonstrably indicate a trend of becoming more high-end and precise, there are increasing demands for specialized productive services. Additionally, there is also a huge increase of foreign investments in knowledge-intensive productive service industries such as financial insurance and technical services. It is agreed that modern service industries' attracting of foreign investments in productive service industries are to be encouraged, and that the transformation and upgrading of the traditional service industries shall be advanced. The structure of those foreign investments preferring manufacturing industries will change gradually, and modern knowledge-intensive service industries will become important fields to which to direct FDI.

Considering the regions in which significant foreign investments in productive service industries can be observed, regional concentration is prominent. That is, productive service industries mainly provide services for producers, and their locations are correspondingly close to manufacturing industry centers. Currently, the regions of high concentrations of manufacturers are mainly along the Yangtze River Delta area centered on Shanghai, the Pearl River Delta centered on Guangzhou, and the Bohai Economic Zone centered around Beijing and Tianjin. Therefore, foreign investments in productive service industries are mainly Guangzhou-centered, Shanghai-centered, Beijing-centered, and Tianjin-centered. Important sectors of productive service industries are selected and analyzed in this sector from the national level. Analysis of their regional distribution, however, will be in the next chapter.

By analyzing relevant statistics, we can see that, following the transition period of entering the WTO in 2005, there has been a strong growth momentum in the service industries, especially the productive service industries' attracting of foreign investments. Although their overall volume is still small, they continue to increase exponentially. Among these industries, especially those concerning computer services, there is a rapid growth in computer system services and data processing; basic software services, application software services, and system integration services in the software industry are also enjoying rapid growth. As the distribution sector of the logistics industry, the wholesaling industry is attracting an increasing number of foreign investments, among which, the wholesaling fields of textiles, garments and articles for daily use, mine products, construction materials and chemical products, mechanical equipment, hardware, and electronic products are hot foreign investment fields.

In the commercial service industry, many segments have performed excellently when attracting foreign investments, however, negative investment growth can nevertheless be observed in legal services and travel agencies, showing an acclimation fever because of differences in the legal system. On the other hand, it shows the slow pace of international operations among China's enterprises, resulting in inadequate demand for international legal services for multinational operations. What's more, the total scale of intellectual property rights services and employment agencies is small and obviously lagging behind that of other commercial service industries in terms of growth rate. The lack of foreign investments in this field shows that China's enterprises have yet to become aware of intellectual property rights protection, and that they have very indifferent attitudes towards integrating global human resources to improve competitiveness, both of which are impassable thresholds for the country's enterprises becoming multinational industries that are able to compete on a global scale.

3.3.2. The Constraints on China's Service Industries' Ability to Attract FDI

Knowledge-intensive direct investments have not only become the main recipient of international direct investments, but also the main direction of direct investment trends within service industries. According to the industrial characteristics of direct investments in international service industries, only host countries with highly developed, knowledge-intensive service industries can attract more FDI. China has a comparatively poor structure set up that features service industries with low levels of development, with traditional service industries remaining dominant and each branch of the service industry featuring low technology. They are mainly labor-intensive or resource-intensive, with catering, retailing and transportation etc. accounting for 40% of all services. The proportion of modern service industries overall, however, is too low, with telecommunication services, IT services, modern logistics, and modern finance accounting for less than 30%. Therefore, compared with the trend of international direct investment in service industries, China's structure and level of development within various service industries is underdeveloped, making it difficult to garner international direct investment.

The following two indicators can be used to measure the level of openness among direct investments: first, the number of multinational enterprises that enter as investment subjects, and second, the contribution rate of international direct investments to domestic industries. By 2006, most of world's top 500 companies had set up headquarters or branches and invested in China. Viewed from industrial distribution, more than 60% of investments flow to the manufacturing industry, followed by infrastructure and the real estate industry. Meanwhile, the service industry, though enjoying rapid growth since the 1990s, accounts for only 6% of investments.

Concerning the contribution rate, the importance of international direct investments in China's economy is increasingly prominent. Still, international direct investments contribute more to the secondary industry than they do to the service industry. The level of globalization and degree of openness to the outside world of China's secondary industries are obviously higher than those of the service industry. The comparatively lower openness level of the service industry imposes constraints on attracting international direct investments. What's more, among service industries, imbalances occur between different segments. The real estate industry, being the most open segment, has a level of openness level around 0.3%, and its contribution rate to the openness level of the service industry is around 50%; the next most open being leasing and the commercial services industry, with an openness level around 0.17%. Other fields like scientific research, technical services, geological investigations, water conservation, environment and public facilities management, resident services and other service industries, education, the health industry, social security and social welfare, culture, PE and the entertainment industry, public management, and social organizations, have openness levels between 0.003% and 0.012%. All of these clearly show a low level of openness and an imbalanced structure.

Institutional factors mainly consist of the following aspects: (1) although the monopoly in the service industry is gradually being broken, certain barriers to entry still exist, especially in those state-owned enterprises where reform progress is slow, with little vitality. (2) Under the pressure of settling surplus employees, many companies keep some service activities internal that would better be done by specialized services. (3) The constraints on the rural population migrating to cities lead to low levels of urbanization and inadequate demands for service industries. Comparing all forms of service expenses, rural expenses are far less than urban ones, as it's generally known that consumption of service is positively correlated with income. The structure of urban and rural populations, people's income, and correlated consumption conditions demonstrably affect the consumption expenses of service industries, and as a result, the attraction of international direct investments to service industries. The lagging urbanization of rural areas has imposed constraints on China's ability to attract international direct investments to service industries.

Additionally, foreign investments flowing into different industries are a result of the combined influence of both the basic investment environment and the policy environment of the government. The view that non-material production does not create new values has long affected China, and China has, as a result, paid inadequate attention to service industries while formulating industrial development policies. The trend of fiscal policy, tax policy, credit policy and other relevant policies preferring the manufacturing industry to the service industry still exists. Specifically regarding the policies of attracting international direct investment, governments of all levels have issued more preferential policies for investments in the manufacturing industry than for service industries, influenced by the following two views: first, that multinational manufacturers have a more mature marketing network, which makes for easy sale of their products on the international market and possesses the capacity for improvement to earn foreign exchanges through export; second, that an investment in the manufacturing industry can extend the industrial chains and promote the development of related industries while increasing employment.

In recent years, China has issued laws and regulations related to investments in its service industries such as the *Maritime Law*, *Law on Commercial Banks*, *Insurance Law*, *Civil Aviation Law, Law on Certified Public Accountants*, *Law on Lawyers*, *Advertising Law*, and *Regulations on Administration of Foreign-Capital Financial Institutions*, under the guiding principles of the *Foreign Trade Law* and similar regulations. These laws play an important role in building an open and unified investment system within the country's service industries. The main focus is on orderly competition and standardized regulation that truly adapt to the country's socialist market economy and common international rules. But China lacks laws specially issued for direct investments in service industries and a unified basic law on the service trade that includes international direct investments in service industries; there is no complete legislation for investments in certain important segments such as tourism and telecommunications. Related stipulations are only present in laws such as the *Joint Venture Law* and *Wholly Owned Enterprise Law*, so a complete legal system is yet to be built.

The formation and development of China's laws concerning foreign investments took a long period of time. Some of them, limited by their respective legislative background, are general, abstract, and deficient in their practical operability. Also, there are no necessary rules and specific individual regulations for their implementation. Additionally, provisions for foreign service industries in China are few. Some provisions are mainly shown as regulations with low levels of legislation, which affects the unification and transparency of laws. Some rules are far different from those of common, comparable international economic and trading rules.

As the service industry has become an important field for international direct investments worldwide, the standardization of the service industry has gradually become an increasingly important subject. In 1998, ISO and the WTO organized symposiums on this subject in various parts of the world and began to prepare for the research into and formulation of service standards, which have become important guarantees for internationalization of service. The standardization of service helps producers to regulate their service quality with unified standards, which reduces repetitive mistakes, reduces costs, and increases competitiveness. As a result, the fact that international standards such as IOS have not been universally adopted in China lessens the attraction of the Chinese market to international direct investments.

3.3.3. The Direction and Trend of the Service Industry's Increasing Efforts towards Attracting FDI

Improvement of the domestic service industry's structure and ability to utilize international direct investments shall be undertaken in the following two aspects: first, to prioritize the development of productive service industries that support the efficient operation of national economy (such as information services, modern finance, modern logistics, e-commerce, etc.), and to vigorously develop intermediate service industries (such as consultancy, legal services, and technical services). Only when these industries are fully developed can a sound structure and system for service industries be formed. Second shall be to take full advantage of all forms of international industrial shifts of the service industry. Generally speaking, the ongoing international industrial shift has three tiers: projects outsourcing, business off-shoring, and FDI, which are concretely measured in new investments, M&A, and venture capital, among other methods. That of the service industry is no exception. A favorable policy climate shall be created to support Chinese enterprises' undertaking of international project outsourcing. Relevant departments shall provide necessary information and consultancy services for enterprises in China and guide them to play an active role in the international project outsourcing market, undertake outsourced projects, and cooperate effectively with foreign service enterprises. Investors shall be permitted and encouraged to invest through mergers and acquisitions, and an institutional climate beneficial for attracting M&A investments shall be created to provide advantageous conditions for multinational enterprises within service industries to participate in enterprises' reorganization and transformation. To achieve this, a platform for attracting international direct investments must be set up; subsequently, channels for international direct investment shall be cleared to provide a practical way for attracting FDI. Only in this way can the industrial structure of China's domestic service industry be improved along with its ability to undertake international direct investments in the service industry.

The service industry's attracting of international direct investment is a systematic project, depending not only on the attraction of the object industries (enterprises), but also on the overall investment environment in China, which involves not only a commitment to the opening of the service industry market, but also to the domestic economic environment. A commitment to a real open service industry market requires not only the formulation of laws and regulations that conform to the *General Agreement on Trade in Service* and are beneficial to the openness of the market, but also formulation of a method by which to practically implement such rules and operable implementing measures. More importantly, the effective implementation of these regulations must be paramount.

As for the domestic economic environment, under certain economic conditions, the determining factor of whether or not foreign investment will be injected into the market is the free competition of object industries, that is, whether there are restrictions for free entry and the extent entry limits. China has fulfilled its commitment under WTO negotiations to opening the service industry market. The expanded, increasingly-open fields include not only industries that have already attracted many investments (such as finance, insurance, trade, retailing and real estate, etc.), but also includes ones with lower degrees of openness (such as communications, the exhibition industry, tourism, and specialized commercial services).

There is higher demand for an environment that attracts international direct investments in China's service industry. Therefore, concerning the construction of legalities regarding how to attract foreign investments. First of all, specialized legislation for FDI should be enacted in conformation to the opening process of the service industry, and the legal system completed. Secondly, for those laws and regulations that lack operability, necessary rules for implementation and clear, supporting individual regulations shall be formulated. Besides, taking into consideration that the level and quality of many services cannot be predetermined and can only be shown during the service process itself, the establishment and completion of industrial standards and operative norm shall be accelerated. The formulation and implementation of technology standards and technical specifications, the establishment of a credit rating system, and the formulation of service standards shall be accelerated, and the certification of International Standard Organization (ISO9000 Series) should be vigorously promoted.

In order to begin constructing a market environment, administrative monopoly over service industry fields like education, the health industry, social security, municipal infrastructure facilities, and urban management shall be broken, while diversified investment subjects should be introduced to improve their development. Secondly, for industries that are essentially monopolistic in nature, such as telecommunications, finance, insurance, railway transportation, and TV broadcasting, reforms shall be advanced and completed, except for those industries related to national security and thus necessarily monopolized by the government.

A favorable investment foundation is the precondition for attracting international direct investments to the service industry. Generally speaking, the basic conditions for service industry investments include two aspects: hardware facilities and a solid software foundation. The former refers to the acquirability of transportation and communication, internet, water, and land resources, which provide facilities for investments. The latter refers to factors such as talented persons, technologies, and an environment of fair competition, which improves efficiency of an investment. Advanced and complete facilities are necessary conditions for attracting foreign investments, while excellent and efficient software foundation makes are appealing to foreign investors. For the purpose of attracting more international direct investments to China, the construction of infrastructure facilities and an investment foundation should be improved. Therefore, more social resources shall be guided to infrastructure facilities needed by the service industry, especially in rural areas and China's underdeveloped central and western regions, to form a convenient network of national transportation, communication, and internet. The education of all talented persons needed to develop the service industry shall be accelerated; the institutions of higher learning and secondary vocational schools shall be guided according to plans to readjust and add majors currently lacking in the service industry and enhance vocational training to improve the quality of service industry employees. What's more, professional personnel from overseas are to be encouraged to work in China, while the professional qualification system shall be comprehensively promoted and a professional qualification standard system for service industry should be established.

Firstly, in order to deepen the reform of enterprise, both "large and inclusive" and "small and inclusive" enterprises shall be transformed into ones that are more specialized, those former internal services shall be transferred outside, that is, to transfer some functional departments and business outside and utilize those companies that are more professional and specialized to increase productive service expenses. For example, specialized service industries such as legal services, accounting and auditing, marketing service industries such as advertising, market research, and consultancy, and technical service industries such as R&D and product design should be treated in this manner. Secondly, to increase residents' income and to improve their ability to increase service consumption should be a goal. Thirdly, these measures should foster increased consumption of service products that fits the general rules of consumption development, for example, consumer electronics and communication devices, auto mobiles, houses, insurance, and educational financing increase as the consumption structure of residents, especially the urban ones, changes. Fourthly, to accelerate the urbanization process, urban areas where service consumption is concentrated and where there is rapid development of urbanization will absolutely push the increase of consumption of services.

The service industry's attracting of foreign investments is another opportunity for the leapfrogging transformation of China's economy, and the international shift in outsourcing services is the ideal point from which to start the process. According to the UNCTD (United Nations Conference on Trade and Development), the global services outsourcing market exceeded 350 billion dollars in 2006, the main fields of which included commercial services, computer and related services, films and culture, Internet-related services, and all kinds of specialized services. As a result, in recent years many countries have prioritized the opening up and development of the service industry, especially the undertaking of global service outsourcing. In 2006, the fields witnessing the most rapid growth in the actual utilization of foreign investments were the service industry, public management and social organizations, residential and other services, transportation and storage, postal services, retailing and wholesaling, and leasing and commercial services, all of which combined utilized 30% of all actual foreign investments. The percentage of foreign investment in scientific research and technical services, geological investigation, information transmission, computer services, and the software industry exceeded 10%. In the fields of software, data processing, commercial agencies, the making, designing, and R&D of cartoons, there were also quite a number of outsourced international services. Therefore, different incentives should be given to foreign investors according to the characteristics of their respective services and service outsourcing industries, as well as their contribution to China's economic development, in order to give them full reign of the new round of economic growth in China.

Chapter 4 The Geographical Distribution of Foreign-Invested Enterprises

Since 2011, the geographical disparities in the distribution of foreign-invested enterprises in the eastern, central, and western areas of China have continuously decreased. The eastern area remains the major focus of foreign investment, yet it is beginning to indicate an economic slow-down; the central area is actively and vigorously attracting foreign investment; while the western area, though developing rather steadily across the board in the attraction of foreign investment, has witnessed a rapid growth in some of its provinces and regions in particular. As regards foreign-invested industries, the eastern area is undergoing the most rapid growth in manufacturing and services industries, with an eye-catching trend of growth in high-end manufacturing and in-depth services; the central area is attracting the majority of its foreign investment in industries of resources-dependent manufacturing and producer services; while the manufacturing industry of the western area attracts foreign investment mainly in resource-intensive industries. One thing worth paying attention to is that the central and western areas have failed to reach their projected growth in foreign-invested, labor-intensive manufacturing. On the one hand, it indicates the improved structure of newly-added foreign investment in China in recent years; and on the other, it means that the transfer of foreign-invested, labor-intensive manufacturing enterprises from the eastern area to the central and western areas has been impeded.

4.1 The Distribution Pattern of Foreign-invested Enterprises in China's Eastern, Central, and Western Regions

By 2008, 355,064 foreign-invested enterprises had been registered in the eastern area, with USD863.9 billion registered in foreign capital; 50,527 foreign-invested enterprises had been registered in the central area, with USD93 billion registered in foreign capital; and 29,110 foreign-invested enterprises had been registered in the western area, with USD47.6 billion registered in foreign capital.

4.1.1. The Industrial Distribution of Foreign-Invested Enterprises in the Eastern Area

According to changes in the number of foreign-invested enterprises and the amount of their investment in all three industries, the primary and secondary industries of the eastern area have a steadily-decreasing share of overall investment in terms of the number of foreign-invested enterprises, registered capital, and paid-in capital, while the tertiary industries are becoming a fast-growing key sector for attracting foreign investment. With increasing industrialization in the eastern area and the apparent trend of industrial structure optimization, the development of the service industry serves as a new boost to economic growth for the eastern area.

According to the structure of foreign-invested enterprises within the secondary industry, manufacturing is the most important sector that attracts foreign investment, within which it is labor-intensive manufacturing industries that are reporting a secure but steadily-decreasing share. From 2005 to 2007, the paid-in foreign capital of the textile industry registered USD 14.284

billion, 16.745 billion, and 18.718 billion, respectively, accounting for 5.73%, 5.78%, and 5.34% of the total paid-in capital of those years; the paid-in foreign capital of apparel, shoes, and hat manufacturing reached USD 14.345 billion, 16.296 billion, and 19.028 billion, respectively, accounting for 5.76%, 5.63%, and 5.43% of the total manufacturing industry. Heavy chemical industries, such as chemical raw materials production and chemical products manufacturing, reported an increasing share. From 2005 to 2007, their paid-in foreign capital reached USD 16.329 billion, 20.399 billion, and 24.872 billion, respectively, accounting for 6.56%, 7.04%, and 7.09% of the total investments in manufacturing industries.

Most equipment industries—general equipment manufacturing excluded—have an increasing share of foreign investment. In the years from 2005 to 2007, general equipment manufacturing took in paid-in foreign capital amounts of USD 14.989 billion, 13.772 billion, and 17.757 billion, respectively, accounting for 6.02%, 4.75%, and 5.06% of the total across all manufacturing industries. As for special equipment manufacturing, paid-in foreign capital amounts of USD 8.956 billion, USD 10.945 billion, and USD 14.029 billion have been reached, accounting for 3.60%, 3.78%, and 4% of the total in manufacturing industries for those years. Transportation equipment manufacturing attracted paid-in foreign capital amounts of USD 14.527 billion, 18.467 billion, and 23.349 billion from 2005 to 2007, accounting for a respective share of 5.84%, 6.37%, and 6.66% of the overall total. Electrical installations and equipment manufacturing attracted paid-in foreign capital of USD 16.281 billion, 18.776 billion, and 23.431 billion from 2005 to 2007, accounting for a respective share of 6.54%, 6.48%, and 6.68% of the total. Communications equipment, computer manufacturing, and other electronic equipment manufacturing attracted paid-in foreign capital of USD 46.286 billion, 56.763 billion, and 70.181 billion from 2005 to 2007, accounting for a respective share of 18.58%, 19.59%, and 20.02%. (See Figure 4-1)[3]

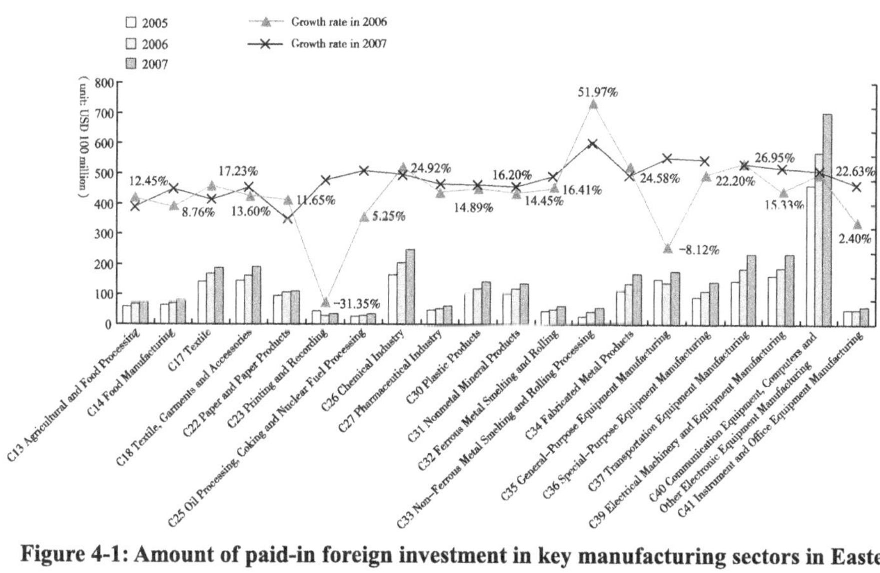

Figure 4-1: Amount of paid-in foreign investment in key manufacturing sectors in Eastern China and changes in growth rates, 2005-2007

Foreign-invested enterprises in the tertiary industry have displayed three major features in terms

[3] Statistics in this article are drawn from the research materials of the Foreign-Invested Enterprises Operation Group under the Institute of Finance and Trade Economics, CASS. Statistics cited below are from the same source.

of internal structure. The real estate industry holds the largest share. It has attracted paid-in foreign capital of USD 38.606 billion, 50.104 billion, and 78.959 billion from 2005 to 2007, accounting for a share of 35.63%, 34.94%, and 38.42%, respectively, of the total paid-in investment in the tertiary industry. Leasing and commercial services are second, attracting paid-in foreign capital in the amounts of USD 23.856 billion, 28.026 billion, and 38.134 billion from 2005 to 2007, accounting for a respective share of 22.02%, 19.55%, and 18.56%. These enterprises are followed by information transmission, computer services, and the software industry, which claim paid-in foreign capital of USD 9.735 billion, 20.921 billion, and 27.077 billion from 2005 to 2007, accounting for respective shares of 8.99%, 14.59%, and 13.18% of the total. Transportation, warehousing, and postal services rank fourth, with paid-in foreign capital of USD 11.193 billion, 14.546 billion, and 19.494 billion from 2005 to 2007, accounting for respective shares of 10.25%, 10.14%, and 9.49% of the total. Wholesaling and retailing represent the fifth largest share, with paid-in foreign capital of USD 9.62 billion, 12.177 billion, and 18.454 billion from 2005 to 2007, accounting for a respective share of 8.88%, 8.49%, and 8.98% of the total. (See Figure 4-2)

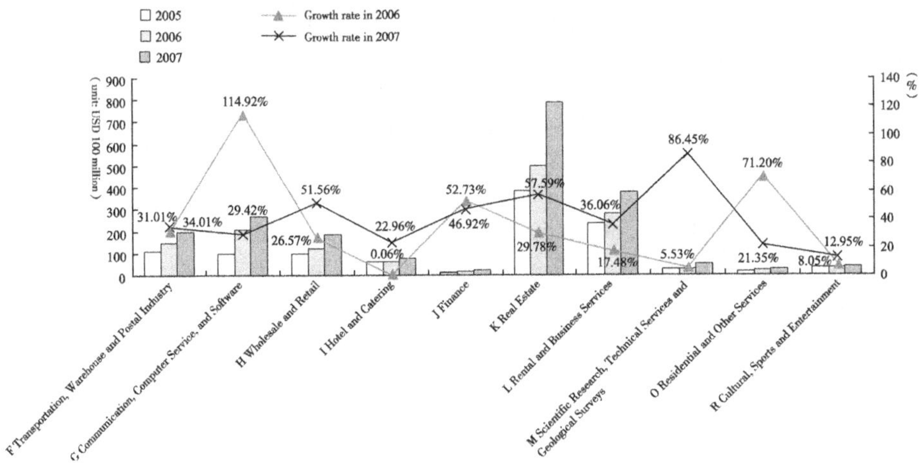

Figure 4-2: Amount of paid-in foreign investment in key service industry sectors in Eastern China and changes in growth rates, 2005-2007

In order to analyze those foreign-invested enterprises in eastern provinces and cities, Figure 4-3 displays the changes in the amount and share of registered foreign capital from 2003 to 2007. We can observe from Figure 4-3 that the share of registered foreign capital in Beijing, Jiangsu, and Zhejiang has increased from 7.81%, 9.46%, and 6.63% in 2003 to 8.93%, 19.90%, and 8.89%, respectively, in 2007, whereas the share of that in Shanghai and Guangdong has dropped from 19.46% and 29.65%, respectively, in 2003 to 15.55% and 23.33% in 2007. Regarding the classification of sectors, Beijing, Shanghai, Guangdong, and some other provinces and cities have been steadily dropping in terms of their share of the manufacturing industries in the eastern area, whereas that of Jiangsu, Zhejiang, Tianjin, and Shandong has been continuously on the rise. The registered foreign capital of the service industry in Shanghai and Guangdong has been declining in terms of the share in the eastern area, while that of Beijing, Jiangsu, Zhejiang, Tianjin, and Shandong has been increasing.

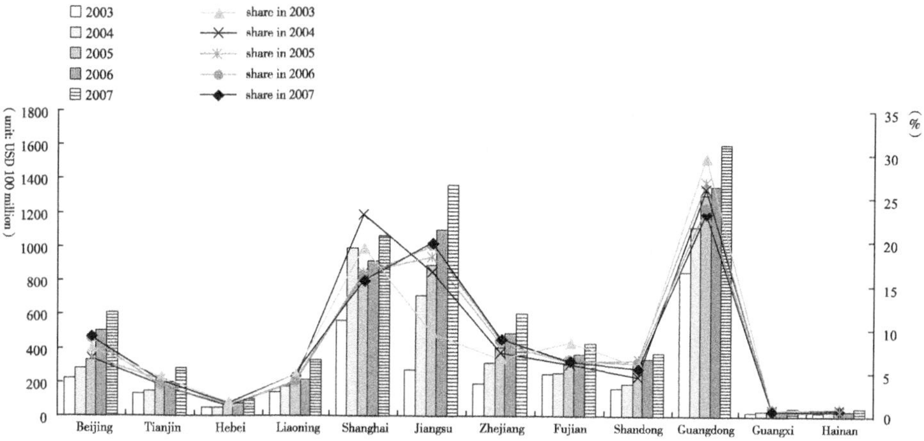

Figure 4-3: Amount of registered foreign capital in Eastern China and changes in growth rate, 2003-2007

4.1.2. The Distribution of Foreign-invested Enterprises in the Central Area

In terms of the distribution of foreign-invested enterprises in the central area, the share of labor-intensive manufacturing has continuously been on the rise among all the foreign-invested enterprises in the secondary industry. To take the period of time between 2005-2007 as an example, farm and non-staple food processing industries have attracted paid-in foreign capital of USD 0.77 billion, 1.056 billion, and 1.665 billion from 2005-2007, respectively, accounting for 4.6%, 5.27%, and 6.4% of the total amount attracted by the manufacturing industry as a whole. Food manufacturing has attracted paid-in foreign capital of USD 0.801 billion, 1.145 billion, and 1.273 billion, accounting for 4.79%, 5.71%, and 4.89%, respectively, of the overall total. The textile industry has attracted paid-in foreign capital of USD 0.568 billion, 0.778 billion, and 0.859 billion, accounting for 3.39%, 3.88%, and 3.3% of the total. Apparel, shoes, and hat manufacturing have attracted paid-in foreign capital of USD 0.427 billion, 0.568 billion, and 0.784 billion, accounting for 2.55%, 2.84%, and 3.01% of the total.

The heavy chemical industry reported an increased share from 2005 to 2007: chemical raw materials production and chemical products manufacturing has attracted paid-in foreign capital of USD 1.098 billion, 1.331 billion, and 1.691 billion, respectively, accounting for 6.56%, 6.64%, and 6.5% of the total of all paid-in foreign capital. The non-metallic mineral products industry has attracted paid-in foreign capital of USD 0.949 billion, 1.15 billion, and 1.536 billion, accounting for 5.67%, 5.74%, and 5.9% of the total. The equipment manufacturing industry—transportation manufacturing excluded—has registered growth to a different extent. Transportation equipment manufacturing, electrical installations and equipment manufacturing, communications equipment, computer equipment, and other electronic equipment manufacturing remain the three largest sectors of manufacturing as a whole. From 2005 to 2007, general equipment manufacturing has attracted paid-in foreign capital of USD 0.321 billion, 0.476 billion, and 0.561 billion, accounting for 1.92%, 2.37%, and 2.15%, respectively, of the total. Special equipment manufacturing has attracted paid-in foreign capital of USD 0.355 billion, 0.408 billion, and 0.611 billion, accounting for 2.12%, 2.03%, and 2.35% of the total. The transportation equipment manufacturing industry has attracted paid-in foreign capital of USD 3.761 billion, 3.994 billion, and 4.467 billion, accounting for 22.46%, 19.93%, and 17.16%, respectively, of the total. Electrical installation and equipment manufacturing has attracted paid-in foreign capital of USD 0.876 billion, 1.225 billion, and 2.17 billion, accounting for 5.23%, 6.11%, and 8.34% of the total. Communications equipment, computer equipment, and other electronic equipment manufacturing has attracted paid-in foreign capital of USD 1.4 billion, 1.853 billion, and 2.53 billion, accounting for 8.36%, 9.25%, and 9.72% of the total. (See Figure 4-4)

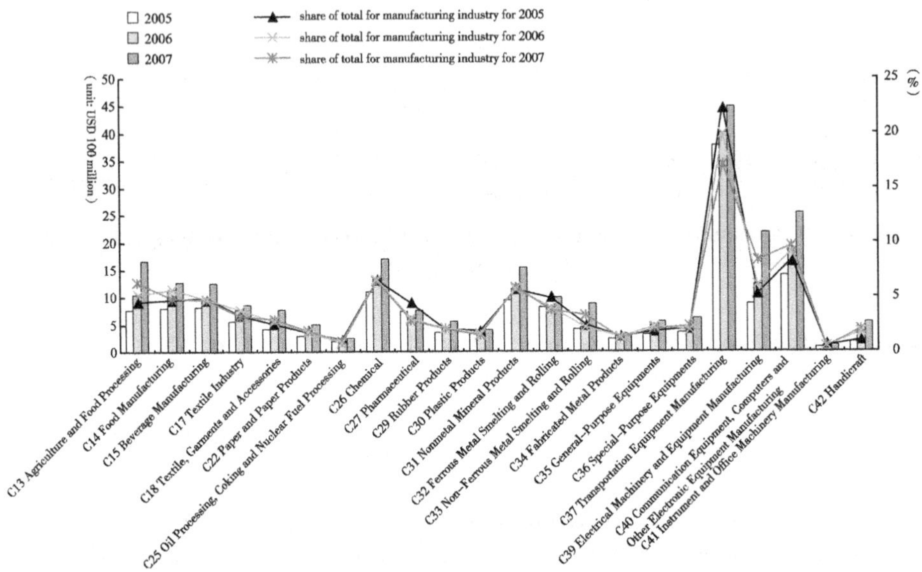

Figure 4-4: Changes in the amount of paid-in foreign investment in select manufacturing sectors as a share of paid-in foreign investment in the manufacturing industry in China's central region, 2005-2007

We are able to observe from the aforementioned statistics on the 2005-2007 distribution and changes in the paid-in foreign capital of manufacturing that, in recent years, the manufacturing industry as a whole has become a hotspot for foreign investment in the central area. As the central area is blessed with an abundant and cheap labor force, rich natural resources, and a sound foundation for the equipment industry, it has successfully brought in large sums of balanced foreign investment with a trend towards such sectors as labor-intensive manufacturing, the heavy chemical industry, and the equipment industry. We should also notice from the statistics, however, that in the context of a deepening optimization of the eastern region's industrial structure, the central area has failed to effectively assume all the transferred industries from the eastern area, such as the textile industry, garment manufacturing, etc. Therefore, future policy regulations towards foreign investment in the central and western areas should be made with an eye towards addressing this problem.

As for the internal structure of foreign-invested enterprises within the tertiary industry, the central area has only attracted Foreign Direct Investment in limited industries, as it is obviously lagged behind in its development of these industrial sectors. As with the eastern area, the real estate industry has the largest share. It has attracted paid-in foreign capital of USD 3.243 billion, 4.296 billion, and 6.604 billion from 2005 to 2007, accounting for a respective share of 25.89%,

37.45%, and 42.16% of the total paid-in investment of the tertiary industry as a whole. This has been followed by the industries of information transmission, computer services, and the software industry, with paid-in foreign capital of USD 4.033 billion, 4.096 billion, and 4.147 billion, respectively, from 2005 to 2007, accounting for shares of 32.2%, 35.7%, and 26.47% of the total.

In recent years, leasing and commercial services, transportation, warehousing and postal services, wholesaling and retailing, accommodation, and catering have all achieved rapid development. Leasing and commercial services have attracted paid-in foreign capital of USD 0.289 billion, 0.648 billion, and 1.499 billion from 2005 to 2007, accounting for a share of 2.31%, 5.64%, and 9.57% of the total. Transportation, warehousing, and postal services have attracted paid-in foreign capital of USD 0.531 billion, 0.594 billion, and 0.758 billion from 2005 to 2007, accounting for shares of 4.24%, 5.18%, and 4.84% of the total. Wholesaling and retailing have attracted paid-in foreign capital of USD 0.25 billion, 0.326 billion, and 0.642 billion from 2005 to 2007, accounting for a respective share of 2%, 2.84%, and 4.1% of the total. Accommodation and catering have attracted paid-in foreign capital of USD 0.767 billion, 0.802 billion, and 1.035 billion from 2005 to 2007, accounting for a respective share of 6.12%, 6.99%, and 18.56% of the total. (See Figure 4-5)

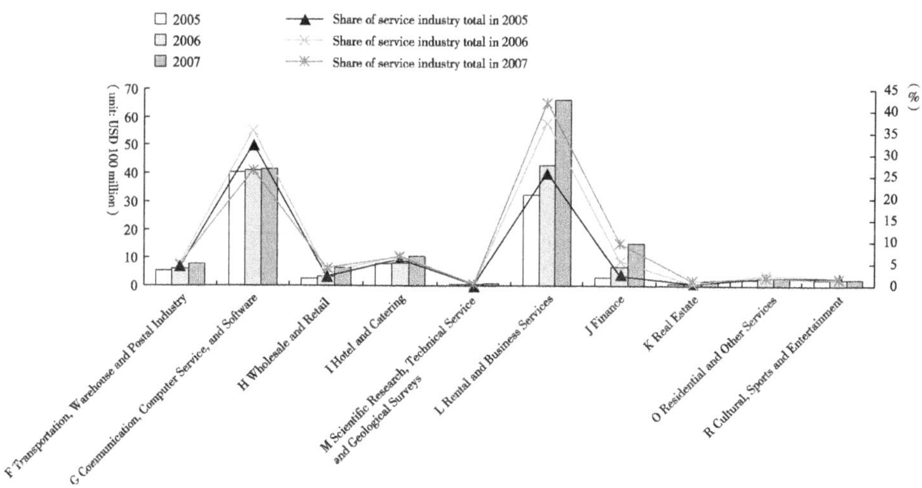

Figure 4-5: Amount of paid-in foreign investment in selected service sectors and changes in its share in the total for the service industry in central China, 2005-2007

By studying the changes that have occurred in the amount and share of registered foreign capital invested by foreign-invested enterprises in the central area, we are able to observe that Anhui, Jiangxi, and Hubei form the first echelon of investment-heavy regions, with the most concentrated amount of foreign-invested enterprises; Jilin, Heilongjiang, Henan, and Hubei belong to the second echelon, with a relatively modest concentration of foreign-invested enterprises; Shanxi and Inner Mongolia belong to the third echelon, with only scattered foreign-invested enterprises. Figure 4-5 displays the changes in the amount and share of registered foreign capital from 2003-2007, from which we can conclude that every province and city has made use of their distinct advantages so as to bear remarkable fruits in attracting foreign investment. The foreign investment in the central area has developed in a rather balanced manner, as the share of Hubei,

Jiangxi, and Anhui—those with the largest proportions of FDI—starts to drop, while Hunan, Henan, Jilin, and Heilongjiang have caught up with the other provinces' rapid growth in terms of the amount of foreign investment, resulting in an increasing share of the central area. (See Figure 4-6)

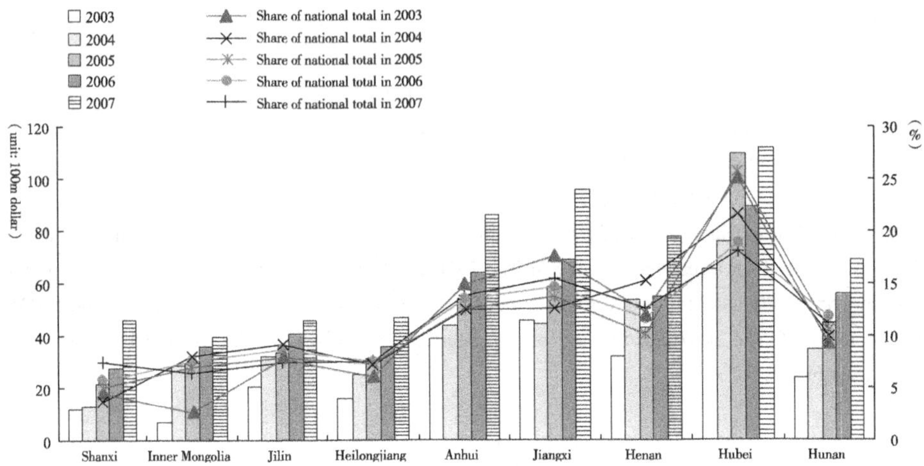

Figure 4-6: Amount of registered foreign capital in central China and changes in its share in national total, 2003-2007

4.1.3. Distribution of Foreign-invested Enterprises in the Western Area

According to the industrial distribution of foreign-invested enterprises in the western area, farm and non-staple food processing, food manufacturing, beverage manufacturing, and papermaking and the paper products industry have become the most significant labor-intensive sectors among the manufacturing industry as a whole in terms of attracting foreign investment. From 2005 to 2007, farm and non-staple food processing has attracted paid-in foreign capital of USD 0.269 billion, 0.331 billion, and 0.381 billion, respectively, accounting for a share of 4.84%, 4.76%, and 3.99% of the total amount of foreign investment attracted by the manufacturing industry overall. Food manufacturing has attracted paid-in foreign capital of USD 0.28 billion, 0.339 billion, and 0.49 billion, accounting for a respective share of 5.04%, 4.89%, and 5.13% of the total. The textile industry has attracted paid-in foreign capital of USD 0.143 billion, 0.169 billion, and 0.19 billion, accounting for a share of 2.57%, 2.43%, and 1.99% of the total. Within the heavy chemical industry over the course of 2005-2007, chemical raw materials production and chemical products manufacturing have attracted paid-in foreign capital of USD 0.516 billion, 0.564 billion, and 0.835 billion, accounting for respective shares of 9.27%, 8.12%, and 8.74% of the total. Pharmaceutical manufacturing has attracted paid-in foreign capital of USD 0.399 billion, 0.47 billion, and 0.576 billion, accounting for a share of 7.18%, 6.76% and 6.04% of the total. The non-metallic mineral products industry has attracted paid-in foreign capital of USD 0.575 billion, 0.752 billion, and 1.151 billion, accounting for a share of 10.34%, 10.83%, and 12.09% of the total. Non-ferrous metal smelting and the rolling processing industry have attracted paid-in foreign capital of USD 0.145 billion, 0.192 billion, and 0.303 billion, accounting for respective shares of 2.61%, 2.76%, and 3.18%. Transportation equipment manufacturing, communications equipment, computer equipment, and other electronic equipment manufacturing remain the largest sectors taken as part of the equipment manufacturing industry as a whole in terms of foreign investment attraction. From 2005 to 2007, general equipment manufacturing has attracted paid-in foreign capital of USD 0.292 billion, 0.349 billion, and 0.405 billion, respectively, accounting for a share of 5.25%, 5.03%, and 4.25% of the total. Special equipment manufacturing has attracted paid-in foreign capital of USD 0.146 billion, 0.227 billion, and 0.348 billion, accounting for a respective share of 2.62%, 3.26%, and 3.65% of the total. Transportation equipment manufacturing has attracted paid-in foreign capital of USD 0.667 billion, 0.899 billion, and 1.233 billion, accounting for a share of 11.99%, 12.95%, and 12.92% of the total. Electrical installations and equipment manufacturing have attracted paid-in foreign capital of USD 0.168 billion, 0.168 billion, and 0.266 billion, accounting for shares of 10.35%, 10.86%, and 10.55% of the total. Communications equipment, computer equipment, and other electronic equipment manufacturing has attracted paid-in foreign capital of USD 0.576 billion, 0.754 billion, and 1.007 billion, accounting for respective shares of 10.35%, 10.86%, and 10.55% of the total. (See Figure 4-7) One thing we can observe from Figure 4-7 is, although almost every manufacturing sector in the western area has been growing with increasing speed in recent years, foreign investments generally still focus on the various mineral resources there, and only enter equipment manufacturing and other equipment-related industries on the basis of those already-invested resources. However, these industries are capital-intensive sectors, requiring relatively larger amounts of capital investment, therefore, their share seems to be rather large considering that the absolute number of foreign investment in the western area is relatively small.

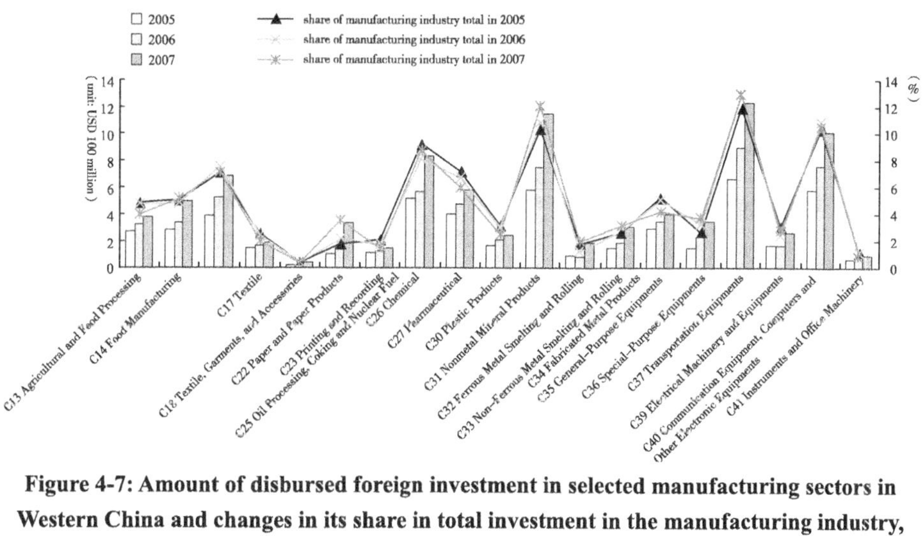

Figure 4-7: Amount of disbursed foreign investment in selected manufacturing sectors in Western China and changes in its share in total investment in the manufacturing industry, 2005-2007

The internal structure of foreign-invested enterprises within the western region's tertiary industry has apparently lagged behind, only attracting Foreign Direct Investment in a few industries, among which the real estate industry accounts for the largest share. From 2005 to 2007, it has attracted paid-in foreign capital of USD 2.101 billion, 3.481 billion, and 7.602 billion, accounting for a respective share of 41.18%, 41.98%, and 57.48% of the total amount of foreign investment attracted by the tertiary industry as a whole. Information transmission, computer services, and the software industry are second, having attracted paid-in foreign capital of USD 1.332 billion, 2.716 billion, and 2.373 billion with a share of 26.11%, 32.77%, and 17.95% of the total. On the other hand, leasing and commercial services, transportation, warehousing and postal services, accommodation, and catering are rapidly losing their shares of paid-in foreign investment. From 2005 to 2007, leasing and commercial services attracted paid-in foreign capital of USD 0.226 billion, 0.227 billion, and 0.473 billion, accounting for respective shares of 4.43%, 2.74%, and 3.58% of the total. Transportation, warehousing, and postal services have attracted paid-in foreign capital of USD 0.332 billion, 0.372 billion, and 0.391 billion, respectively, from 2005-2007, accounting for decreasing shares of 6.51%, 4.49%, and 2.96% of the total. Accommodation and catering have attracted paid-in foreign capital of USD 0.495 billion, 0.646 billion, and 0.805 billion, accounting for shares of 9.69%, 7.79%, and 6.09% of the total.

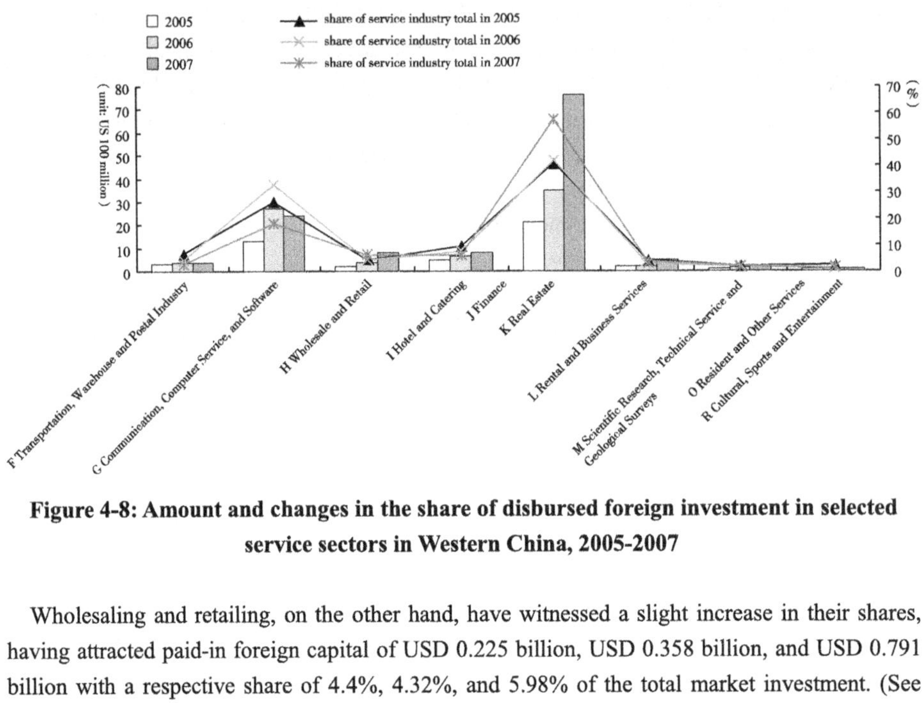

Figure 4-8: Amount and changes in the share of disbursed foreign investment in selected service sectors in Western China, 2005-2007

Wholesaling and retailing, on the other hand, have witnessed a slight increase in their shares, having attracted paid-in foreign capital of USD 0.225 billion, USD 0.358 billion, and USD 0.791 billion with a respective share of 4.4%, 4.32%, and 5.98% of the total market investment. (See Figure 4-8) Though the tertiary industry has achieved an overall increase in terms of both the number of foreign-invested enterprises and the amount of paid-in foreign capital, it should be acknowledged that the unconventional development of foreign investment in the real estate industry has played a vital role, which is to say, both the expanding number of foreign-invested real estate enterprises and the increasing amount of foreign investment overall have been key contributing factors to the large increase of foreign shares in the tertiary industry of the western area. This is a vitally important point.

When considering changes in the amount and share of foreign-invested enterprises in the western area, we shall observe that Chongqing, Sichuan, Yunnan, and Shaanxi form the first echelon, or those with the most concentrated amount of foreign-invested enterprises; Guizhou and Xinjiang Uyghur Autonomous Region belong to the second echelon, with a moderate concentration of foreign-invested enterprises; and Qinghai and Ningxia Hui Autonomous Region belong to the third echelon, with only scattered foreign-invested enterprises. Figure 4-9 displays the changes in the amount and share of registered foreign capital from 2003-2007 in these provinces, from which we can conclude that every province and city has made use of their distinct advantages so as to bear remarkable fruits in foreign investment attraction. However, the whole area attracts foreign investment in a fairly imbalanced way: Chongqing and Sichuan, which used to have large shares, still tend to account for the largest shares; whereas other provinces and regions, though growing rapidly in their attraction of foreign investment, are losing their shares in the western area.

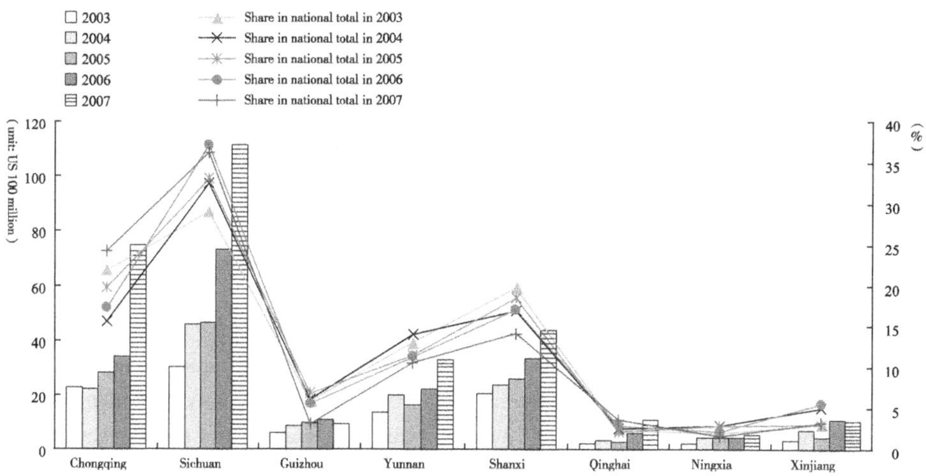

Figure 4-9: Amount of registered foreign investment in Western China and changes in its share in national total, 2003-2007

4.2 The Industrial Distribution of Foreign-Invested Enterprises in the Pearl River Delta and the Yangtze River Delta Regions[4]

4.2.1. The Industrial Distribution of Foreign-invested Enterprises in the Pearl River Delta Region (Guangdong Province)

The Pearl River Delta has traditionally held a dominant role in the textile industry as well as in the garment, shoe, and hat manufacturing industries. Industries that attract huge foreign investments are those of synthetic textile products manufacturing and knitted and crocheted articles, as well as their synthetic article manufacturing, along with the textile and clothing industry overall. In the synthetic textile products manufacturing industry, the number of foreign-invested enterprises was

[4]The Yangtze River Delta region, in the narrowest sense, includes 16 cities: Nanjing, Shanghai, Zhoushan, Suzhou, Changzhou, Jiaxing, Wuxi, Huzhou, Ningbo, Shaoxing, Zhenjiang, Hangzhou, Taizhou, Nantong, Yangzhou, and Taizhou, while the Pearl River Delta region, in its narrowest sense, includes nine cities: Dongguan, Foshan, Guangzhou, Huizhou, Jiangmen, Shenzhen, Zhaoqing, Zhongshan, and Zhuhai. In a broader sense, however, the Yangtze River Delta region can be understood to include Shanghai Municipality, Jiangsu Province, and Zhejiang Province, while the Pearl River Delta region can incorporate all of Guangdong Province. This book intends to study and analyze the two above-mentioned regions in their broader sense.

652 and 655, respectively, in 2005 and 2007; the amount of registered foreign capital increased by 3.78%, rising from USD 1.604 billion in 2005 to USD 1.667 billion in 2007, while the disbursed foreign capital increased by 8.61%, rising from USD 1.313 billion to USD 1.426 billion . In the knitted and crocheted articles and their related synthetic articles manufacturing industry, the number of foreign-invested enterprises totaled 520 and 544, respectively, in 2005 and 2007; the amount of registered foreign capital increased by 9.68%, rising from USD 1.198 billion in 2005 to USD 1.314 billion in 2007, while the amount of paid-in foreign capital increased by 19.17%, rising from USD 939 million to USD1,119 million. In the textiles and clothing industry, the number of foreign-invested enterprises weighed in at 3515 and 3653, respectively, in 2005 and 2007, with the paid-in foreign capital rising from USD 3.762 billion to USD 4.107 billion, an increase of 9.17%.[5]

In the dedicated equipment manufacturing industry, the number of foreign-invested enterprises engaging in the manufacture of dedicated equipment for chemical, wood, and non-metal processing was 799 and 871, respectively, in 2005 and 2007; the amount of registered foreign capital in this industry increased by 12.91%, rising from USD 1.495 billion to USD 1.688 billion , with paid-in foreign capital increasing by 24.46%, rising from USD 1.104 billion to USD 1.374 billion. The number of foreign-invested enterprises engaging in the manufacture of dedicated equipment for printing, pharmaceuticals, and daily chemical production totaled 142 and 129 in 2005 and 2007; the registered foreign capital in this industry increased by 0.7%, rising from USD 268 million to USD 270 million, while the amount of paid-in foreign capital increased by 6.33%, rising from USD 221 million to USD 235 million. The number of foreign-invested enterprises in medical equipment and the manufacture of medical instruments was 119 and 122, respectively, in 2005 and 2007; registered foreign capital increased by 64.54%, rising from USD 141 million to USD 232 million, while paid-in foreign capital increased by 81.98%, rising from USD 111 million to USD 202 million. There were, respectively, 108 and 153 foreign-invested enterprises engaging in the manufacture of equipment dedicated to environmental protection, public social security, and other related fields in 2005 and 2007; their registered foreign capital increased by 288.24%, rising from 102 million USD, with paid-in foreign capital increasing by 222.78%, rising from USD 79 million to USD 255 million.

In the transportation equipment industry, the situations of different sectors in 2005 and 2007 were as follows: the number of foreign-invested enterprises in the automobile industry was 492 and 544, respectively; the registered foreign capital in this industry increased by 34.03%, rising from USD 2.389 billion to USD 3.202 billion, with the disbursed foreign capital increasing by 40.12%, from USD 2.009 billion to USD 2.815 billion. Ships and the maritime industry attracted 92 and 97 foreign-invested enterprises, respectively, in these two years, with their registered foreign capital increasing by 39.30%, an increase from USD 257 million to USD 358 million. Meanwhile, the paid-in foreign capital in this industry increased by 38.99%, rising from USD 218

[5]In this comparative data analysis, we compare and contrast two particular periods of time: in the year 2005, a year before the transition period of China's accession to the WTO ended, the business strategies adopted by foreign-invested enterprises basically resumed the patterns that existed before China's WTO entry. However, the year 2007 was a year after the transition period of China's accession to the WTO ended, as a result, foreign-invested enterprises had adjusted their business strategies at this period to fit into the altered operating environment brought about by the WTO. Due to the significant difference in the operating environment for foreign-invested enterprises between these two years, by comparing the data, the changes in investment methods and the strategies adopted by foreign-invested enterprises against different industries can be clearly reflected, and thus we can grasp the changing trend of the industrial distribution of foreign-invested enterprises in a relatively accurate way.

million to USD 303 million. In the aerospace vehicle industry, there were seven and nine foreign-invested enterprises, respectively, which brought about a 53.74% increase in registered foreign capital from USD 52,572,800 to USD 80,824,400 , with paid-in foreign capital increasing by 51.66%, rising from USD 52,521,400 to USD 79,655,900.

In the fields of electrical equipment and machinery manufacturing, the situation regarding foreign investment in 2005 and 2007 was as follows: the number of foreign-invested enterprises in electric manufacturing was 150 and 166, respectively; the registered foreign capital in this industry increased by 37.72%, rising from USD 342 million to USD 471 million, while the paid-in foreign capital increased by 37.88%, rising from USD 293 million to USD 404 million . There were 757 and 839 foreign-invested enterprises engaged in power transmission, distribution, and control equipment manufacturing during these two years; their registered foreign capital increased by 35.27%, rising from USD 1.735 billion to USD 2.347 billion, while their paid-in foreign capital increased by 36.88%, rising from USD 1.456 billion to USD 1.993 billion.

In the communications equipment, computer, and other electronic equipment manufacturing industry, the foreign investment situations across different sectors in 2005 and 2007 were as follows: 382 and 377 foreign-invested enterprises were engaged in communications equipment manufacturing in 2005 and 2007; the amount of registered foreign capital increased by 14.93%, rising from USD 1.641 billionto USD 1.886 billion, with paid-in foreign capital increasing by 18.11%, rising from USD 1.364 billion to USD 1.611 billion. Thirty-two and 30 foreign-invested enterprises were involved in broadcast and TV manufacturing, with registered foreign capital increasing by 2.52%, which rose from USD 82,684,800 to USD 84,768,600. The paid-in foreign capital of this industry increased by 8.73%, rising from USD 70,180,300 to USD 76,306,600. The number of foreign-invested enterprises in electronic computer manufacturing was 536 and 515 respectively; registered foreign capital increased by 33.33%, rising from USD 2.574 billion to USD 3.432 billion, and their paid-in foreign capital increased by 41.76%, rising from USD 2.191 billion to USD 3.106 billion. The number of foreign-invested enterprises engaging in electronic device manufacturing was 411 and 478, respectively, during the years 2005 and 2007, with their registered foreign capital increasing by 52.73%, rising from USD 2.693 billion to USD 4.113 billion, and their paid-in foreign capital increasing by 69.01%, rising from USD 2.017 billion to USD 3.409 billion.

In the manufacture of instruments, meters, and machinery for cultural and office use, the foreign investment situations of different sectors in 2005 and 2007 were as follows: there were 97 and 78 foreign-invested enterprises engaging in general instrument manufacturing during these two years; their registered foreign capital decreased by 18.31%, dropping from USD 118 million to USD 96.3729 million, and their paid-in foreign capital also decreased (by 17.79%), dropping from USD 104 million to 85.5063 USD million. The number of foreign-invested enterprises in dedicated instrument manufacturing was 102 and 101, respectively; registered foreign capital increased by 43.49%, rising from 98.9643 million USD to 142 million USD, while paid-in foreign capital increased by 66.3%, rising from 72.7631 million USD to 121 million USD. One hundred and fifty-eight and 156 foreign-invested enterprises engaged in optical instrument and glasses manufacturing, respectively, in these two years, with their registered foreign capital decreasing by 18.27%, dropping from USD 520 million to USD 425 million, and paid-in foreign capital decreasing by 9.58%, dropping from USD 428 million to USD 387 million. Foreign-invested enterprises engaging in the manufacture of machinery for cultural and office use totaled 214 and

188, respectively, with paid-in foreign capital increasing by 7.24%, rising from USD 912 million to USD 978 million.

The number of foreign-invested enterprises engaged in the freight forwarding industry in 2005 and 2007 was 134 and 310, respectively. Their registered foreign capital increased by 146.54%, surging from USD 159 million to USD 392 million, while their paid-in foreign capital increased by 150.79%, surging from USD 126 million to USD 316 million.

There were, respectively, 285 and 316 foreign-invested enterprises in the warehousing industry in 2005 and 2007. The amount of their registered foreign capital increased by 57.84%, rising from 733 million USD to 1157 million USD, and their paid-in foreign capital increased by 54.97%, rising from 604 million USD to 936 million USD.

The number of foreign-invested enterprises in telecommunications and other information transmission services in 2005 and 2007 was 48 and 46, respectively; registered foreign capital increased by 352.88%, surging from USD 191 million to USD 8,645 million, with disbursed foreign capital increasing by 364.52%, rising from USD 186 million to USD 864 million.

Ninety-one and 172 foreign-invested enterprises were engaged in computer services in 2005 and 2007, respectively. Their registered foreign capital enjoyed a 244.44% increase, rising from USD 63.03 million to USD 217 million, and paid-in foreign capital increased by 196.44%, rising from USD 58.37 million to USD 173 million.

There were 965 and 1008 foreign-invested enterprises in the software industry, respectively, in 2005 and 2007. Their registered foreign capital increased by 83.71%, rising from USD 1,099 million to USD 2,019 million, with their paid-in foreign capital increasing by 91.91%, rising from USD 977 million to USD 1,875 million.

Six hundred and ninety-five foreign-invested enterprises were engaged in the wholesale industry in 2005, with an aggregate investment of USD 1.134 billion. Registered foreign capital reached USD 680 million and disbursed foreign capital was USD 533 million. By contrast, there were 3584 foreign-invested enterprises in this industry in 2007, with total aggregate investment surging to USD 5.42 billion, a 377.95% increase from that of 2005. Registered foreign capital increased by 446.18%, reaching USD 3.714 billion, and paid-in foreign capital also increased by 495.12%, reaching USD 3.172 billion. Among these enterprises, 239 and 241 engaged in trade brokerage and agency services in 2005 and 2007, respectively. The registered foreign capital in this field increased by 11.45%, rising from USD 131 million to USD 146 million, and the amount of paid-in foreign capital increased by 20.69%, rising from USD 116 million to USD 140 million.

One hundred ninety-one and 291 foreign-invested enterprises engaged in the retail industry in 2005 and 2007, respectively. The amount of registered foreign capital increased by 48.46%, rising from USD 813 million to USD 1,207 million, and the disbursed foreign capital increased by 77.22%, rising from 632 million USD to USD 1,120 million.

The number of foreign-invested enterprises in the accommodation industry was 205 and 251, respectively, in 2005 and 2007. The registered foreign capital in this field increased by 58.27%, rising from USD 1.234 billion to USD 1.953 billion, and the paid-in foreign capital increased by 62.77%, rising from USD 983 million to USD 1.6 billion.

Four hundred fourteen and 468 foreign-invested enterprises engaged in catering in 2005 and 2007, respectively. Their registered foreign capital decreased by 7.89%, dropping from USD 634 million to USD 5.84 million, and their paid-in foreign capital decreased by 2.68%, dropping from USD 522 million to USD 508 million.

Nineteen and 37 foreign-invested enterprises were engaged in finance in 2005 and 2007, respectively. The amount of their registered foreign capital increased by 38.46%, rising from USD 299 million to USD 414 million, and their paid-in foreign capital increased by 30.77%, rising from USD 299 million to USD 391 million.

There were 1777 and 2198 foreign-invested enterprises in the real estate industry in 2005 and 2007. The registered foreign capital sunk into these enterprises enjoyed a growth rate of 90.92%, rising from USD 10.931 billion to USD 20.87 billion, and the amount of disbursed foreign capital also increased, by 93.82%, surging from USD 9.063 billion to USD 17.566 billion.

One thousand six hundred and thirty-eight foreign-invested enterprises engaged in the financial services industry in 2005, with an aggregate investment of USD 6.061 billion. Registered foreign capital reached USD 3.699 billion and paid-in foreign capital was USD 3.09 billion. By contrast, there were 2246 foreign-invested enterprises in this industry in 2007, with aggregate investment surging to USD 8.048 billion, a 32.78% increase from that of 2005. Registered foreign capital increased by 48.28%, reaching USD 5.485 billion, and paid-in foreign capital increased by 51.68%, reaching USD 4.687 billion. Among these enterprises, 48 and 92 were involved in the enterprise management service industry in 2005 and 2007, respectively, with their registered foreign capital increasing by 64.17%, a rise from USD 240 million to USD 394 million. Paid-in foreign capital also increased by 69.27%, rising from 179 million USD to 303 million USD. Three hundred thirty-five and 252 enterprises, respectively, engaged in the legal service industry in these two years, with registered foreign capital increasing by 10.95%, rising from USD 557 million to USD 618 million. Their paid-in foreign capital increased by 9.28%, rising from 485 million USD to USD 530 million. Seven hundred ten and 1398 enterprises engaged in the consultancy and research industry in 2005 and 2007, respectively. Their registered foreign capital increased by 300.75%, surging from USD 532 million to USD 2,132 million, and the paid-in foreign capital increased by 386.5%, surging from USD 363 million to USD 1,766 million. Forty-seven and 61 enterprises were involved in the advertising industry in 2005 and 2007. The amount of registered foreign capital in this field has increased by 19.61%, rising from USD 44.2029 million to USD 52.8729 million. There were 2 and 7 enterprises in intermediary job services in these two years. The registered foreign capital sunk into this field increased by 6.23%, rising from USD 2.17 million to USD 2.3052 million, and the paid-in foreign capital basically remained the same, with only a slight increase from USD 2.17 million to USD 2.1767 million. Thirty-five and 23 enterprises engaged in the travel agency service in 2005 and 2007. The amount of registered foreign capital actually decreased by 49.4%, dropping from USD 185 million to USD 93.6208 million, and the paid-in foreign capital also suffered a decrease of 41.19%, dropping from USD 120 million to USD 70.571 million. Other commercial services attracted 445 and 392 foreign-invested enterprises, respectively, in 2005 and 2007. Their registered foreign capital increased by 7.18%, rising from USD 1.965 billion to 2.106 billion USD, and the paid-in foreign capital increased by 7.62%, rising from USD 1.746 billion to USD 1.879 billion. Ten and 22 foreign-invested enterprises were engaged in conference and exhibition services, the registered foreign capital of which increased by 113.65%, rising from USD 9.953 million to USD 21.2647 million, and the paid-in foreign capital of which increased by 146.01%, rising from USD 8.6307 million to USD 21.2325 million.

From the above data, we can see that the industrial distribution of foreign-invested enterprises in the Pearl River Delta is basically in line with that of the overall situation in China. As far as manufacturing is concerned, although the textile industry and the garment, shoe, and hat industry have large foreign investment stocks, foreign-invested enterprises are continuing to grow at a low rate in terms of quantity and capital. In the important sector of equipment manufacturing, foreign-invested enterprises engaging in dedicated equipment manufacturing and the transportation equipment industry have developed relatively slowly, for which the historical pattern of industrial formation in Guangdong Province was partly responsible. The automobile industry, however, was an exception, and it has managed to maintain a rapid, large-scale growth rate. The Pearl River Delta has an edge in the manufacturing of communications equipment, computers, and other electronic equipment, of which the electronic computer manufacturing and electronic device manufacturing hold the largest shares. By maintaining a high growth rate, they are gradually shifting to the high-end parts of the communication/computer industry, such as digital network equipment manufacturing, integrated circuit manufacturing, and optoelectronic device manufacturing. In addition, Guangdong is still in the fledging period of attracting foreign-invested enterprises to its high-end and precision manufacturing sectors, and the development of such areas as precision instruments has even been in decline recent years. In the service industry, foreign-invested enterprises in the Pearl River Delta mainly engage in such sectors as transportation, telecommunication, wholesaling, finance, commercial services, science and technology services, and real estate. The volume of foreign investment is growing at an accelerated speed compared to that of the service industry overall. Foreign-invested enterprises have developed slowly in the area of computer services. The real estate industry has enjoyed the fastest growth by making itself the most open sector of the service industry in the Pearl River Delta. What's more, commercial services have also developed very rapidly, and both the enterprise management service industry and the consultancy and research industry hold majority shares. By contrast, the scale of new services—such as the legal service industry, intellectual property services, job intermediary services, and conference and exhibition services—is relatively small even as it continues to shrink.

4.2.2. The Industrial Distribution of Foreign-Invested Enterprises in the Yangtze River Delta Region (with a Focus on Shanghai Municipality, Jiangsu Province, and Zhejiang Province)

In the textile industry as well as the garment, shoe, and hat manufacturing industry, the foreign investment situation of different sectors in 2005 and 2007, respectively, were as follows: in the synthetic textile products manufacturing industry, the number of foreign-invested enterprises was 2164 and 2279, respectively, in these two years; The registered foreign capital increased by 21.02%, rising from USD 4.729 billion in 2005 to USD 5.723 billion in 2007, while the paid-in foreign capital increased by 41.54%, rising from USD 3.262 billion to 4.617 billion USD. In the knitted and crocheted articles and associated synthetic articles manufacturing industry, the number of foreign-invested enterprises was 919 and 996, respectively, in 2005 and 2007; the registered foreign capital increased by 35.29%, rising from USD 1.295 billion in 2005 to USD 1.752 billion in 2007, while the amount of paid-in foreign capital increased by 47.07%, rising from 939 million USD to USD 1381million. In the textiles and clothing industry, foreign-invested enterprises numbered 6072 and 6519, respectively, in 2005 and 2007; their registered foreign capital increased by 34.38%, rising from USD 6.72 billion to USD 9.03 billion, while their paid-in foreign capital decreased by 14.2%, dropping from USD 4.667 billion to USD 4.005 billion.

In the field of dedicated equipment manufacturing, 201 and 278 foreign-invested enterprises were engaged in the manufacture of dedicated equipment for mining, metallurgy, and construction in 2005 and 2007. Their registered foreign capital increased by 64.86%, rising from USD 609 million to USD 1,004 million, and their paid-in foreign capital increased by 76.67%, rising from 463 million USD to USD 818 million. The number of foreign-invested enterprises engaging in the manufacture of dedicated equipment for chemical, wood, and non-metal processing was 1179 and 1310, respectively, in 2005 and 2007; the registered foreign capital in this industry increased by 22.06%, rising from USD 2.851 billion to 3.48 billion USD, with paid-in foreign capital increasing by 42.56%, rising from USD 1.753 billion to USD 2.499 billion. The number of foreign-invested enterprises engaging in the manufacture of dedicated equipment for textiles, clothing, and the leather industry totaled 309 and 379, respectively, in 2005 and 2007; the registered foreign capital in this industry increased by 58.19%, rising from USD 708 million to USD 1,120 million, while the amount of paid-in foreign capital increased by 60.66%, rising from USD 572 million to USD 919 million. Four hundred and one and 457 foreign-invested enterprises were involved in the electrical and electronic machinery industry in 2005 and 2007. Their registered foreign capital increased by 20.57%, rising from USD 943 million to USD 1,137 million, and their paid-in foreign capital increased by 40.72%, rising from USD 609 million to USD 857 million. The number of foreign-invested enterprises in the medical equipment and instrument manufacturing field was 256 and 302, respectively, in 2005 and 2007; the amount of registered foreign capital in this sector increased by 45.9%, rising from USD 586 million to USD 855 million, while the paid-in foreign capital increased by 84.14%, rising from USD 372 million to USD 685 million.

In the transportation equipment industry, the foreign investment situation of different sectors in 2005 and 2007 were as follows: 52 and 45 foreign-invested enterprises were engaged in the railway transportation equipment manufacturing industry during these two years. Their registered foreign capital decreased by 20.57%, dropping from 141 million USD to 112 million USD, and the paid-in foreign capital decreased by 18.03%, dropping from 122 million USD to 100 million USD. The number of foreign-invested enterprises in the automobile industry was 1454 and 1883, respectively; registered foreign capital in this industry increased by 49.14%, rising from 6.901 billion USD to USD 10.292 billion, with the paid-in foreign capital increasing by 58.46%, rising from USD 5.327 billion to USD 8.441 billion. In the aerospace vehicle industry, there were 12 and 16 foreign-invested enterprises, respectively, over the course of these two years, which brought a 193.66% increase in registered foreign capital that rose from USD 51.0795 million to USD 150 million, and the corresponding amount of paid-in foreign capital increased by 326.53%, surging from USD 32.1227 million to USD 137 million. Transport devices and the associated manufacture of transport and communication facilities attracted 54 and 90 foreign-invested enterprises; their registered foreign capital increased by 99.29%, rising from USD 141 million to USD 281 million, and their paid-in foreign capital increased by 139.75%, rising from USD 82.1791 million to USD 197 million.

In regards to electrical equipment and machinery manufacturing, the foreign investment situation of different sectors in 2005 and 2007 were as follows: the number of foreign-invested enterprises involved in electric manufacturing was 318 and 382, respectively; the registered foreign capital in this industry increased by 76.49%, rising from USD 774 million to USD 1366 million, while paid-in foreign capital increased by 96.03%, rising from USD 579 million to USD 1,135 million. There were 1062 and 1220 foreign-invested enterprises engaging in power transmission and distribution and control equipment manufacturing, respectively; the amount of their registered foreign capital increased by 42.66%, rising from 3.397 billion USD to 4.846 billion USD, while the disbursedforeign capital increased by 66.89%, rising from USD 1.945 billion to USD 3.246 billion. The electrical wire and cable, optical fiber cable, and electrical equipment industry attracted 399 and 497 foreign-invested enterprises, respectively; their registered foreign capital increased by 38.72%, rising from USD 1.09 billion to USD 1.512 billion, and their disbursed foreign capital increased by 43.86%, rising from USD 847 million to USD 1,217 million.

In the fields of communication equipment, computers, and other electronic equipment manufacturing, the foreign investment situations of different sectors in 2005 and 2007 were as follows: 409 and 439 foreign-invested enterprises engaged in communication equipment manufacturing in 2005 and 2007, respectively; the registered foreign capital of these enterprises increased by 31.82%, rising from USD 2.109 billion to USD 2.78 billion, with paid-in foreign capital increasing by 30.33%, a rise from USD 1.843 billion to USD 2.402 billion. The number of foreign-invested enterprises in the field of electronic computer manufacturing was 449 and 449, respectively, in 2005 and 2007. Registered foreign capital increased by 37.91%, rising from USD 3.82 billion to USD 5.268 billion, and paid-in foreign capital increased by 55.5%, rising from USD 2.993 billion to USD 4.654 billion. The number of foreign-invested enterprises engaging in electronic device manufacturing was 638 and 827, respectively; their registered foreign capital increased by 20.16%, rising from USD 10.949 billion to USD 13.156 billion, and their paid-in foreign capital increased by 31.1%, rising from USD 8.03 billion to USD 10.527 billion.

In the manufacture of instruments, meters, and machinery for cultural and office use, the foreign investment situation of different sectors in 2005 and 2007 were as follows: there were 359 and 402 foreign-invested enterprises engaging in general instrument manufacturing in these two years; the registered foreign capital associated with them increased by 8.25%, rising from USD 727 million to USD 787 million, and the paid-in foreign capital increased by 8.75%, rising from USD 560 million to USD 609 million. The number of foreign-invested enterprises in the field of dedicated instrument manufacturing was 256 and 285, respectively, and their registered foreign capital increased by 44.28%, rising from 411 million USD to USD 593 million. Meanwhile, paid-in foreign capital increased by 39.3%, rising from USD 313 million to USD 436 million.

The number of foreign-invested enterprises engaging in the freight forwarding industry in 2005 and 2007 was, respectively, 311 and 484. The registered foreign capital associated with this industry increased by 67.99%, surging from USD 453 million to 761 million USD, while the paid-in foreign capital increased by 55.28%, surging from USD 398 million to USD 618 million.

There were, respectively, 1103 and 1111 foreign-invested enterprises in the warehousing industry in 2005 and 2007. Their registered foreign capital increased by 69.31%, rising from USD 1.828 billion to USD 3.095 billion, and their disbursed foreign capital increased by 71.28%, rising from USD 1.309 billion to USD 2.242 billion.

The number of foreign-invested enterprises in telecommunications and other information transmission services in 2005 and 2007 was 30 and 48, respectively; the registered foreign capital of these services increased by 48.34%, surging from USD 1.084 billion to 1.608 billion USD, while the disbursed foreign capital increased by 46.99%, rising from USD 1.083 billion to USD 1.592 billion.

One hundred sixty and 301 foreign-invested enterprises were engaged in computer services in 2005 and 2007. The amount of their registered foreign capital enjoyed a 106.26% increase during that time, rising from 361 million USD to 741 million USD, and the paid-in foreign capital increased by 103.91%, rising from 281 million USD to 573 million USD.

There were 1756 and 2081 foreign-invested enterprises in the software industry in 2005 and 2007. Registered foreign capital associated with this industry increased by 87.17%, rising from USD 2.034 billion to USD 3.807 billion, with the associated paid-in foreign capital increasing by 92.66%, rising from USD 1.69 billion to USD 3.256 billion.

Four thousand and six foreign-invested enterprises were engaged in the wholesale industry in 2005, with an aggregate investment of 4.478 billion USD. Their registered foreign capital reached USD 2.84 billion and their paid-in foreign capital was USD 2.399 billion. By contrast, there were 7415 foreign-invested enterprises involved in this industry in 2007, with overall aggregate investment surging to USD 13.901 billion, a 210.43% increase from that of 2005. The registered foreign capital increased by 182.57%, reaching USD 8.025 billion, and paid-in foreign capital similarly increased by 193.58%, reaching USD 7.043 billion. Among these enterprises, 164 and 372, respectively, were engaged in trade brokerage and agency services in 2005 and 2007. The registered foreign capital in this field increased by 146.58%, rising from USD 146 million to USD 360 million, and the paid-in foreign capital increased by 125.81%, rising from USD 124 million to USD 280 million.

Three hundred eighty-two and 556 foreign-invested enterprises were engaged in the retail industry in 2005 and 2007, respectively. Their registered foreign capital increased by 66.51%, rising from USD 1.696 billion to USD 2.824 billion, and disbursed foreign capital increased by 82.42%, rising from USD 1.445 billion to USD 2.636 billion.

The number of foreign-invested enterprises in the accommodations industry was 218 and 271, respectively, in 2005 and 2007. Their registered foreign capital increased by 24.97%, rising from USD 1.57 billion to USD 1.962 billion, and their paid-in foreign capital increased by 35.91%, rising from USD 1.242 billion to USD 1.688 billion.

Seven hundred seventy-five and 895 foreign-invested enterprises engaged in catering in 2005 and 2007, respectively. The amount of registered foreign capital increased by 57.59%, rising from USD 764 million to USD 1.204 billion, and the amount of paid-in foreign capital increased by 69.69%, rising from USD 584 million to USD 991 million.

Thirty-six and 59 foreign-invested enterprises were engaged in finance in 2005 and 2007, respectively. The registered foreign capital of these enterprises increased by 23.49%, rising from USD 711 million to USD 878 million, and the disbursed foreign capital increased by 26.93%, rising from USD 583 million to USD 740 million.

There were 2183 and 2597 foreign-invested enterprises in the real estate industry in 2005 and 2007, respectively. Registered foreign capital enjoyed a 89.08% growth, rising from USD 19.388 billion to USD 36.659 billion, and paid-in foreign capital also increased, by 103.95%, surging from USD 16.081 billion to USD 32.797 billion.

Three thousand eight hundred and forty-two foreign-invested enterprises were engaged in the financial service industry in 2005, with an aggregate investment of USD 15.416 billion. The amount of their registered foreign capital reached USD 11.409 billion, and paid-in foreign capital was USD 9.324 billion. By contrast, there were 4949 foreign-invested enterprises in this industry in 2007, with aggregate investment surging to USD 25.978 billion, a 68.51% increase from that of 2005. Registered foreign capital increased by 72.46%, reaching USD 19.676 billion, while paid-in foreign capital increased by 84.89%, reaching USD 17.239 billion. Among these enterprises, 143 and 321 were involved in the enterprise management service industry in 2005 and 2007, respectively, with an increase in registered foreign capital of 237.41%, rising from USD 1.575 billion to USD 5.655 billion. Their disbursed foreign capital also increased, by 290.0%, rising from USD 1.289 billion to USD 4.992 billion. Seven hundred ninety-eight and 374 enterprises, respectively, engaged in the legal service industry in these two years, with registered foreign capital decreasing by 53.72%, dropping from USD 430 million to USD 199 million. The amount of paid-in foreign capital decreased by 46.29%, declining from USD 350 million to USD 188 million. Two thousand two hundred twenty-eight and 3484 enterprises were engaged in the consultancy and research industry in 2005 and 2007, respectively. Their registered foreign capital increased by 197.39%, surging from USD 1.342 billion to USD 3.991 billion, with disbursed foreign capital increasing by 174.55%, surging from USD 1.061 billion to USD 2.913 billion. Sixty-seven and 107 enterprises were involved in the advertising industry in 2005 and 2007, respectively. The registered foreign capital in this field has increased by 131.66%, rising from USD 83.3176 million in 2005 to USD 193 million in 2007, and disbursed foreign capital increased by 132.11%, rising from USD 77.1278 million to USD 179 million.

From the above data, we can see that the garment, shoe, and hat manufacturing industries, along with the textile industry, remain the most advantageous enterprises in the Yangtze River Delta, with a steady growth in the number of foreign-invested enterprises in recent years. Yet foreign investment tends to focus on high-end products like textile fabrics, while the amount of foreign investment in textile services and manufacturing has begun to shrink under the influence of outside investment in fabrics. In addition to textiles, the Yangtze River Delta also features a significant number of industries dealing with equipment manufacturing. Within the sub-sector of special equipment manufacturing, advanced equipment manufacturing (which includes electronic and electrical machinery manufacturing, medical equipment and instrument manufacturing, and environmental protection equipment manufacturing) has maintain a high level of rapid growth in terms of both size and the speed.

Within the sub-sector of transportation equipment manufacturing, apart from the traditionally rapid growth still maintained by the automobile manufacturing industry, other industries—such as the manufacture of ships and floating devices and aerospace aircraft manufacturing—have also experienced remarkable development. Communications equipment, computer equipment, and other electronic equipment manufacturing is another profitable industry of the Yangtze River Delta, of which computer manufacturing and electronic devices manufacturing have both the largest shares and relatively rapid growth. In the meantime, however, enterprises are gradually transferring to the fields of computer network equipment manufacturing, integrated circuit manufacturing, optoelectronic devices, and other high-end areas of communications manufacturing and computer manufacturing. What's more, the Yangtze River Delta has also exhibited outstanding operations in the manufacture of instruments, meters, and machinery, which shows that the Yangtze River Delta has obvious advantages in attracting foreign investment over other regions.

In the tertiary industry, warehousing, computer services, wholesaling, real estate, and commercial services are the chief fields in terms of attracting foreign investment. However, within the commercial services industry, legal services, advertisement services, IPR services, professional intermediary services, and exhibition services still need further improvement in order to attract significant foreign investment. From this division within the Yangtze River Delta region, we can see that it has an orderly division characterized by cooperation and coordination. The FDI of Jiangsu and Zhejiang focuses mainly on the manufacturing industry, whose actual utilization of foreign capital accounts for over 75% of the aggregate amount of foreign capital. Foreign capital has a larger share of the manufacturing industry in Jiangsu province compared with that of Zhejiang province. In Shanghai, FDI focuses mainly on the high-end fields of the manufacturing industry and on the service industry, while the service sectors that attract FDI has been continuously increasing in number and sophistication. For example, Shanghai exhibits a strong momentum towards developing a "Headquarters Economy," meaning that it is focused on becoming the city that attracts the most knowledge-intensive business service enterprises, such as the regional headquarters of multinational companies, investment companies, and foreign-invested R&D centers in China's mainland. Shanghai has been focusing its financial services towards opening up to the outside, attracting the most financial institutions of any region in China's mainland. Consequently, Shanghai has witnessed impressive results in attracting multinational purchasing centers, leading the whole country in wholesaling, retailing, and other commercial fields. By relying on its distinctive location, advantageous market, and promising future prospects, modern logistics have always been one of the major foreign-invested sectors in the tertiary industry. By relying on the excellent business environment in Shanghai—and based on the manufacturing industry of Jiangsu and Zhejiang—accounting, legal, consulting, real estate broking, and other commercial intermediary services are attracting foreign investment to China while increasing Chinese industry's openness to the outside world.

4.2.3. The Reasons for and Development Trends of the Foreign Investment Landscape in the Pearl River Delta and Yangtze River Delta Regions

The Pearl River Delta and the Yangtze River Delta Regions are the two regions exhibiting the earliest openness to the outside, as well as the two with the most complete development of their economic sectors. Foreign-invested enterprises are distributed similarly between these two regions, and they have become the central focus of foreign investment in the country—which to some extent determines the landscape of foreign-invested enterprises in China overall. According to the above analysis, the distribution of foreign-invested enterprises across these two regions is generally similar, resulting in similar industrial structures. However, the changes to foreign investment in recent years show that the Pearl River Delta is increasing its development of electronic and information products, while the Yangtze River Delta is deepening its development of high-precision equipment manufacturing. Regarding the service industry, both regions' real estate industry and producer services are hotspots for foreign investment, with Shanghai bringing in the majority of foreign capital in fields such as finance, wholesaling, transportation, and warehousing.

Conversely, foreign-invested enterprises that provide IPR, legal services, and professional intermediary services are in their infancy in both regions, but Shanghai is developing faster than Guangdong, meaning that enterprises in the former have a better degree of internationalization and stronger concepts of international operations than those of the latter.

There are many reasons for the current landscape of foreign investment in these two regions, with a few of them worth paying special attention to, the first of which is their observably advantageous locations. Both regions are blessed with numerous harbors and other useful infrastructure, which is coupled with convenient transportation. Second, the regions feature coordinated and reasonable industrial distribution and a strong basis for the manufacturing industry. Both regions have established economic circles centering on Shanghai and Guangzhou-Shenzhen, each with reasonable inter-industrial and intra-industrial distribution. Third, the establishment of a harmonious and honest business environment is a central feature of the regions. The idea of such a business environment refers to not only the accessibility of capital and human resources for production and investment, but also includes soft indicators such as government services, the legal environment, IPR, market maturity, degree of internationalization, international trade facilitation, cost of logistics, quality of talent, level of information, industrial support, the establishment of a social credit system, and more. Through decades of reform and opening up, both regions have established Shanghai or Guangzhou-Shenzhen centered business circles that cover the whole Yangtze River Delta and the Pearl River Delta, improving their attractiveness to foreign-invested enterprises.

At present, the State Council has approved a development plan for the Yangtze River Delta region, clarifying Shanghai's strategic status as the center of international shipping and finance. In order to position Shanghai in such a way, the plan requires that industries be displayed in accordance with their corresponding industrial levels, so that industries such as logistics and transportation, warehousing, etc., promote the integration of land transportation, airlift, ocean and river shipping. This has the effect of Shanghai exerting its influence on neighboring regions and to effectively take the leading role within the whole country. Shanghai shall expand its openness in the areas of financial services, accelerate the development of financial services such as bonds, futures, and insurances, and attract foreign investment to financial business developments and various financial expansion. The city should attract functional projects such as the global headquarters of multinational companies, regional headquarters, functional headquarters (R&D, procurement, training, finance, etc.), investment companies, etc., in an effort to promote the aggregated effect of multinational companies among regional headquarters.

As for Jiangsu and Zhejiang, these two provinces should accelerate the reform and upgrading of their current manufacturing industry, promote the overall industrial level of the manufacturing industry, and vigorously develop producer and production services such as legal services, advertising, accounting, consulting, exhibitions, information services, construction planning, engineering design, credit ratings, and marketing. Central provinces like Anhui, Jiangxi, Hubei, and Henan should, on the other hand, grasp the opportunity to acquire the traditional industries being transferred out of Jiangsu and Zhejiang. Similarly, the task of transforming the industrial structure and of transferring certain industries towards the Guangxi Zhuang Autonomous Region, Hunan, and Jiangxi also exists in the Pearl River Delta region, and is, in fact, part of the plan for attracting foreign investment. The landscape of foreign-invested enterprises will definitely be changed as a result.

4.3 The Distribution of Foreign-Invested Enterprises in the Eastern, Central, and Western Areas, as well as Trends in Development

FDI has brought changes to the industrial structures of the eastern, central, and western areas of China by affecting their capital formation, export size, and industrial structure. These changes are expressed as differentiating tendencies brought about in the pursuit of overall optimization. Foreign investment in the eastern area has primarily focused on the manufacturing sector of the secondary industry and the real estate sector, and the leasing and commercial services of the tertiary industry. Foreign investment in the central area, compared with that of the eastern area, has focused more on manufacturing, real estate, and the production and supply of electricity, gas, and water, with an absolute gap in the overall amount of investment. Though the concentration of the tertiary industry in the central area has certain advantages, a huge gap exists between the number of enterprises concentrated in the two areas. Foreign investment in the western area, much like the central area, focuses on manufacturing, real estate, the production and supply of electricity, gas, and water, residential services, and other related services.

According to analyses of certain indicators—including the number of foreign-invested enterprises, aggregate investment, registered capital, and paid-in capital in the eastern, central, and western areas of China in recent years—the author discovered that China is characteristic of the ladder-type structure for the regional attraction of foreign investment. The eastern area remains the key region for foreign investment; the central area, though growing rapidly in foreign investment, remains at a relatively low level; the western area mostly staggers along at a relatively low level of foreign investment attraction, with the exception of rapid growth in a few select provinces and regions. Foreign-invested enterprises often serve as the weather vanes of economic structure and economic benefits, so the regional and industrial distribution of foreign-invested enterprises acts as a strong indicator of China's regional economic structure and benefits overall. In general, although foreign investment in primary industries has witnessed some slow growth, the manufacturing industry and service industry are still the key focal points of foreign investment. The manufacturing industry of the eastern area is transitioning to a higher level of structure with obvious improvements in equipment manufacturing; whereas labor-intensive manufacturing and the heavy chemical industry are tending towards slow growth in most provinces and cities. The service industry is growing rapidly in the eastern area, as is the real estate industry and transportation services, wholesaling and retailing, leasing and commercial services, accommodation, and catering.

Chapter 5 The Geographic Distribution of the Sources of Foreign Investment Companies

Based on both the amount and scale of investment coming from foreign companies, our sources of FDI can be identified as coming from mainly ten regions. The investment activities of countries and regions which are major sources of FDI in China share some obvious features: foreign investment mainly flows into the manufacturing industry and only gradually extends to manufacturing-related services; in the short-term, wholly-owned enterprise is preferred when organizing enterprises with foreign capital while joint-venture firms are increasingly falling out of favor; and the choice of investment areas is resistant to change even as the Yangtze River Delta region becomes a new focal point for attracting foreign investment.

5.1 The Geographic Distribution of the Sources of Foreign Investment Companies

The implementation of policies on foreign investment utilization plays a positive role in attracting foreign capital, forming a basic pattern of sources of FDI.

5.1.1. The Sources of FDI are highly Concentrated and Generally Stable

Based on the number of foreign-invested enterprises in China, the top ten countries and regions play a leading role in China's economy: in 2003, there were a total of 143 thousand foreign-invested companies in China, with 118 thousand coming from the world's top countries and regions, accounting for 82.9% of the total investors; in 2004, the total amount rose to 171 thousand, with about 147 thousand from the top countries and regions (accounting for 85.5%). In 2005, there were a total of 190 thousand foreign-invested companies with 162 thousand from the top ten primary countries and regions, which accounts for 85.4% of total amount; in 2006, the total amount was 207 thousand, about 178 thousand of which were from the top countries and regions, accounting for 85.8%. Finally, in 2007, the total number of foreign-invested enterprises numbered 220 thousand, with about 188 thousand from the top countries and regions, which accounts for 85.5%. From 2004 to 2007, the percentage of foreign-invested companies in China from the top countries and regions held steady at 85% or above of all foreign-invested enterprises.

From 2003 to 2007, there were 14 major sources of foreign investment, including Hong Kong, Taiwan, the United States, Japan, Korea, the British Virgin Islands, Singapore, Canada, the Philippines, Australia, Samoa, Macao, and investment companies established by the transnational corporations of China and Germany. The first eight countries and regions have consistently ranked among China's top ten foreign investors.

From 2003 to 2007, the ranking of China's top ten investing countries and regions can be divided to two groups. The first part includes those countries and regions that rank from first to seventh as far as number of investors, for instance, Hong Kong, Taiwan, the United States, Japan, Korea, the British Virgin Islands, and Singapore. Their rankings remained the same during this time period, except that the United States and Japan changed places after 2003. Hong Kong is consistently the top investor in China, since the number of companies in which it invested accounts for over 35% of the total number of companies that were invested in by foreigners; Taiwan, Japan, the United States, and Korea rank from the second to the fifth, successively, forming the second-tier investors' group that accounts for roughly 6% to 11% of the total number of foreign-invested companies. The rankings of the British Virgin Islands and Singapore were unchanged during this time, but their proportional investment decreased by 2% to 3%.

The second group includes countries and regions that rank from eighth to tenth, and includes seven countries and regions with frequently-changing rankings in their overall proportion of investment (for example, Canada ranked eighth, ninth, and thirteenth over a period of five years). What's more, none of these countries or regions account for more than 2 percent of total foreign investment.

From 2003 to 2007, the proportion of investment from the top five countries and regions witnessed a slight drop in the total number of overseas-funded enterprises, falling from 72.1% to 71.3%, but the overall situation remained stable; during the same period, the proportion of investment by the top ten countries and regions rose compared to the total amount of overseas-funded enterprises, from 82.9% to 85.5%. The concentrated ratio of the top five countries and regions decreased while the top ten countries increased, so that generally speaking, the proportion of investment by certain companies increased while the total number of investors in the community expanded.

5.1.2. The Diversification of the Sources of Foreign-Invested Enterprises

In 2003, 91.9% of foreign-invested enterprises had only one foreign investor, 5.9% had two foreign investors, and 2.2% had three foreign investors. In 2007, the proportion changed to 89.6%, 6.2%, and 4.2%, respectively. There was a slight change, but the general pattern was still one where a single foreign-investor model accounted for about 90% and other models accounted for about 10%.

From 2003 to 2007, foreign-invested enterprises with only one foreign investor witnessed a slight decrease, falling from 91.9% to 89.6%, while there was a small increase from 5.9% to 6.2% for enterprises with two foreign investors and the proportion of enterprises with three foreign investors increased relatively quickly, from 2.2% to 4.2%.

In 2003, 8425 foreign-invested enterprises had two foreign investors, but only 3093 foreign-invested enterprises had three. In 2007, the figures changed to 13750 and 9348, respectively. Although the total amount of enterprises with two foreign investors was still larger than the amount of those with three investors, the increased number of enterprises with two foreign investors was 5324, smaller than that of those with three investors, which numbered 6255.

From the perspective of the development and management efficiency of these enterprises, foreign-invested enterprises with only one foreign investor are preferred by both Chinese law and common practice because it minimizes the cost of coordination and management for all property owners, as well as providing sufficient space for enterprises to make decisions efficiently. From the perspective of risk control and the scale of capital, however, the diversification of property owners is helpful in sharing investment risks and for acquiring further financing.

5.1.3. The Scale of Investment by Investment-Oriented Companies is Broader than the Average Number of Foreign Investors

The investment-oriented companies founded by multi-national corporations within China's borders (called IO companies below) have become an important source of foreign investment for the mainland. From 2003 to 2007, the number of IO companies reached 767 in 2003, 391 in 2004,

294 in 2005, 491 in 2006, and 605 in 2007, showing a V-type move. However, in regards to gross totals, the number of invested IO companies accounted for less than 1% of total foreign investment, and the investment volume of IO companies was less than 2%. From 2003 to 2007, the number of IO companies accounted for 0.005%, 0.002%, 0.002%, 0.002%, and 0.003% of total FDI companies in each respective year, and the corresponding investment volume accounted for 0.011%, 0.005%, 0.018%, 0.007%, and 0.008% of total foreign investment volume over the course of five years, respectively. Although this currently shows that the proportion of IO companies is quite small, its average investment level is higher than the average level of foreign investment enterprises. In 2003, foreign investment enterprises invested 2.26 million US dollars overall, while IO companies invested USD 4.68 million. In 2007, the investments increased to USD 3.53 million and USD 9.75 million, respectively. In addition, the emergence and development of IO companies marked the fact that China's foreign investment policy has the ability to explore a new financing channel.

5.2 Country-Wide and Regional Distribution of the Total Volume of Foreign Investment

The top ten countries and regions investing in China have remained roughly the same for the last five years, and play an important role in China's utilization of FDI. As the analysis in last section shows, investments from the top ten countries and regions account for about 85% of total foreign-invested enterprises, which is to say, their behaviors demonstrate basic features of FDI in China. As far as actually using FDI, Hong Kong, Taiwan, the United States, Japan, and Korea are the main sources, although the additional previously-mentioned five countries have also contributed a lot towards investment. For the sake of research convenience, this report mainly focuses on the top five countries and regions as the primary focus of research.

5.2.1. The Volume of Foreign Investment is Highly Concentrated

From 2003 to 2007, the investment from the top ten countries and regions accounted for 77.9%, 75.5%, 78.3%, 80.8%, and 82.6% of total foreign investment volume, respective with year, with the proportion at the end of the period being 4.7% higher than in the beginning. This indicates that the ratio of concentration by the top ten countries and regions is gradually increasing.

From 2003 to 2007, investment from the top five countries and regions accounted for 60.6%, 55.8%, 54.7%, 56.5%, and 58.3% of total foreign investment, respectively. While the proportion initially decreased only to increase again, generally speaking, it slid down by 2.3%, indicating that the concentrated ratio of the top five countries and regions is decreasing overall. However, although the concentrated ratio of the top five countries and regions decreased, more than 50% of total foreign investment still came from those top five countries and regions.

5.2.2. Rankings by Investment Volume of the Top Countries and Regions are Relatively Stable

Between 2003 and 2007, the ranking of the top seven countries and regions—Hong Kong, Taiwan, the United States, Japan, Korea, the British Virgin Islands and Singapore— remained relatively stable. The rank among the following countries and regions was subject to frequent change, however: Canada, the Philippines, Australia, Samoa, Macao, and Germany. For example, Canada belonged in the top ten foreign economies investing in China for five years; it then ranked eighth for the two years, ranked tenth in the subsequent year, and finally ranked ninth in the latter two years. As for Singapore and Australia, both made the top ten list in 2003 only; Macao entered the top ten in 2004 and 2006; Samoa ranked ninth in 2004 and 2005 and eighth in 2006 and 2007; while Germany started to appear in the top ten countries only in 2007.

5.3.3. The Changing Ratio of Foreign Investment Volume and Its Influence

Based on the ratio of their registered foreign capital to total registered capital, the countries and regions making major investments exhibit the following features:

First of all, the proportion of registered capital of Samoa has been as high as 93% of a company's total registered capital. Since Samoa entered the top ten in 2004, its investment volume has risen from USD 8.2 billion to USD 17.4 billion in 2007, with a growth rate of 112%. The registered foreign capital invested in enterprises established by Samoa take up to 93% of its total registered capital, which is rare among other top ten countries and regions.

Secondly, there are four countries and regions whose registered foreign capital accounts for up to 80% to 90% of total registered capital, and the proportions of which remain relatively stable: Taiwan, the British Virgin Islands, Korea, and Singapore. The proportion of registered foreign capital from Taiwan is maintained at or above 80%; its peak was at 86.4% in 2003 and 2004, and its bottom was no lower than 81.3% in 2005. The proportion of registered foreign capital from the British Virgin Islands stayed basically at over 82% with a rise to 85.3% in 2005. Singapore exhibited only minor fluctuations during this time, from 81% to 83%. The proportion invested by Korea fell to 78.2% in 2004, but in other years, it wavered between 82% and 84%.

Thirdly, there are three countries and regions whose registered foreign capital accounts for up to 70% to 80% of total registered capital, which includes Hong Kong, the United States, and Japan. Hong Kong's scale of investment is the largest, reaching USD 121.9 billion in 2004, and then rocketing up to USD 307.6 billion in 2007—an increase of 152%. Furthermore, the proportion of registered foreign capital from Hong Kong has been steadily increasing, from 71.7% in 2003 to 76.6% in 2007. Investment from the United States rose by 67%, from USD 23 billion in 2003 to USD 38.3 billion in 2007, with the proportion of registered foreign capital from the US rising slightly, from 72.3% in 2003 to 73.6% in 2007. Investment from Japan, meanwhile, increased from USD 24.3 billion in 2003 to USD 58 billion in 2007, with a rate of increase of 139%, with its proportion increasing from 72.1% in 2003 to 77.9% in 2007.

Fourthly, Canada remains waveringly among the bottom three on the list. It ranked seventh in 2003 and 2004 and fell to tenth among major foreign investors in 2005; it was then restored to ninth in 2006 and 2007. It invested a relatively lower proportion of registered capital, roughly 65%, overall, except in 2007, when its proportion exceeded 70% to reach 72.9%.

There are many ways to analyze the proportion of registered foreign capital to domestic capital; in this section, the focus is on the ability of major investment countries to stimulate domestic investment and their need for domestic capital support. Obviously, areas exhibiting lower proportions—such as the enterprises invested in by Canada—need more support from domestic capital; while those industries with higher proportions of foreign investment—such as those enterprises invested in by Samoa—need, perhaps, only 6% to 7% domestic financing. Different ratios differently influence the stimulation of domestic capital operations, the efficiency of domestic capital, and marketization.

5.3 The Industrial Distribution of Countries and Regions that are Major Sources of Investment in China

The industrial distribution of major FDI sources—including Hong Kong, Taiwan, the United States, Japan, and Korea—can, to a great extent, reflect the basic distribution pattern of all foreign-invested enterprises.

5.3.1. The Enterprises Invested in by Hong Kong are Mainly Concentrated in the Manufacturing Industry, with a Secondary Emphasis on Real Estate

Across all industries, the number of Hong Kong-invested enterprises as a proportion of the total number of foreign-invested enterprises demonstrates certain specific features.

Firstly, the manufacturing industry is the top priority for Hong Kong-invested enterprises. In 2003, 38,957 out of 55,026 Hong Kong-invested enterprises were in the manufacturing industry, accounting for 70.8% of all investments. This proportion was maintained through 2004 and 2005, at 70.2% and 71.1%, respectively, and dropped only slightly, to 69.6%, in the following year. In 2007, the total number of Hong Kong-invested enterprises reached 84,127, with the proportion of Hong Kong-invested enterprises in manufacturing decreasing to 66.3%. In general, Hong Kong-invested manufacturing enterprises accounted for about 70% of all total Hong Kong-invested enterprises over the past five years, with the proportion dropping slightly in the later years.

Real estate, however, is the second choice of investment for Hong Kong-invested enterprises. In 2003, 4,448 out of 55,026 Hong Kong-invested enterprises were in real estate enterprises, taking up to 8.1% of the total amount. This proportion slid slightly over the next four years, to 7.7%, 7.8%, 7.7%, and 7.5%, respectively. In general, about 78% of Hong Kong-invested enterprises are real estate enterprises, with their overall proportion slightly dropping within in a narrow range.

What's more, there are multiple industries where the proportion of Hong Kong-invested enterprises exceeds 1% of total investments, including the fields of agriculture, architecture, transportation, warehousing and postal services, information transmission, computer services and the software industry, retail and wholesale operations, the accommodation and catering industry, leasing and business services, culture, sports and recreational services, etc. Two newly-added industries in 2007 were electricity, the production and supply of gas and water, and technical service for scientific research and geological prospecting, while the proportion of enterprises providing culture, sports and recreational services fell below 1%.

Finally, Hong Kong-invested enterprises in the fields of retail and wholesale operations and leasing and business services have grown rapidly in the last five years; the number of enterprises in these two industries increased from 1694 and 1,717 to 5,381 and 3,769, respectively, between 2003 and 2007, with a net increase of 3,687 and 2,052 for a rate of increase of 217.7% and 119.5%.

According to the analysis above, the industrial structure of foreign-invested enterprises can be regarded as an independent industrial system. Hong Kong, as one of the major sources of foreign investment, occupies an important role in that system.

Firstly, Hong Kong-invested enterprises account for a significant proportion of nearly all industries. In 2003, Hong Kong-invested enterprises played a more important role than other foreign-invested enterprises in all industries except for the financial industry; the highest proportion of their involvement in Chinese enterprises was 58.2%, while at their lowest level of involvement they still made up 25% of the total (excluding the financial industry, in which their investment was only 7.2%). In 2007, however, Hong Kong-invested enterprises withdrew from the public management and social/international organization industry, while simultaneously greatly improving their status in the financial sector, increasing from 22 companies in 2003 to 61 companies in 2007 for an increase of 38.3%. The proportion of Hong Kong-invested enterprises in twenty industrial divisions[6] rose from the twentieth place to the twelfth.

Secondly, the types of industries in which over 50% of enterprises were Hong Kong-invested experienced a gradual reduction. In 2003, the proportion of Hong Kong-invested enterprises in the real estate industry was 58.2%, 56.4% of transportation, warehousing, and postal services, and 52% of electricity, gas, and water production and supply, while in the fields of cultural, sports, and recreational services, the proportion reached to 49.4%, with 49.2% of architecture. In 2007, however, the proportion of Hong Kong-invested enterprises in real estate, transportation, warehousing, and postal service made up over 50% of the total industry, reaching 60% and 57.5%, respectively, while in electricity, gas, and water production and supply, it decreased to 46.8%.

5.3.2. Taiwanese-Invested Enterprises Highly Favor the Manufacturing Industry and the Number of Logistical Enterprises Doubled.

Across all industries, the number of Taiwanese-invested enterprises as a proportion of the total number of foreign-invested enterprises demonstrates certain specific features.

Firstly, the country's investment in the manufacturing industry accounts for 80% of Taiwan's total investment. In 2003, 12,589 Taiwanese companies were involved in the manufacturing business, making up to 81% of all Taiwanese companies; only 636 Taiwanese companies were in the agricultural business, a little more than 4%. No other industries exceeded 3% of total Taiwanese investment. The sharp difference between the manufacturing industry and other industries indicates the preferences of Taiwanese-invested enterprises. Similarly, in 2007, the manufacturing industry accounted for 78.1% of the industrial distribution of Taiwanese-invested companies, a slight decrease from 2003; the proportional ratio of agricultural investment fell from 4% to 3.8%.

Conversely, the retail and wholesale companies developed rapidly. In 2003, there were 378 retail and wholesale Taiwanese companies, while in 2007, the number rose to 1,120, for a net increase of 742 at a rate of 196.3%. The proportion of Taiwan's retail and wholesale companies increased more than 3 %, from 2.4% to 5.6%, exceeding the agricultural industry and ranking

[6]The twenty industrial divisions are: 1) agriculture, 2) mining, 3) manufacturing, 4) electricity, gas, and water production, supply, and technical services, 5) architecture, 6) transportation, warehousing, and postal services, 7) information transmission, computer services, and the software industry, 8) retail and wholesale operations, 9) accommodations and the catering industry, 10) the financial industry, 11) real estate, 12) leasing and business services, 13) technical services for scientific research and geological prospecting, 14) water conservancy and environmental and public facilities management, 15) residential and other services, 16) education, 17) health, social security, and social welfare, 18) cultural, sport, and recreational services, 19) public management and social organization, and 20) international organization.

second on Taiwan's list of invested distribution across industries.

Among all foreign-invested enterprises, Taiwanese-invested enterprises played an important role in agricultural production and operational industries, maintaining a rate of over 20% between 2003 and 2007 to become a major feature of Taiwanese companies. Other industries that exceeded 10% included manufacturing, resident and related services, and cultural, sport, and recreational services.

5.3.3. The United States Invests Mainly in the Manufacturing Industry, but at a Low Overall Proportion of all Investment

Much like Taiwanese-invested and Hong Kong-invested enterprises, across all industries in China, the proportion of United States-invested enterprises to the total number of foreign-invested enterprises is indicative of specific trends in the country's method of investment.

To begin with, manufacturing is still the leading industrial choice. In 2003, 8,993 out of 12593 American enterprises were in the manufacturing industry, accounting for 71.4% of all total American-invested enterprises; in 2007, the number of American-invested manufacturing enterprises increased to 12,001, for a net increase of 3008. While the total number of American-invested enterprises increased rapidly—to 17,578—the overall proportion decreased to 68.3%.

In addition to manufacturing, the number of American-invested enterprises in three industries—information transmission, computer services, and the software industry, retail and wholesale operations, and leasing and business services—were 589, 663, and 628, respectively, in 2003; in 2007, the number increased to 1,107, 1,129, and 1190, with a net increase of 518, 466, and 562 new enterprises in each field. With proportional rates of increase of 6.3%, 6.4%, and 6.8%, respectively, the three industries have become the largest three industries of American investment in mainland China, notwithstanding manufacturing.

Regarding the industrial distribution of FDI, the industrial proportion of American-invested enterprises has the following features:

To begin with, the proportion of investment in the manufacturing industry remains at a low level. Although the United States invests in many manufacturing enterprises and its industrial proportion is high among total American investments, this ratio is not significant compared to other foreign-invested enterprises, always wavering between 8% and 9% with a trend of further decrease, from 8.7% in 2003 to 8% in 2007.

The industry in which the United States actually invested the most is that of health, social security, and social welfare. From 2003 to 2007, its proportion remained above 20%, at a peak of 27.8% when the number of invested enterprises reached 40 in 2005, highlighting in the industrial distribution of American-invested enterprises.

What's more, in 2003, industries where the proportion of American-invested enterprises exceeded 10% were: retail and wholesale operations; leasing and business services; technical services for scientific research and geological prospecting; water conservancy, environmental, and public facilities management; and international organizations. In 2007, the proportion invested in information transmission, computer services, and the software industry, leasing and business services, technical services for scientific research and geological prospecting, and international organizations remained above 10%, but the proportion of investment in retail and wholesale operations fell to 6.9%, the proportion in the financing industry increased to 10.5%, and education increased to 10.6%. In conclusion, there are seven out of twenty industrial divisions where the proportion of American-invested enterprises exceeded 10%.

5.3.4. The Proportion of Japanese-Invested Enterprises in the Manufacturing Industry is gradually decreasing, but it still has an Edge in Retail and Wholesale Operations

The ratio of Japanese-invested enterprises to the total number of all foreign-invested enterprises in mainland China is revealing of certain investment preferences.

First of all, the concentration ratio of Japanese-invested enterprise in the manufacturing industry is gradually decreasing. From 2003 to 2007, the proportion of Japanese-invested enterprises in the manufacturing industry went from 75.1%, 74.6%, 73.2%, 71.6%, down to 69.3% across five years. While the actual number of companies increased (there were 13398 companies in 2007, 5309 more than in 2003), the ratio decreased year by year. Even so, manufacturing is still the top choice for Japanese-invested enterprises. Among the 8,558 newly-established Japanese enterprises, 5,309 entered the manufacturing field, which indicates that over 60% of newly-increased Japanese-invested enterprises chose to enter the manufacturing industry.

Secondly, retail and wholesale operations are the strength of Japanese-invested enterprises. In 2003, 7.4% of Japanese-invested enterprises were in retail and wholesale operations, and this proportion rose to 11.3% in 2007. When the amount increased to 2,188 from 792, the net increase was 1,396 at an increased rate of 176.3%. Similarly, Japanese companies in leasing and business services increased from 396 in 2003 to 946 in 2007, with a net increase of 550 companies at a rate of increase of 138.9%.

The industrial proportion of Japanese-invested enterprises is not particularly high compared to other foreign-invested enterprises. In 2003, Japan only accounted for 12.9% of retail and wholesale operations, and less than 10% across other industries; in 2007, the amount of industries in which the Japanese proportion was over 10% increased to three, including information transmission and the computer service and software industry, retail and wholesale operations, and residential and related services; the proportion of Japanese-invested enterprises was 12.7%, 13.4%, and 11.7%, respectively. Additionally, Japanese-invested enterprises demonstrated some unique features in the field of residential and related services, where companies increased by 105 in 5 years at a rate of over 100%.

5.3.5. 80% of Korean Investment is Concentrated in Manufacturing, but its Expansion into the Productive Service Industry is Remarkable

Across all industries, the proportion of Korean-invested enterprises in China, when compared to the number of foreign-invested enterprises overall, demonstrates the defining features of Korean-invested enterprises from 2003 to 2007.

To begin with, the proportion of Korean-invested enterprises has consistently maintained a high level. From 2003 to 2007, there were 8067, 10483, 12160, 12580, and 12494 Korean-invested manufacturing enterprises in China, accounting for 86%, 85.2%, 83.4%, 80.7%, and 77.7% of total Korean-invested enterprises, respectively, every year. While the amount of manufacturing enterprises has soared—from 9377 to 16073 enterprises with Korean investment—its proportion of total investment has decreased yearly. In the last 5 years, the amount of new manufacturing enterprises was up 4427, 66.1% of the 6696 Korean-invested enterprises total, which means that two-thirds of new Korean investment is in manufacturing, an obvious industrial preference.

Secondly, the development of Korean-invested enterprises in the productive service industry is remarkable. When viewed from the number of new enterprises, this development is much more obvious, up from 273 in 2003 to 1231 in 2007; this net increase of 958 newly-invested enterprises accounts for 14.3% of the 6696 total. In leasing and business services, there were 156 enterprises in 2003 and 503 in 2007, with a net increase of 347, accounting for 5.2% of total newly-established enterprises. These fields have become second only to manufacturing from the perspective of Korean investment preferences.

The other industries in which Korea had a sizeable preference were in the accommodation and catering industry (11.5%), education (9.9%), residential and related services (9.2%), cultural, sport, and recreational services (9.2%) and manufacturing (8.3%). This shows the competitive edge of Korean-invested enterprises.

In general, FDI from Hong Kong, Taiwan, the United States, Japan, and Korea primarily flows into the manufacturing industry, which strongly boosts the development of China's manufacturing enterprises and improves competitiveness; the corresponding increase of enterprises investing in real is negligible with the exception Hong Kong, which, for its part, shows gains in certain productive service industries such as retail, wholesale, leasing, and business services.

5.4 The Investment Forms of Countries and Regions that are Major Sources of FDI

The five major suppliers of FDI indicate the overall trend of forms of investment for all foreign investment enterprises.

5.4.1. The Forms of Investment by Hong Kong in Mainland China have Undergone Structural Adjustments.

Firstly, individual proprietorship has doubled and redoubled. In terms of the amount, both individual proprietorship and joint venture Hong Kong-invested enterprises grew between 2003 and 2007, however, due to their different rates of growth, the gap between them was and is widening sharply. Hong Kong-invested enterprises following a model of individual proprietorship increased from 25610 in 2003 to 51887 in 2007, at a rate of 102.6%. In the same period, joint venture enterprises increased from 22834 to 26908. This overall increase in numbers rose by just 17.8%, much lower than the growth rate, which made up 52.9% of all total Hong Kong-invested enterprises. In 2003, there were just minor differences between the two forms of investment; the number of enterprises under individual proprietorship was 2776 more than that of joint venture enterprises, a difference of just 13%; in 2007, the number of enterprises with individual proprietorship was two times that of joint venture enterprises, increasing by 24979 new enterprises, or 93% (Figure 5-1).

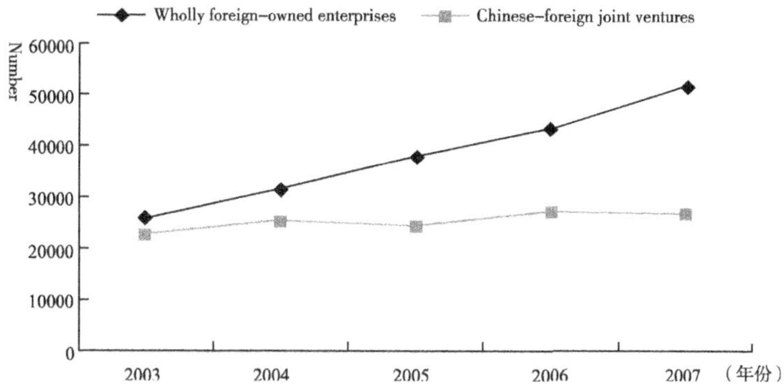

Figure 5-1: Number of wholly Hong Kong-owned enterprises and Chinese-Hong Kong joint ventures, 2003 - 2007

Secondly, individual proprietorship accounts for 60% of all Hong Kong-invested enterprises in China. In terms of structure, there has been significant change in Hong Kong's investment in mainland China. While individual proprietorship is increasing steadily, both joint venture and cooperatives are decreasing. The proportion of individual proprietorship has risen slightly on a year-to-year basis, from 46.5% in 2003 to 61.7% in 2007, an increase of 15%. Meanwhile, the proportion of joint venture enterprises dropped from 41.5% in 2003 to 32% in 2007, decreasing by 9%; at the same time, the proportion of cooperative models declined from 11.7% in 2003 to 6% in 2007, decreasing by half. The decrease in the proportion of joint venture corporations is because its quantitative growth was lower than that of newly-established Hong Kong-invested enterprises as a whole, meaning that although the proportional rate is decreasing, the actual number of joint venture corporations is increasing. However, the reduction in the number of cooperatives is absolute. In 2003, there were 6646 Hong Kong cooperatives, but in 2007 the amount was reduced to 5032, decreasing by 1414. In 2003, only 134 enterprises had adopted the investment form of joint-equity, but this number rose to 302 in 2007, increasing by 125%. However, its relatively small numbers only account for a minor fraction of all the Hong Kong-invested enterprises (Figure 5-2).

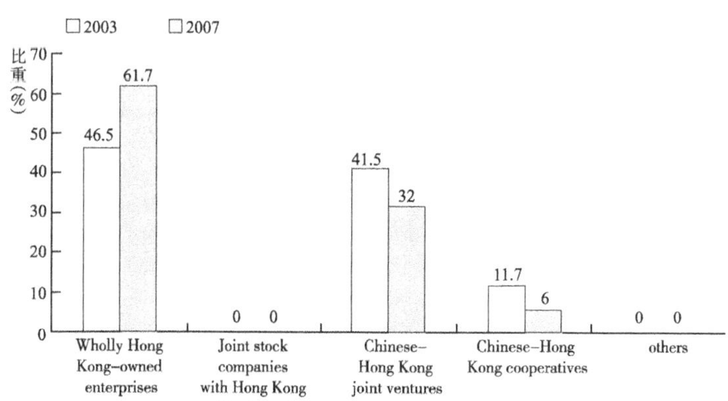

Figure 5-2: Share of different types of enterprises with investment from Hong Kong in mainland China, 2003-2007

In 2007, more than 60% of Hong Kong-invested enterprises in mainland China had adopted individual proprietorship models, and over five years, over 15% Hong Kong enterprises chose individual proprietorship, including both newly-established enterprises and existing enterprises that shifted their former forms of investment. This trend is significant in interpreting the capitalistic activities of Hong Kong-invested enterprises.

5.4.2. The Investment Form of the United States Invested Enterprises is going through a Structural Reverse

American-invested enterprises developed quickly from 2003 to 2007, and exhibited great diversity of investment forms.

Firstly, the number of enterprises based on a model of individual proprietorship grew very quickly, triggering qualitative changes in American investment structures. In 2003, the major form of American-invested enterprises was that of a joint venture model, which accounted for 49.2% of the total number of American-invested enterprises; at that time, the number of individual proprietorship enterprises accounted for 45.1%, with both forms basically balancing out. In the following years, the individual proprietorship enterprises developed rapidly, increasing from 5,684 in 2003 to 10,007 in 2007, with a net increase of 4,323 and a growth rate of 76.1%. In the same period, the number of joint venture enterprises only increased by 771 with a growth rate of 12.4%. In 2007, the proportion of individual proprietorship enterprises was 56.9%, increasing by 10%; while the proportion of joint venture enterprises fell to 39.7%, decreasing by 10%. In 2003, the proportion of individual proprietorship enterprises was 4% lower than that of joint venture enterprises; in 2007, however, the proportion of individual proprietorship enterprises was 17% more than that of joint venture enterprises (Figure 5-3, 5-4).

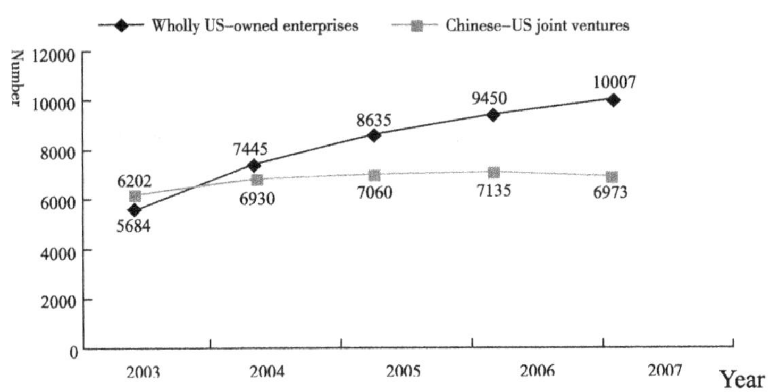

Figure 5-3: Number of wholly US-owned enterprises and Chinese-US joint ventures in mainland China, 2003-2007

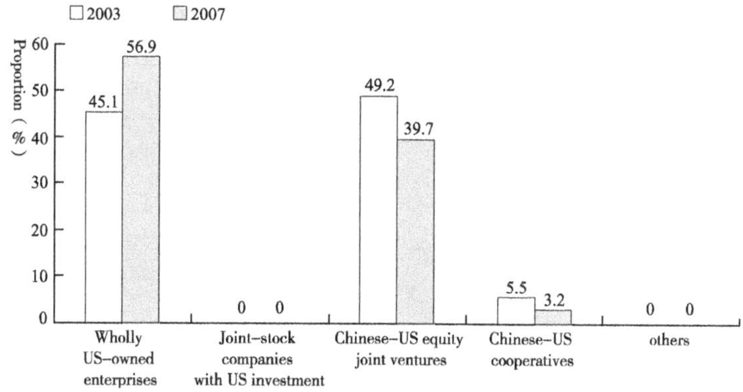

Figure 5-4: Share of different types of enterprises in mainland China with investment from the US, 2003-2007

Secondly, individual proprietorship has been the predominant investment choice for newly-established American enterprises. From 2003 to 2007, there were 4,983 newly-established American-invested enterprises. In consideration of the decrease in cooperatives and the increase of stock corporations, there were actually 5,094 new enterprises that chose between individual proprietorship and joint-venture models. Among those newly-created enterprises, 84.9% of them chose individual proprietorship as an investment model, but only 15.1% chose the form of joint venture.

5.4.3. The Preference of Japanese-Invested enterprises Shifts to a Model of Individual Proprietorship

The number of Japanese-invested enterprises in China has increased rapidly over the last five years, with a net growth of 8,858 enterprises at a rate of 79.5%. The dominant forms of investment were in individual proprietorship and joint venture enterprises, with the preferred proportion gradually shifting more to individual proprietorship.

Firstly, the growth of individual proprietorship and joint venture enterprises were markedly different. In 2003, there were 5,179 individual proprietorship enterprises and 5005 joint venture enterprises; in 2007, there were 11,342 individual proprietorship enterprises, an increase of 6,136 at a growth rate exceeding 119%. On the other hand, there were 7,324 joint venture enterprises in 2007, increasing by 2,319 at a rate of 46%, which is 75% less than the increased rate of enterprises relying on individual proprietorship (Figure 5-5).

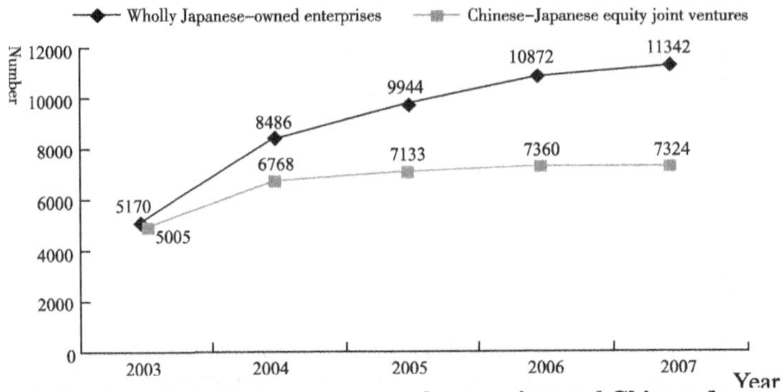

Figure 5-5: Number of wholly Japanese-owned enterprises and Chinese-Japanese joint ventures, 2003-2007

Secondly, the number of individual proprietorship enterprises is now much greater than that of joint venture enterprises. In 2003, the proportion of Japanese-invested individual proprietorships was 48.1%, quite close to the proportion of joint venture enterprises, which was 46.5%. In 2007, however, the two figures became 58.7% and 37.9%, respectively, enlarging the difference between individual proprietorship and joint venture enterprises from 1.6% to 20% (Figure 5-5).

Finally, the number of cooperatives increased even while its proportion decreased. It rose from 569 enterprises in 2003 to 621 enterprises in 2007, for a net increase of 52 and a growth rate of 9.1%, much lower than the growth rate of 79.5% for all total Japanese-invested enterprises. Thus, the proportion of cooperatives declined from 5.3% in 2003 to 3.2% in 2007, decreasing by 2.1% for a decline of nearly 40% (Figure 5-6).

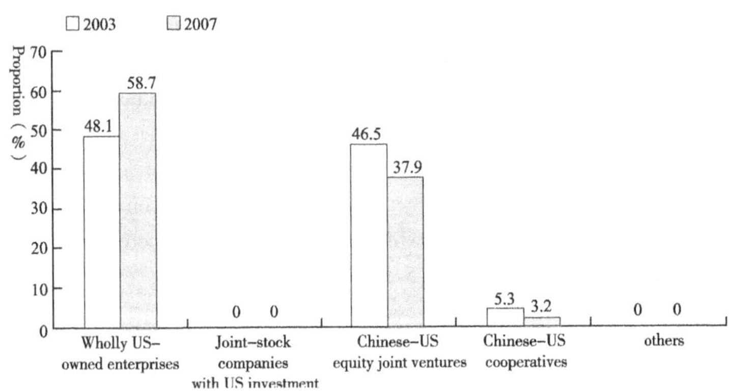

Figure 5-6: Shares of different types of enterprises in mainland China with investment from Japan, 2003-2007

5.4.4. The Basic Pattern of Taiwan's Investment Structure is Relatively Stable.

Firstly, the majority of Taiwanese-invested enterprises in mainland China have been established in the form of individual proprietorship. In 2003, there were a total of 15,550 Taiwanese-invested enterprises, among which 10,435 were individual proprietorships, accounting for 67.1% of the total amount and serving as the major investment model. In 2007, that amount increased to 20,089, with 14,579 enterprises adopting a structure of individual proprietorship. This accounted for 72.5% of total growth, further enhancing the dominance of this investment pattern. (Figure 5-7)

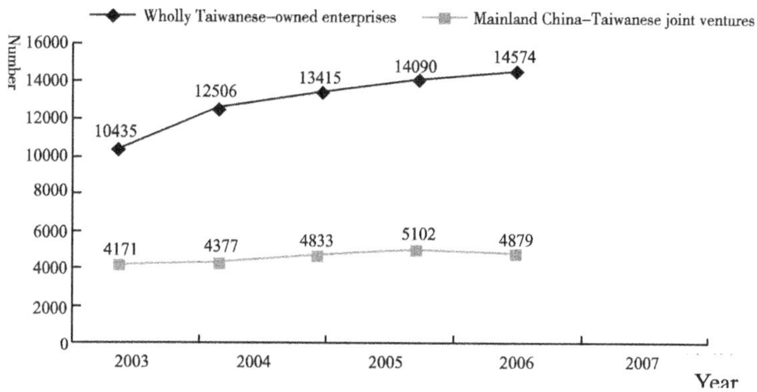

Figure 5-7: Number of wholly Taiwanese-owned enterprises and mainland China –Taiwanese joint ventures in mainland China, 2003-2007

Secondly, the proportion of individual proprietorship has risen while the proportion of joint venture enterprises has decreased. From 2003-2007, the proportion of individual proprietorship increased continually at a stable rate of almost 2% every year. The proportion of joint venture enterprises decreased, however, except in 2007, around 1%. Therefore, on one hand, the proportion of individual proprietorship rose by 5.3%, but on the other hand, the proportion of joint venture enterprises decreased by 2.5%, making Taiwan the country among China's five major investors with the least variation in growth (Figure 5-8).

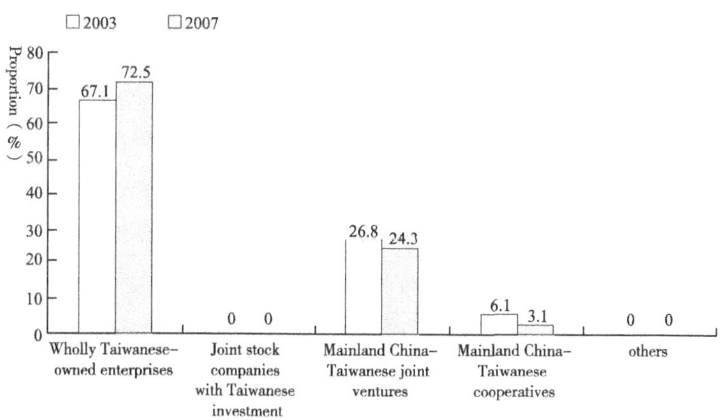

Figure 5-8: Shares of different types of enterprises in mainland China with investment from Taiwan, 2003-2007

Thirdly, both the amount and proportion of joint venture enterprises has decreased. There were over 940 Taiwanese cooperatives, accounting for 6.1% of total Taiwanese enterprises in 2003, but the proportion has decreased every year. In 2007, there were only 628 cooperatives, and the proportion declined to 3.1%. What's more, Taiwanese-invested enterprises seldom adopted other investment patterns, such as stock corporations.

5.4.5. Korean Enterprises' Investments in China are Highly Concentrated on I Wholly Foreign-owned Enterprises

Korea's primary investiture in China is in the form of wholly Korean-owned enterprises. Among all Korean investments in mainland China, the proportion of enterprises with wholly Korean-owned enterprises rose from 70.4% in 2003 to 77.2% in 2007. This proportion is higher than that of any of the other four major investors in mainland China (Hong Kong: 46.5% in 2003, 61.7% in 2007; Taiwan: 67.1% in 2003, 72.5% in 2007; Japan: 48.1% in 2003, 58.7% in 2007; the United States: 45.1% in 2003, 56.9% in 2007). It rose by nearly 7 % in five years, with the most rapid growth rate—2.7 %—occurring in 2005, a rate occupying 39.7% of the total increase over five years. Among the 2,281 new investing enterprises in 2005, 2,054 of them adopted a model based on wholly foreign-owned, accounting for over 90% of total Korean investment that year.

Secondly, the gap between the increasingly rapid net growth of wholly Korean-owned enterprises and joint ventures is huge. In five years, the number of wholly Korean-owned enterprises increased from 6603 to 12,415, for a net growth of 5,812 enterprises (an increase of 88%). The number of Chinese-Korean joint ventures increased from 2,500 to 3,366, with a net growth of 866, reaching 34.6% in terms of the overall growth rate. The number of joint ventures lagged far behind that of the wholly Korean-owned enterprises when considering net growth, and was 53 % behind in terms of comparable growth rates (Figure 5-9).

The analysis of the preferred investment forms of these five FDI-sourced countries and regions clearly shows that, from 2003 to 2007 (the five-year period before the international financial crisis), there was a growing disposition towards wholly foreign-owned enterprises (Figure 5-10).

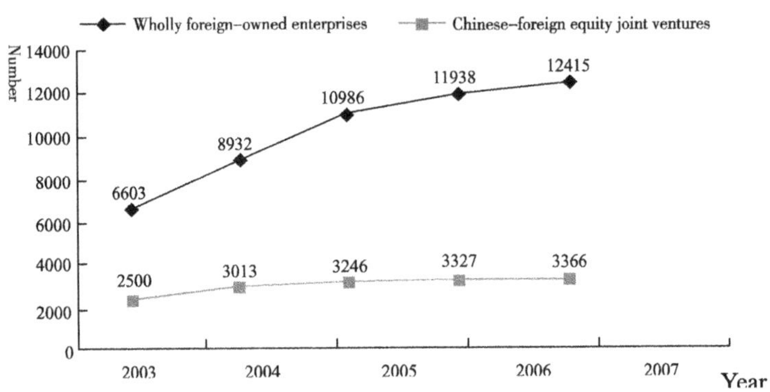

Figure 5-9: Numbers of wholly South Korean-owned enterprises and Chinese-South Korean equity joint ventures in China, 2003 - 2007

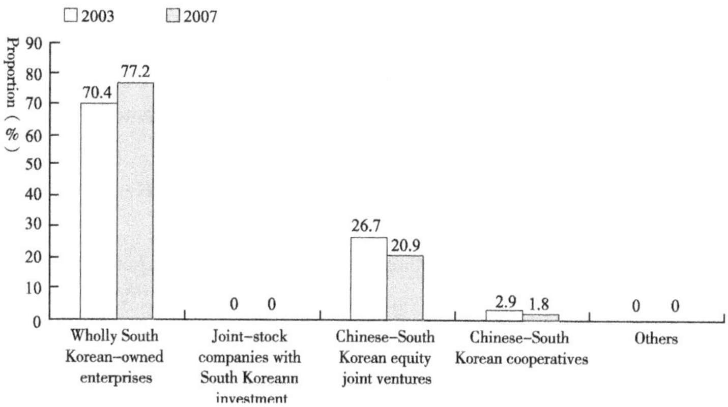

Figure 5-10: Break-down of South Korean Investment in China by type of enterprise, 2003 - 2007

5.4.6. Joint Ventures are less favored than Shareholding

The five major sources of FDI—namely, Hong Kong, Taiwan, the United States, Japan, and Korea—have shown certain changes in their shareholding requirements when establishing joint ventures.

Firstly, the number of joint ventures has, in general, increased steadily. From 2003 to 2007, the number of joint ventures demonstrated a yearly increase, with the exception of certain years (Hong Kong in 2005 and Taiwan, the United States, and Japan in 2007). The number of joint ventures in 2007 was higher than that in 2003, during which time investments from Taiwan, the United States, Japan, and Korea increased by 17%, 12.4%, 46.3%, and 34.6%, respectively.

Secondly, the shareholding patterns of joint ventures structurally show two opposing trends. With the number of joint ventures rising in general, the proportion of joint ventures holding 50% or more in particular stocks has been declining, while the proportion of joint ventures holding less than 50% of stocks increased. From 2003 to 2007, the proportion of Hong Kong-invested joint ventures holding 50% or higher in stocks decreased from 44% to 41%, while that of the Taiwanese ventures declined from 43% to 37%. The percentage of American-invested companies holding a majority share declined from 39% to 36%, Japan from 48% to 43%, and South Korea from 43% to 36%. By contrast, the proportions of joint ventures invested in by the five major investors that held less than 50% of stocks rose from 56% to 59%, 57% to 63%, 61% to 64%, 52% to 57%, and 57% to 64%, respective to Hong Kong, Taiwan, the United States, Japan, and Korea. It indicates that, for whatever reason, more foreign-managed ventures, old or new, chose not to have or to give up the majority share of their establishment.

Thirdly, investors' preferences regarding shareholding differ. In terms of their preference in 2003, Japan ranked top, with a rate of 48% of enterprises engaged with shareholding, while the United States was the lowest, with a rate of 39%. Hong Kong, Taiwan, and South Korea, whose rates ranged from 43% to 44%, ranked in the middle. In 2007, Japan remained the country with the highest rate of shareholding, with a rate of 43%. Next came the 41% of Hong Kong, which didn't change much compared with its rate in 2003. The rates of Taiwan, the United States, and Korea ranged from 36% to 37% in 2007, with low rates of shareholding among major foreign investors. Hong Kong had the smallest drop, just 2 % from 2003 to 2007, followed by the United States' 3 %. Japan ranked third as far as decreasing in shareholding, with a drop of 5 %, while

Taiwan and South Korea had the largest drop, from 6 to 7 %. The last two clearly demonstrate the investors' weakening preference for shareholding. Meanwhile, though the United States and Korea were roughly on par in terms of preferences for shareholding in 2007, the proportion didn't change much compared with that of 2003. Therefore, little change can be assessed in terms of the US's preference for shareholding one way or another.

5.4.7. The Number of Corporate and Cooperative Enterprises Remain Few, with Slow Growth

Corporate enterprises, cooperatives, and other forms of investment experienced little change in terms of either growth in overall number or proportion of growth from 2003 to 2007. Hong Kong was the exception, with numerous cooperatives. Apart from owning a large number of wholly foreign-owned enterprises and joint ventures, Hong Kong had 1.6 times and 1.4 times more cooperatives in 2003 and 2007, respectively, than other four major foreign investors.

During 2003 and 2007, despite small increases in the number of Japanese and Korean cooperatives (increasing by 52 companies and 16 companies, respectively), the number of cooperatives of the other three major investors declined, with Hong Kong decreasing by 1414 companies, the US by 124 companies, and Taiwan by 312 companies.

In 2003 and 2007, the number of Hong Kong corporate enterprises invested in mainland China was 134 and 302, respectively. Meanwhile, the number of American and Japanese corporate enterprises increased from over 10 companies to over 30 companies during these five years. However, the number of Taiwanese and Korean corporate enterprises remained fewer than ten. As a result, it is hardly convincing to draw any conclusions of practical significance based on either the numbers or the proportions discussed above.

5.5 The Geographical Distribution of Investments by Major Investors

Hong Kong, Taiwan, the United States, Japan, and Korea are the five major regions and countries investing directly in mainland China. From 2003 to 2007, 67%~72% of Hong Kong enterprises, 58%~64% of Taiwanese enterprises, 55%~65% of American enterprises, 60%~63% of Japanese enterprises, and 20%~30% of Korean enterprises were concentrated in Beijing, Shanghai, Guangdong, Jiangsu, and Zhejiang provinces. It can be concluded that those five Chinese municipalities and provinces have become home to the majority of the enterprises of the five major foreign investors.

Moreover, three features are consistently demonstrated in terms of the geographical choices made by the five foreign investors in the five Chinese municipalities and provinces. First of all, Hong Kong investments show distinctive geographical features. Secondly, Shanghai is largely favored by foreign direct investments. Finally, no significant change is seen in terms of the basic methods of absorbing foreign investment across the five municipalities and provinces.

5.5.1. Hong Kong Investments: Distinctive Geographical Features are Maintained by more Investments going North

Guangdong province is a key destination for Hong Kong investment due to its adjacent location to Hong Kong. This geographical preference has weakened in recent years, however. From 2003 to

2007, over 40% of Hong Kong enterprises invested in Guangdong. The proportion was 42% in 2003, which subsequently varied regularly with the rapid growth of Hong Kong investment in other provinces and municipalities, such as Shanghai, Jiangsu, and Zhejiang, only to ultimately stabilize at about 40% (Figure 5-11).

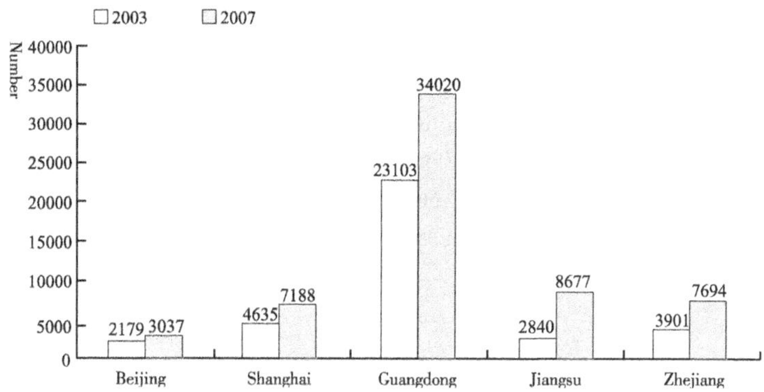

Figure 5-11: Number of companies with investment from Hong Kong in mainland China, 2003 - 2007

At the same time, more Hong Kong investments are moving northward, and Shanghai, Jiangsu, and Zhejiang have become new points of Hong Kong-supplied FDI growth in recent years. In 2007, 7,188 Hong Kong companies invested in Shanghai, increasing by 55% compared with 2003. The numbers of Hong Kong companies invested in Jiangsu and Zhejiang in 2007 were 8,677 and 7694, respectively, with an increase of 205% and 97%. During the same period of time, 34020 Hong Kong companies invested in Guangdong, increasing their numbers by 47%. In terms of absolute numbers, Guangdong remains the key destination for Hong Kong capital. However, in terms of growth rates, the new investments by Hong Kong enterprises in the Pearl River Delta have apparently lagged behind that in Yangtze River Delta. In addition, investment in Guangdong declined by 2%, from 42% in 2003 to 40% in 2007.

The changes to the geographical choices of Hong Kong capital show that, on the one hand, the Yangtze River Delta is becoming a new focal point for China's export-oriented economy. On the other hand, Hong Kong investment in the mainland is becoming more mature, which goes beyond any single geographical factor and begins to take into consideration the comprehensive economic advantages of a given region when choosing their investment destination.

5.5.2. Taiwanese Investment in Zhejiang and Jiangsu Grows Rapidly

From 2003 to 2007, Taiwan witnessed dramatic changes in its investment structure across the five major investment destinations in mainland China.

First, in 2003, Taiwanese companies were mainly concentrated in Guangdong and Shanghai, making up 59.4% of all Taiwanese companies invested in the five major provinces and municipalities of mainland China. However, this proportion dropped to 48.9% in 2007, decreasing by more than 10 %. In contrast, the number of Taiwanese companies invested in Jiangsu reached 4071, increasing by 2,433 companies at a growth rate of 148.5%. This increase accounted for 53.6% of all 4539 new Taiwanese companies investing in the mainland from 2003 to 2007, to surpass Guangdong and Shanghai in becoming the province most favored by Taiwanese investment.

Secondly, great proliferation has been witnessed in terms of Taiwanese companies' investment in Zhejiang. In five years, 440 new Taiwanese companies invested in Zhejiang. Though the total number is still behind the number of Taiwanese companies in Guangdong and Shanghai, the rate of growth reached 27.7%, higher than Guangdong's 15.7% and Shanghai's 21.3%. The growing trend of new Taiwanese investment in Jiangsu and Zhejiang shows the strong agglomerative effect of Taiwanese investment in Zhejiang and Jiangsu, which has the potential to stimulate economic development in the two provinces.

Thirdly, Taiwanese investment in Beijing leveled out over the course of these five years. From 2003 to 2007, only 46 more Taiwanese companies invested in the city municipality, steadily increasing by about 11%. Among the total number of Taiwanese enterprises investing in the five main destinations, the proportion of Taiwanese enterprises in Beijing dropped from 4.9% in 2003 to 3.8% in 2007.

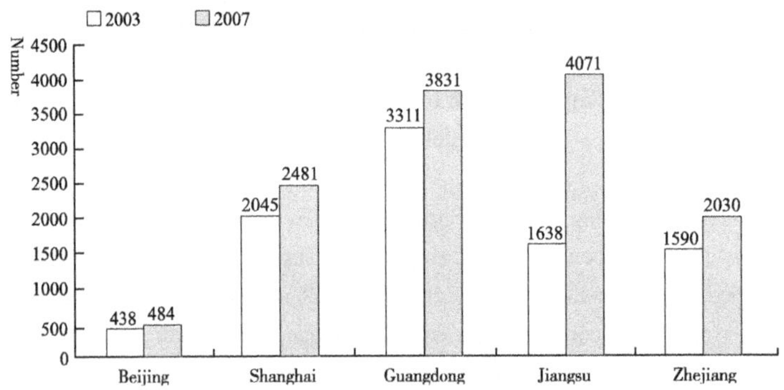

Figure 5-12: Number of companies with investment from Taiwan in mainland China, 2003 - 2007

5.5.3. The United States' Investment in China Remains Largely Balanced, with Jiangsu as New Focal Point

The number of American companies invested in the five most heavily-invested municipalities and provinces of China increased from 6,929 in 2003 to 11384 in 2007, for a net growth of 4455 companies, reaching 64.3% in terms of growth rate. It accounted for 89.4% of all American companies invested in China, indicating that the five municipalities and provinces are the key recipients of American investment. Statistics show that, in terms of new American enterprises invested in the five regions, Beijing increased by 429 companies with a growth rate of 26.1%, Shanghai increased by 1,097 companies with a growth rate of 51.2%, Guangdong increased by 646 companies with a growth rate of 64.7%, Jiangsu increased by 1652 companies with a growth rate of 131.1%, and Zhejiang increased by 631 companies with a growth rate of 47%. The growth in Jiangsu is, frankly, amazing, almost doubling in five years. What's more, it accounts for 33.2% of all the net growth of American investment in China (Figure 5-13).

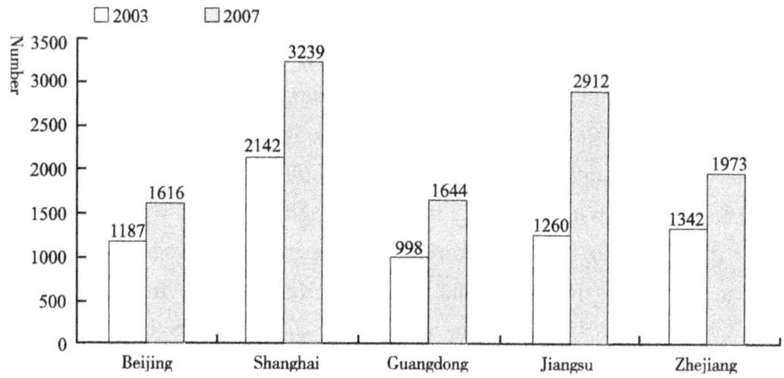

Figure 5-13: Number of enterprises with investment from the US in mainland China, 2003 - 2007

5.5.4. Shanghai Remains the Favorite Focus of Japanese Investment, with Jiangsu Experiencing New Growth

Japanese investments in China have historically been highly concentrated in Shanghai. In 2003, 3,145 Japanese enterprises invested in Shanghai, making up 48.5% of all Japanese enterprises invested in the five regions of China. Though this proportion declined to 43.2% in 2007, the total number of Japanese enterprises there increased to 5240 companies.

Across the span of five years, the net growth of the number of Japanese enterprises invested in China's five most prominent provinces totaled 5634 new enterprises: an increase of 86.9%. Among these, the growth rate of those in Guangdong and Jiangsu surpassed 100%, reaching 110.5% and 179.1%, respectively. Beijing enjoyed an increase of 44.5%; Zhejiang, 54.9%; and Shanghai, 66.6%.

In terms of the geographical distribution of new Japanese companies in these five regions, Jiangsu had 2,146 more companies, an increase of 38.1%; Shanghai gained 2,095 more companies, accounting for 37.2%; Guangdong had 570 more companies, accounting for 10.1%; Zhejiang attracted 526 more companies, accounting for a 9.3% increase; and Beijing had 297 more companies, accounting for 5.3%. New Japanese enterprises in Jiangsu and Shanghai occupied 3/4 of the total in the five regions, indicating that Jiangsu and Shanghai have become the major investment destinations of Japanese capital (Figure 5-14).

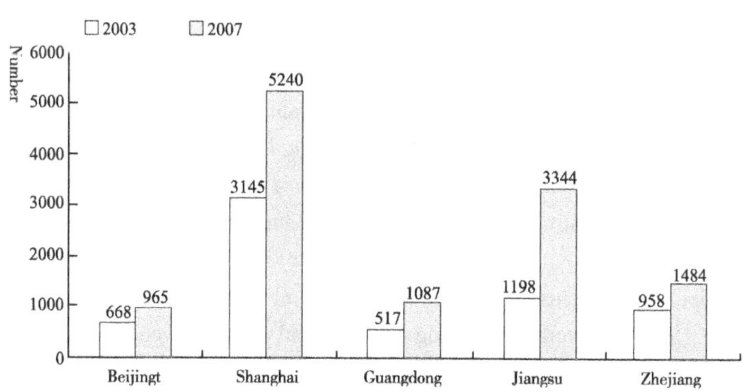

Figure 5-14: Number of enterprises with investment from Japan in mainland China, 2003 - 2007

5.5.5. Korean Investment Focuses on Shanghai and Jiangsu

Firstly, the geographical distribution of Korean investment in China is largely balanced. From 2003 to 2007, Korean companies in Beijing, Shanghai, Guangdong, Jiangsu, and Zhejiang numbered 1,898, 3,061, 3,679, 4,281, and 4,769, respectively, accounting for 20%, 25%, 25%, 27%, and 30% of the total number of Korean companies in China. Compared with the other four major investors, South Korean investment is the most geographically diffuse.

However, the geographical focus of Korean investment has changed greatly. In 2003, the number of Korean companies invested in the five most prominent provinces and municipalities in China was: 447 in Beijing, 418 in Shanghai, 382 in Jiangsu, 378 in Zhejiang, and 273 in Guangdong. In 2007, Korean companies began to focus primarily on Shanghai and Jiangsu, with an increase of 585 and 1184 companies, respectively, in the two regions. This was a growth rate of 140% and 310%. The investment structure in the five regions thus changed from 23.6%, 22%, 14.4%, 20.1%, and 19.9% in 2003 into 20.8%, 21%, 11.4%, 32.8%, and 13.9% in 2007, with declines in the proportions allotted to Beijing and Shanghai and a sharp increase in that of Jiangsu. The proportion of Korean foreign investment in Guangdong and Zhejiang decreased moderately. The largest gap among the five regions was the rise in the investment structure from a 9% increase in 2003 to a 21% growth increase in 2007. Changes largely took place in 2004, when Korean enterprises in Jiangsu increased by 661, an increase of 173% in terms of growth rate. In 2007, the number of Korean enterprises in Shanghai increased by 168, with a growth rate of 20.1%. Thus, the overall structure of Korean investment in China changed dramatically (Figure 5-15).

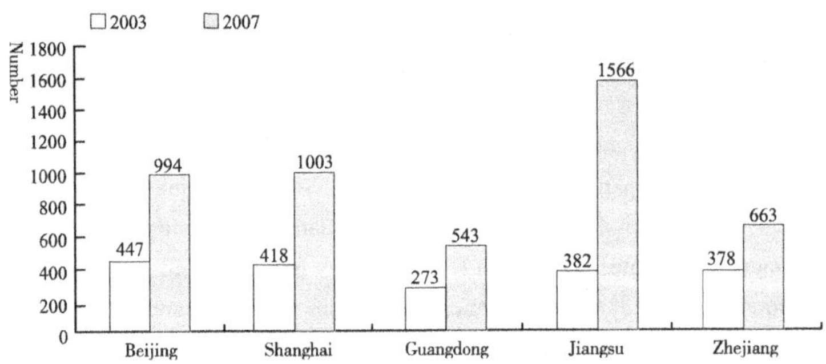

Figure 5-15: Number of enterprises with investment from South Korea in mainland China, 2003 - 2007

Through an analysis of the investment patterns of these five FDI source countries and regions, we can draw the following conclusions: firstly, the geographical structure of the five major source countries and regions remains, basically, unchanged; Hong Kong's investment in China has strong geographical features; new enterprises in Taiwan and Korea are primarily concentrated in Jiangsu; American investment is relatively balanced, while Japanese companies favors Shanghai; and Shanghai and Jiangsu are becoming the new focal points of foreign direct investment. This shift in geographical importance is closely related to the rapid economic growth of the Yangtze River Delta since the 1990s, as well as growing international competitiveness strengthened by the development of associated industries and the improvement of public infrastructure.

Chapter 6 The Operation of Foreign-Invested Enterprises, their Profitability, and Tariffs

China's utilization of foreign direct investment (FDI) still lags behind the average level of the rest of the world. Chinese foreign direct investment enterprises not only constitute a significant component of Chinese enterprises and the national economy, but are also integral to the global economy and transnational enterprises, which may reflect the special characteristics of the Chinese economy as well as the general trend of changes in the world economy as a whole. Foreign investment enterprises are characterized by their rapid development and the structural inequality in their industrial and regional development, particularly in China.

The decreased contribution of imports and exports to the economy and the growth rate of foreign investment enterprises in China indicates the gradual diminishment of the traditional economic strategy in which a sizeable labor force is the sole advantage. Expanding the proportion of daily sales in the domestic market reflects the fact that, now, foreign investment is increasingly being drawn to the other attractions of the Chinese market. The property scale of foreign investment enterprises in China has increased both rapidly and steadily, contrasting with the trend by which foreign direct investment primarily flows into the service industry. The Chinese manufacturing industry attracts a comparatively large proportion of foreign investment, while, for all its growth, the service industry attracts a comparatively small one. Foreign investment enterprises in China reflect the trend in which the turnover of assets and the earnings power of real assets increase year by year; conversely, in foreign investment enterprises in the United States and the rest of the world, the speed of asset turnover and the earnings power of real assets continues to diminish. In terms of the growth rate of assets, asset utilization, and the growth rate of assets earned, foreign investments in China show an obvious inclination towards wholly foreign-owned enterprises. Other investment methods are all less efficient and profitable than wholly foreign-owned enterprises, as foreign investment enterprises in China have a comparatively light tax burden. The trend in which both overall profits and the overall loss of foreign investment enterprises in China are increasing, and the scale by which profits increase rapidly every year,is on par with the rest of the world.The average social net profit margin of foreign investment enterprises in China, however, differs from that of the US, as well as the world. The average social return on the total assets of foreign investment enterprises in China increases yearly, corresponding with that of the profit ratio of industrial capital in China and the net profit margin of foreign investment in the US. The rate of return on foreign investment capital in China is also increasing, and is characterized by regional distribution.

6.1 Foreign Investment Enterprises in China are Developing Rapidly

In the past thirty years, foreign investment enterprises in China have made great contributions to the country's trade, which plays an important role in economic development. In recent years, the proportion of foreign direct investment in China in fixed assets investment, as well as in the proportion of foreign-funded enterprises' assets to the total assets of the same industry, has been increasing.The scale of foreign-funded enterprises in China has also been increasing. Additionally, due to the sustained reconstruction of recent years, both the competence and efficiency of foreign-funded enterprises have increased greatly. Foreign-funded enterprises have transformed from their initial beginnings as production factories into modern enterprises incorporating various functions like production, sales, research, finance, and capital operations. Additionally, systematic coordination between different enterprises has been strengthened greatly. Those changes have a great influence on entities within the economy, such as production, distribution, and technology.This promotes the growth of the Chinese economy, raises the level of technology, improves the quality of capital, cultivates human resources, and increases the competitiveness of the Chinese market economy. These changes allow technologies and knowledge from foreign-funded enterprises to rapidly saturate the market, from which the Chinese economy greatly benefits. However, up until recently, Chinese economic development and technology remained at a low level. The scale of capital was also comparatively small, as economic development still depends greatly on foreign direct investment. China's utilization of foreign capital is not commensurate with the proportion of the total economy to China's population, such that China's utilization of FDI is far from the global average. The time has not yet come when China can develop autonomously without the aid of FDI.

According to statistics released by the Chinese Ministry of Commerce, from the years 1979 to 2008, the overall use of actual foreign capital was USD 902.661 billion, of which the actual use of incoming foreign capital from 2003 to 2008 by year was USD 56.140 billion , USD 64.072 billion, USD 63.805 billion , USD 67.076 billion, USD 78.339 billion, and USD 95.253 billion, respectively. The overall actual use of foreign capital from these six years was a collective USD 424.685 billion, almost accounting for half of the actual use of foreign capital investments in the past thirty years overall. Even though the actual use of incoming foreign capital in 2008 was USD 95.253 billion (the highest amount on record at that time), the actual ratio of the utilization of foreign capital per capita in China was only USD 70, while the average use of foreign capital per capita in the world was around USD 280 , and the average use of foreign capital per capita in the United States was USD 1,036 . When viewed in these terms, there is a significant gap not only between China and the United States, but also between China and the average economic level of the rest of the world. China's actual use of foreign capital is still far from sufficient.

According to statistics from the United Nations Conference on Trade and Development, from 2006 to 2008, the world's incoming FDI was 1411 billion dollars, 1979 billion dollars, and USD 1,697 billion, respectively, with a growth rate of 50.1%, 35.4%, and 14.2%. In the year 2008, however, influenced by the international financial crisis, foreign direct investment shrank by a large margin (See Table 6-1).

Table 6-1: Indexes of Global Foreign Direct Investment and International Production between1982 and 2008

	Values at Current Price (*One Billion Dollars)					Annual Growth Rate (%)							
Year	1982	1990	2006	2007	2008	86-90	91-95	96-00	2004	2005	2006	2007	2008
FDI inflow	58	207	1411	1979	1697	23.6	22.1	39.4	30.0	32.4	50.1	35.4	-14.2
FDI outflow	27	239	1323	2147	1858	25.9	16.5	35.6	65.0	-5.4	58.9	53.7	-13.5
Inward FDI stocks	790	1942	12470	15660	14909	15.1	8.6	16.0	17.7	4.6	23.4	26.2	-4.8
Outward FDI Stocks	579	1786	12756	16227	16206	18.1	10.6	16.9	16.8	5.1	22.2	25.3	-0.1
Inward FDI Stocks Income	44	74	950	1 182	1171	10.2	35.3	13.3	33.4	32.8	23.3	21.9	-0.9
Outward FDI Stocks Income	46	120	1038	1 252	1273	18.7	20.2	10.3	42.3	28.4	18.4	18.5	1.7
Cross-Border Mergers and Acquisitions	..	112	1118	1031	673	32.0	15.7	62.9	28.4	91.1	38.1	62.1	-34.7
Sales of Foreign Subsidiaries	2530	6026	25844	31764	30311	19.7	8.8	8.1	26.8	5.4	18.9	23.6	-4.6
Gross Product of Foreign Subsidiaries	623	1477	5049	6295	6020	17.4	6.8	6.9	13.4	12.9	21.8	20.1	-4.4
Total Assets of Foreign Subsidiaries	2036	5938	55818	73457	69771	18.1	13.7	18.9	4.8	20.5	23.9	20.8	-5.0
Export Value of Foreign Subsidiaries Sales	635	1498	4950	5775	6664	22.2	8.6	3.6	21.3	13.8	15.0	16.3	15.4
Employees of Foreign Subsidiaries Sales(*1000)	19864	24476	70003	80396	77386	5.5	5.5	9.7	12.2	8.5	11.4	25.4	-3.7
Gross Domestic Product (at Current Price)	11963	22121	48925	55114	60780	9.5	5.9	1.3	12.6	8.4	8.2	12.5	10.3
Gross Fixed Assets Formation	2795	5099	10922	12399	13824	10.0	5.4	1.1	15.4	11.8	10.9	13.8	11.5
Charge for Chartered Rights and Licenses	9	29	142	163	177	21.1	14.6	8.1	23.7	10.6	9.1	16.1	8.6
Export of Goods and Non-Factored Service □	2395	4414	14848	17321	19990	11.6	7.9	3.7	21.3	13.8	15.0	16.3	15.4

Data Source: The United Nations Conference on Trade and Development (UNCTAD)

In 2006 and 2007, foreign investment coming into China was USD 72.715 billion and USD 83.521 billion, respectively, which only made up 5.1% and 4.2% of the world's total incoming foreign investment. In 2006 and 2007, foreign investment coming into the United States was USD 236.719 billion and USD 232.865 billion, accounting for 16.8% and 11.8%, respectively, of the world's incoming foreign investment. Although the growth rate by which China's absorbs foreign investment is increasing comparatively quickly, when compared with world superpowers'use of foreign investment, foreign investment inflow in China accounts for a comparatively small proportion of the world foreign investment inflow.

In terms of FDI stocks, the scale of China's use of foreign investment to the proportion of that ofthe world is also comparatively low. According to statistics from the United Nations Conference on Trade and Development, at the end of 2006 and 2007, China's use of foreign investment stocks were around USD 292.56 billion and USD 327.09 billion, respectively, while the use of foreign investment stocks of the United States were around USD 1,843.89 billion and USD 2,093.05 billion, respectively.At the same time in the United Kingdom, the numbers were USD 1,133.44 billion and USD 1347.69 billion , respectively. In 2006 and 2007, global inward FDI stocks were USD 12,470 billion and USD 15,660 billion. China's use of inward FDI stocks only accounted for 2.3% and 2.1% of the global total, while the use of inward FDI stocks by the United States accounted for 14.8% and 13.4% of the world's, respectively, and the figures for the United Kingdom came up at 9.1% and 8.6%. In terms of foreign investment stocks, China's proportion of the world still has a great gap with that of other national powers.

From 2006 to 2008, the world's inward FDI flow accounted for 13.4%, 16.0%, and 12.3%, respectively, of all fixed assets, while in those three years, China's inward FDI flow only accounted for 6.4%, 6.0%, and 6.0%, respectively, of fixed assets. The gap between China and the world's average level was 7%, 10%, and 6% (See Table 6-2 and Table 6-3), which demonstrates a significant extant gap. China's use of foreign investment as fixed assets still makes up quite a small proportion of its total use of FDI. The majority of fixed assets are not foreign-owned, and in terms of the proportion of outward FDI stocks in fixed assets, China makes up a small proportion. As such, China's foreign direct investment lags behind.

Table 6-2: The Combined Proportion of Total Global FDI (%)

	Percent of FDI Flow in the Formation of Fixed Assets			Percent of FDI Stocks in GDP		
	2006	2007	2008	1990	2000	2008
Inward	13.4	16.0	12.3	9.1	18.1	24.5
Outward	12.9	17.4	13.5	8.5	19.2	26.9

Data source: UNCTAD, FDI/TNC database

Table 6-3: The Combined Proportion of China's FDI (%)

	Percent of FDI Flow in the Formation of Fixed Assets			Percent of FDI Stocks in GDP		
	2006	2007	2008	1990	2000	2008
Inward	6.4	6.0	6.0	5.1	16.2	8.7
Outward	1.9	1.6	2.9	1.1	2.3	3.4

Data source: UNCTAD, FDI/TNC database

In terms of the proportion of inward-directed FDI stocks to overall GDP, in 1990, 2000, and 2008, the average global level was at 9.1%, 18.1%, and then 24.5%, presenting an upward trend and demonstrating that the contribution FDI stocks make to GDP has increased continuously. In1990, 2000, and 2008, China's inward-flowing FDI stocks accounted for 5.1%, 16.2%, and 8.7%, respectively, of GDP. Except for 2000, the proportion of China's FDI stocks was slightly lower than the average global level; the low level seen in 1990 was due to the fact that China was not economically open at that time.The proportion of China's FDI stocks to overall GDP in 2008 was notably lower than average global level, which shows that the status of China's foreign investment stocks contributing to GDP has continued to decrease.

When considering the proportion of foreign investment per capita, incoming foreign investment,and stocks in the global marketplace, the proportion of foreign investment in fixed assets formation and the proportion of foreign investment stocks in GDP is significantly lower in China than in the rest of the world. China has great potential to expand the scale of its use of foreign investment,but currently has never had the opportunity. Theory and policies should not be influenced by the rumors regarding reducing external dependence, which stress relying on China's own efforts and transforming the country's economic development into one that mainly relies on domestic demand. As for policies, it is necessary to maintain an open road of economic development, to keep expanding the scale of foreign investment utilization, to adjust the spatial layout and industrial structure of foreign investment use, to improve the quality of foreign investment utilization, and to increase the level at which foreign investment is used. Before both the private economy and market economy disappear in China, in order to improve the efficiency of resource distribution, China should not reject foreign investment, but make use of it in order to improve economic efficiency and imbue new energy into its current economy.

6.2 The Speed and Structural Characteristics of Foreign Investment Enterprises

In recent years, economic development in China has been characterized both by high speed and structural imbalances. Those two characteristics are also fully embodied in the foreign investment enterprises of China.

6.2.1. The Number of Foreign-Invested Business Enterprises in China are Increasing Rapidly

According to certain statistics, in 2003, there were more than 140,000 foreign investment enterprises in China with combined sales incomes of 5,784.9 billion *yuan*. In 2004, the number of foreign investment enterprises in China expanded to 170,000, increasing by 19.7%, with sales income of 8,540.5 billion *yuan*, increasing by 47.6%. In 2005, the number of foreign investment enterprises in China increased to 190,000, increasing by 10.8%, with a sales income of 10,665.1 billion *yuan*, increasing by 24.8%. In 2006, the number of foreign investment enterprises in China expanded to 207,000, increasing by 9%, with a sales income of 13,737.1 billion *yuan*, increasing by 28.8%. In 2007, the number of foreign investment enterprises in China expanded to 220,000, increasing by 6.2%, with a sales income of 17308.4 billion *yuan*, increasing by 26%. The increased rate of the number of foreign investment enterprises in China gradually slowed, while sales incomes maintained an annual rate of increase of more than 20%.

On the whole, the businesses of foreign investment enterprises in China maintained a high momentum of development, but the individual speed differed across various types of enterprises. From 2003 to 2007, in terms of the changes in sales income of foreign investment enterprises in China and classed by type of enterprise, the proportion of sales income of wholly foreign-owned enterprises to overall sales income increased gradually, while the proportion of sales income of foreign-owned joint venture enterprises decreased. The proportion of sales income of wholly foreign-owned enterprises increased from 41.5% in 2003 to 50.6% in 2007 for a rapid increase in business. The development of Chinese-foreign joint ventures and Chinese foreign cooperatives steadily increased at a comparatively low rate. From the year 2004 to 2007, the increased rate of sales income of Chinese-foreign joint ventures was 36.2%, 18.1%, 26%, and 26.3%, respectively. However, the proportion of sales income of Chinese-foreign joint ventures to the overall sales of foreign investment enterprises decreased, from 45% in 2003 to 38.5% in 2007. From 2004 to 2007, the increased rate of sales income of Chinese foreign cooperatives was 12%, 9.7%, 10.9%, and 9.2%, respectively. Comparatively speaking, the speed of development of joint-equity foreign investment enterprises was more rapid than that of other investment models. From 2004 to 2007, the rate of increase was 28.9%, 49.6%, 39.8%, and 34%.

The development of foreign investment enterprises was not steady, however. At present, Chinese-foreign joint ventures and Chinese foreign cooperatives are still the two main models of foreign investment enterprises. Wholly foreign-owned enterprises, with the fastest growth rate, are more suitable to being managed by foreign investment enterprises and have subsequently become the dominant type of enterprise in the foreign investment economy, indicating a trend towards wholly foreign-owned enterprises. In the future, except for the war industry, China's foreign investment policy should give foreign investors greater autonomy in choosing the organizational form of their enterprises and improve the level of freedom of investment. The government should not require that foreign investors invest in an enterprise with the form of Chinese-foreign joint ventures or Chinese foreign cooperatives.7

6.2.2. Regional Development in China and the Industrial Development of Foreign Investment Enterprises are Imbalanced

The sales income brought in by foreign investment enterprises in China has a high rate of increase, and the share of foreign investment economics in the national economy is also gradually growing more dominant. However, there are imbalances in the regional and industrial development of foreign investment enterprises, which may bring structural problems of imbalance in regional and industrial development to the whole country (not just to foreign investment enterprises).

The businesses of foreign investment enterprises in China are mainly located in the eastern provinces and cities along the coast or Yangtze River. In terms of the sales income of foreign investment enterprises in other areas in China, provinces and cities such as Guangdong, Jiangsu, and Zhejiang Provinces—as well as Beijing and Shanghai—contain the majority of foreign investment enterprises with the largest scale of sales income. In 2007, sales income from Guangdong, Jiangsu, Zhejiang, Beijing, and Shanghai accounted for 22.4%,16.8%, 15.6%, 8.3%, and 6.8%, respectively,of sales income overall, and,taken together, collectively made up 70% of the overall sales income of foreign investment enterprises in China.In comparatively

[7]Data were drawn from the Chinese Academy of Social Sciences' Research Group on Foreign Investment and Trade Enterprises with Foreign Investment survey results. Similarly hereinafter.

less-developed provinces and areas in western China, however, such as Guizhou, Yunnan, Gansu, and Qinghai provinces, as well as the Xinjiang Uygur and Ningxia Hui autonomous regions and Tibet, due to a lack of advantages in attracting investment, foreign investment enterprises remain few, and the scale of their sales income also only accounts for a small proportion of the overall sales income of foreign investment enterprises in the entire country. As a result, foreign investment enterprises still do not have any obvious positive influences on the local economic society of those regions. Those areas still need to open wider to the outside of the world in order to improve the role the foreign investment economy plays in the national economy. Meanwhile, they should open the market to domestic private investment, use the private economy to attract foreign investment, and promote the development of a multi-economy.

Firstly, those businesses of foreign investment enterprises already in China mainly focused on the manufacturing industry. In the years between 2003 and 2007, the sales income of foreign investment enterprises in China's manufacturing industry accounted for a large proportion of the overall sales income of foreign investment enterprises, at 74.4%, 76.2%, 77%, 75.4%, and 73.7%, respectively, of the sales income of foreign investment enterprises overall. From 2004 to 2007, however, the increased rate of sales income of foreign investment enterprises in the manufacturing industry decreased yearly, at 51.1%, 26.1%, 26.1%, and 23.1%, respectively.

Secondly, the sales income of foreign investment enterprises in wholesaling and retail also accounted for a significant proportion in the overall sales income of foreign investment enterprises, at 7.4%, 6.3%, 6.1%, 6.9%, and 8.5% of all income, respectively, and with annual rates of increase of 25.4%, 21.7%, 45.1%, and 56%. The increase of sales in education, water conservancy, the environment and public facility management industry, the residential and related service industry, culture, the sports and entertainment industry, health, the social security and social welfare industry, public management and social organization, and the international organization service industry was not steady. Businesses of foreign investment enterprises invested in architecture, the transportation industry, storage and the postal service industry, information transmission, the computer service and software industry, the accommodation and catering industry, the production and supply of power, gas and water, the financial industry, the realty industry, the leasing and commercial services industry, scientific research, technology services, and the geological survey industry increased steadily at a comparatively high speed. Foreign investment enterprises in the mining industry increased rapidly, from 2003 to 2007, however, the increase of sales income in foreign investment enterprises from agriculture, forestry, stock farming and the fishery industry was not steady. Between year 2005 and 2007, there was also a significant drop in sales.

6.3 The Operational and Strategic Transition of Foreign Investment Enterprises

6.3.1. The Decline of Imports,Exports,and the Growth Rate of Foreign Investment Enterprises in China Highlights the Gradual Decline of the Strategy by which a Large Labor Force is the Sole Advantage

Foreign investment enterprises in China are an important component of the national economy and make great contributions to Chinese economic development. Foreign investment enterprises, along with various economic sectors—such as the state-owned economy, collective economy, private economy and stock economy—work together to promote the long-term and sustainable development of the Chinese economy, which has positive influences on the Chinese macro economy as a whole. The primary contribution made by foreign investment enterprises is that of promoting the development of the Chinese export-oriented economy, especially the development of the import and export trade of Chinese commodities. Foreign-invested enterprises play vital roles in the import and export trade and are themselves an indispensable component. Contributions made by foreign investment enterprises are embodied in many important aspects of the economy, such as the increase of GDP, the improvement of technology and industrial structural upgrading, expanding exports and improving the production structure of exports, as well as strengthening the competence of research and development. (Jiang Xiaojuan, 2002a)[8]Trade from foreign investment enterprises accounts for more than half of the overall import and export volume of the whole country. However, the annual rate of increase has been declining in recent years. Foreign investment enterprises are heavily involved in the export of goods and services, which promotes the development of the national economy and foreign trade.

In 2005, the total value of the import and export of foreign investment enterprises in China accounted for 58.48% of the overall macro-economic value of the whole country. The total value of exports accounted for 58.3% of the overall value of the whole country, while the total value of imports accounted for 58.7% of the overall value of the whole country. The rate of increase from 2005 to 2007 was 25.42%, 31.19%, and 19.4%, respectively, compared with 2008. (See Table 6-4) The proportions and growth rates of 2006 and 2007 declined. In 2008, the total value of the import and export of foreign investment enterprises in China accounted for 55.07% of the overall value of the whole country. The total value of exports accounted for 55.34% of the overall value of the whole country, and the total value of imports accounted for 54.71% of the overall value of the whole country. The growth rate was 12.4%, 13.67%, and 10.82%, respectively.Therefore, foreign investment enterprises accounted for more than half of the overall value of import and export of the whole country. Foreign investment enterprises have a positive trade effect on China. They push forward the growth of exportsin China, raise the level of competitive power of Chinese products, and bring along the competition in which Chinese enterprises participate in the global value chain. (Xian Guoming, 2002[9]; Zhan Xiaoning and Chen Jianguo, 2002[10]; Dai Jinping, 2003[11]) Foreign investment enterprises make a significant contribution towards expanding the scale of exports in China and improving the structure of Chinese export commodities. (Jiang Xiaojuan, 2002b)[12]

---

[8]Jiang Xiaojuan, "Contributions Made by Foreign Investment Economy in China to Increase, Structural Upgrading and Competitive Power,"*Social Sciences in China No. 6*(2002)

[9] Xian Guoming, "Promoting Linkages Becomes a New Trend of Host Countries' Policies to Attract Foreign Direct Investments,"*International Economic Cooperation No.1*(2002)

[10] Zhan Xiaoning and Chen Jianguo, "Export Competitive Power and the Function of FDI in Transnational Corporations,"*The Journal of World Economy No.11*(2002)

[11] Dai Jinping, "Foreign Direct Investment and Chinese Export Competitive Power,"*Nankai Economic Studies No.5*(2003)

[12] Jiang Xiaojuan,"Chinese Export Growth and Structural Changes: The Contributions Made by Foreign Investment Enterprises,"*Nankai Economic Studies No.2*(2002)

Table 6-4: The Proportion and Growth of Imported and Exported Goods of Foreign Investment Enterprises in China

Year	Type of Growth	Amount (in Billions of U.S. Dollars)	Country-Wide Proportion (%)	Yearly Growth(%)
2005	Total Combined Value of Imports and Exports	8317.26	58.48	25.42
	Total Value of Exports	4442.1	58.30	31.19
	Total Value of Imports	3875.16	58.70	19.40
2006	Total Combined Value of Imports and Exports	10364.51	58.87	24.61
	Total Value of Exports	5838.35	58.18	26.93
	Total Value of Imports	4726.16	59.70	21.96
2007	Total Combined Value of Imports and Exports	12549.28	57.73	21.08
	Total Value of Exports	6955.2	57.10	23.36
	Total Value of Imports	5594.08	58.53	18.36
2008	Total Combined Value of Imports and Exports	14105.76	55.07	12.40
	Total Value of Exports	7906.20	55.34	13.67
	Total Value of Imports	6199.56	54.71	10.82

Data were drawn from the Chinese Academy of Social Sciences' Research Group on Foreign Investment and Trade Enterprises with Foreign Investment survey results. Similarly hereinafter.

The tendency of foreign investment enterprises towards a high volume of imports and exports has begun to decline, however. The annual growth rate of imports and exports has decreased, which shows the comparative advantage of a cheap labor force in foreign investment. Foreign investment enterprises have placed an increasing emphasis on the Chinese domestic market. Chinese domestic enterprises and foreign trade have gradually grown. Foreign investment enterprises have different export tendencies in different types of enterprises, as well as different impacts on the economies of various industries and regions in China. They fully reflect the comparative advantage of the cheap Chinese labor force as utilized by foreign investment enterprises. They maximize interests by taking advantage of their respective capitals, technologies, marketing, and management, and by making savvy choices about the different types of enterprises, different geographical positions, and different industries.

In terms of the type of enterprise, in contrast to the decreasing proportion of export-based income of Chinese foreign equity joint ventures to the overall export of foreign investment enterprises and the decreasing scale of exports, the proportion of export-based income of wholly owned foreign enterprises to the overall export of foreign investment enterprises is steadily increasing. In 2005 and 2007, the export value of Chinese foreign equity joint ventures was USD 1440.4 billion, USD 1,784.6 billion, and USD 1,763.8 billion, respectively, accounting for 28.7%, 29.1%, and 27.2% of the overall value of the export of foreign investment in those years. It increased by 23.9% in 2006 and decreased the following year by 1.2%. (See Table 6-5) From 2005 to 2007, the value of the exports of wholly foreign-owned enterprises was USD 3,189 billion, USD 3,893.7 billion, and USD 4,177.6 billion, respectively, accounting for 63.5%, 63.5%, and 64.5%of the overall value of the export of foreign investment. The rate of increase in 2006 and 2007 was 22.1% and 7.3%. In 2006, cooperative foreign investment enterprises grew slightly. In 2007, there was a big drop of 25.9%. In 2006 and 2007, the exports of joint-stock enterprises increased greatly. The rate of increase over these two years was27.5% and 53.4%, respectively. Different types of foreign investment enterprises, therefore,had different influences on Chinese foreign investment imports and exports.

Table 6-5: The Scale of Exports by Foreign Investment Enterprises in China as Classified by Type of Enterprise

Unit: *100 million yuan

Type of Enterprises by Year	2005	2006	2007
Wholly Foreign-owned	31890	38937	41776
Joint-Stock	1971	2514	3856
Joint Venture	14404	17846	17638
Cooperative	1919	2022	1499
Other	11	0.2	0
Total	**50195**	**61319**	**64769**

Data were drawn from the Chinese Academy of Social Sciences' Research Group on Foreign Investment and Trade Enterprises with Foreign Investment survey results. Similarly hereinafter.

In terms of the industrial distribution of foreign investment enterprises' exports in China, the manufacturing industry, wholesaling, retail, and the transportation industry, as well as the storage and postal industry, are the largest industries with the broadest scale of exports, accounting for 92% to 96% of exports across all industries. From 2005 to 2007, the exports of foreign investment enterprises in manufacturing industries were 4,316 billion *yuan*, 5,249.4 billion *yuan*, and 5691.7 billion *yuan*, respectively, accounting for 86%, 85.6%, and 87.9% of all exports. The rate of increase in 2006 and 2007 was 21.6% and 8.4%, respectively. Foreign direct investment has had positive influences on the import and export trade in China, especially the import and export of industrial products. (Mo Junyang and Liu Weijiang, 2001)13 From 2005 to 2007, the exports of foreign investment enterprises in the wholesale and retail industry accounted for 3%, 4.1%, and

[13]Mo Junyang and Liu Weijiang, "The Empirical Analysis on Trade Effect of Foreign Direct Investment,"*The Journal of Shanghai University of Finance No.3*(2001)

4.2%, respectively, of the overall export of foreign investment enterprises. In 2006 and 2007, the rate of increase was 70.9% and 7.8%, respectively. From 2005 to 2007, the scale of exports of transport, storage, and the postal industry was 155.4 billion *yuan*, 199.1 billion *yuan*, and 251.8 billion *yuan*, accounting for 3.1%, 3.2%, and 3.9% of the overall export of foreign investment across all industries. The increase in the export of foreign investment enterprises in other industries was not steady, however. Sharp declines in exports appeared in 2006 and 2007.

The role played by foreign investment enterprises in China differs from area to area of investment, as does its role in the steady increase of exports. Even though foreign investment has greatly improved the competitiveness of exports in the eastern areas, it has had no obvious influence on the western areas and may have even had some negative effects on the central areas.(Yan Bing, 2006)14 More than 30% of exports were due to foreign investment enterprises in Guangdong. From 2005 to 2007, exports of foreign investment enterprises in Guangdong was 1,600.67 billion *yuan*, 1,904.24 billion *yuan*, and 1,966.94 billion *yuan*, accounting for 31.9%, 31.1%, and 30.4%, respectively, of the overall export of foreign investment enterprises. In 2006 and 2007, the rates of increase were 19% and 3.3%, respectively. The scale of exports and the growth of foreign investment enterprises were equal in influence and power. The proportion of the exports of foreign investment enterprises in Beijing, Zhejiang, Shandong, Tianjin, Fujian, and Liaoning decreased successively. The export growth of foreign investment enterprises in Beijing, Tianjin, and Inner Mongolia was not steady, while the growth of foreign investment enterprises' exports in other provinces and cities was. The export scale of foreign investment enterprises in the central and western areas was comparatively small, with unsteady growth.

6.3.2. The Expansion of Domestic Sales by Foreign Investment Enterprises in China Reflects that the Chinese Market has begun Attracting Foreign Investment

In the past, foreign investment enterprises took advantage of the cheap materials and labor force offered by China to improve their competitive power on the international market and to then sell products back to both the market and the secondary market, where capital originated, to make a profit.As the Chinese market gradually became increasingly open, the purchasing power of domestic consumers has gradually increased. Foreign investment enterprises have noticed the potentially huge consumer market with its population of 1.3 billion. They have strengthened the sales of products, established sales channels, and improved the share of the domestic market.

In 2005, 167,000 foreign investment enterprises in China had reached a sales income of 10,665.1 billion *yuan*, among which domestic sales were 5,645.6 billion *yuan*, accounting for 53% of total sales, and export sales were 5,019.5 billion *yuan*, accounting for 47%. The ratio of domestic to export sales was 100 to 88.9. In 2006, 187,000 foreign investment enterprises in China had reached a sales income of 13737.1 billion *yuan*, of which domestic sales were 7605.2 billion *yuan*, accounting for 55.4%, and export sales were 6131.9 billion *yuan*, accounting for 44.6%. The ratio of domestic to export sales was 100 to 80.6. In 2007, 203,000 foreign investment enterprises in China had reached a sales income of 17,308.4 billion *yuan*, among which domestic sales were 10,831.5 billion *yuan*, accounting for 58.8%, and export sales were 6476.9 billion *yuan*, accounting for 41.2%. The ratio of domestic to export sales was 100 to 70.2.

In 2006, the domestic sales of foreign investment enterprises increased by 34.7% and export sales of foreign investment enterprises increased by 22.2%. In 2007, the domestic sales of foreign investment enterprises increased by 42.4%, and export sales of foreign investment enterprises

[14] Yan Bing, "FDI and Chinese Export Competitive Power," *Finance and Trade Economics No.8*(2006)

increased by 5.6%. The share of the domestic sales of foreign investment enterprises has been increasing gradually, while export tendencies have been declining every year. Foreign investment enterprises have been transforming from a development model that mainly relies on exportsinto a development mode increasingly focused on the domestic market. Most of the increase in the sales income of foreign investment enterprises comes from increases in domestic sales, while export sales are gradually slowing down. In 2006, domestic sales of the world's largest 100 transnational companies accounted for 58% of total exports—61% and 61% of the market in 2007 and 2008—which were much higher than the proportion of export sales being made by foreign investment enterprises in China. (See Table 6-7)

As a result, large transnational companies have been making transnational investments with the purpose of getting more access to the profits of the Chinese market, instead of pursuing their own local market. However, the foreign investment enterprises in China still export much more than do foreign investment enterprises in the United States. In 2000, the ratio of domestic and export sales was 100 to 7.9. Export sales only accounted for 7.3% of the market. In 2005, the ratio of domestic and export sales was 100 to 7.5. Export sales accounted for about 7%. (See Table 6-6) In the United States, foreign investment enterprises mainly relied on domestic sales, with exports only a subsidiary.

Table 6-6: Details about the Operation of Foreign Investment Enterprises in the United States

Unit: *100 million dollars

Year	Total Assets	Sales	Net Income	Gross Product	Compensation and Welfare	Employment(*10000)	Exports of Branch Agencies	Imports of Branch Agencies	Research of branch Agencies
2000	42163.49	20518.78	254.38	4472.87	2927.26	565.65	1509.11	3546.13	261.80
2001	47606.42	20702.34	-517.74	4171.22	3100.15	559.43	1455.25	3338.55	264.63
2002	45731.39	20309.62	-549.73	4606.09	3157.79	542.54	1405.10	3350.21	275.07
2003	51007.96	21226.83	304.16	4750.62	3163.69	524.44	1476.43	3567.56	298.03
2004	55403.50	22929.31	715.23	5114.74	3237.93	513.15	1555.07	3944.63	300.83
2005	59520.52	25095.75	987.08	5495.69	3361.25	520.16	1743.18	4489.11	310.99
2006	68076.54	27951.43	1342.57	6146.85	3641.62	533.05	1952.92	4823.63	342.57

Data resources: Bureau of Economic Analysis of Department of Commerce

The sales model relying on the domestic sales of foreign investment enterprises in the United States is in contrast to that of foreign investment enterprises in China, which rely mainly on export sales.This adequately reflects the contrastive differences in the economic structures of China and United States. China utilizes an economic development model that relies primarily on exports and investment, while the United States relies mainly on domestic consumption. Meanwhile, the Chinese advantage of a large labor force remains an important factor in attracting foreign investment.

6.4 The Scale of Assets, Structures, and the Flow of Funds in Foreign Investment Enterprises

6.4.1. The Scale of Assets of Foreign Investment Enterprises in China is steadily and rapidly increasing

As assets increase, the accumulation and expansion of foreign investment enterprises in China has also increased. According to related statistics, in 2003, the total assets of foreign investment enterprises were 8,413.46 billion *yuan*. In 2004, the assets scale of foreign investment enterprises expanded to 11,862.7 billion *yuan*, increasing by 41% compared with that of the previous year. In 2005, the total assets of foreign investment enterprises accounted for 13317.8 billion *yuan*, increasing by 12.3% compared with that of 2004. In 2006, the assets scale of foreign investment enterprises expanded to 16,104.68 billion *yuan*, increasing by 20.9% from the year before. The scale of the assets of foreign investment enterprises in 2006 had almost doubled since 2003. In 2007, the assets of foreign investment enterprises continued to increase, amounting to 20,295.8 billion *yuan*, increasing by 26% compared to that of 2006. Compared to the increase rate—15.8%—of the world's 100 largest transnational companies from 2006 to 2007, the rate of increase by foreign investment enterprises in China was 10% higher. (See Table 6-7) The conclusion can therefore be drawn that, according to the statistics, the rate of foreign investment enterprises' assets was higher than that of the world's 100 largest transnational companies. Therefore, the business development of foreign investment in China is very successful. China is an ideal place for foreign investment.

Table 6-7: The World's Top 100 Largest Transnational Corporations

		2006	2007	2008	Change percentage from 2006 to 2007	Change percentage from 2007 to 2008
Assets (*one billion dollars)	Foreign Assets	5245	6116	6094	16.6	-0.4
	Total Assets	9239	10702	10687	15.8	-0.1
	Foreign Assets/Total Assets	57	57	57	0.4	-0.1
Sales (*one billion dollars)	Foreign Sales	4078	4936	5208	21.0	5.5
	Total Sales	7088	8078	8518	14.0	5.5
	Foreign Sales/Total Sales	58	61	61	3.6	0.0
Employment (*1000)	Foreign Employment	8582	8440	8898	-1.66	5.4
	Total Employment	15388	14870	15302	-3.4	2.9
	Foreign Employment /Total Employment	56	57	58	0.98	1.4

Data Resources: UNCTAD

The global financial crisis in 2008 severely impacted business development and the assets growth of large global transnational corporations. Both foreign sales and the total sales of the world's 100 largest transnational corporations only increased by 5.5% compared to the year before.

In 2008, foreign assets and total assets decreased by 0.4% and 0.1%, respectively. The global financial crisis' blow to foreign investment enterprises in China was far lighter than the influence on transnational corporations in other regions in the world. Since only the Chinese market still experienced any growth during the crisis, many large transnational corporations considered China a port of refuge.

6.4.2. The Assets Industry of Foreign Investment Enterprises in China is Distributed Differently than in the Rest of the World

The assets of foreign investment enterprises in China are mainly focused on the manufacturing industry, while the scale of the service industry using foreign investment is comparatively small. The proportion of the manufacturing industry in China is the greatest among all industries as far as total assets of foreign investment enterprises. Accordingly, from 2003 to 2007, the scale of the assets of foreign investment enterprises in the manufacturing industry reached 4,821.2 billion *yuan*, 7,236 billion *yuan*, 8,143.7 billion *yuan*, 9546.3 billion *yuan*, and 11,592.9 billion *yuan*, respectively, accounting for 57.3%, 61%, 61.1%, 59.3%, and 57.1% of the total assets of foreign investment enterprises in those years; during the same five-year period, the average proportion of foreign investment in the manufacturing industry compared to total foreign investment was 59.16%. From 2004 to 2007, the rate of increase was 50.1%, 12.5%, 17.2%, and 21.4%. In those four years, the assets of foreign investment enterprises in the manufacturing industry increased 1.4 times. On the whole, the proportion of the Chinese manufacturing industry that attracted foreign investment was comparatively large, while the proportion of the service industry correspondingly attracting foreign investment was comparatively small.

In terms of the industrial distribution of global foreign direct investment stocks, the manufacturing industry accounted for a comparatively small part, while the service industry accounted for a comparatively large part. In 1990, global FDI stocks sunk into the manufacturing industry were worth 798.598 billion dollars, accounting for 41.1% of the total FDI stocks, or 1,942.116 billion dollars in that year. FDI stock invested in the service industry was 947.701 billion dollars, accounting for 48.8% of total stocks. (See Table 6-8)

Table 6-8: Global FDI Stocks in 1990 and 2007 across Different Industries

Unit: *100 million dollars

Industry	1990	2007	Industry	1990	2007
Primary Industries	1818.54	1 1724.36	Other Secondary Industries	744.30	6916.46
Agriculture, Forestry, Fishery and Hunting	80.36	320.10	Service Industries	9477.01	100204.83
Ore mining and Petroleum Exploitation	1717.89	11404.26	Electricity, Water, and CNG Supply	101.34	3448.55
Other	20.28		Construction	221.71	1358.07
Manufacturing Industries	7985.98	4 2458.34	Trade	2281.97	16602.15
Food, Beverages, and Tobacco	803.41	4500.30	Inns and Hotels	258.50	1066.80

Textiles, Clothing, and Leather	286.97	902.54	Transport, Storage, and Communications	295.77	9204.66
Wood and Wood Products	250.32	1418.00	Finance	3840.35	30418.94
Media Publishing, Printing, and Duplicates	156.43	772.71	Mercantilism	1392.85	29256.68
Coal, Petroleum Products, and Nuclear Fuel	576.66	1471.69	Public Management and Defense	0.59	220.09
Chemistry and Chemicals	1719.50	8419.29	Education	0.94	87.97
Rubber and Plastic Product	148.59	760.76	Public Health and Social Services	9.92	311.52
Nonmetal Mineral Products	198.41	1416.42	Community, Social,and Individual Services	133.52	475.61
Metal and Metal Products	676.13	3698.78	Other Services	744.03	2059.41
Machinery and Equipment	634.49	2453.12	Other Tertiary Industries	195.51	5694.37
Electric Power and Electronic Equipment	893.16	3995.23	Private Property Businesses	-	60.43
Precision Instruments	122.84	936.86	Other Industries	139.63	2520.79
Automobiles and other Vehicles	552.02	3700.39	Total	1 9421.16	156968.76
Other Manufactures	222.74	1095.79			

Data Source: UNCTAD

In 2007, global FDI stocks in the manufacturing industry was USD 4245.834 billion, accounting for 27% of all total FDI stocks.The 15696.876 billion dollars accrued in that year representeda decline of13.1% compared to that of the previous year, and was also 30% lower than the proportion of assets of foreign investment enterprises in China in the manufacturing industry,which accounted for 57% of the market in 2007. FDI stocks in the service industry was 10020.483 billion dollars, accounting for 63.8% and increasing by 15% compared to that of the year 1990. Therefore, while foreign direct investment in China mainly flows into the manufacturing industry, the overall situation of the world finds foreign direct investment mainly flowing into the service industry.

The scale of foreign investment assets in the real estate industry in China accounts for the second-largest proportion of all assets. From2003 to 2007, the scale of assets of foreign investment in the real estate industry reached 1258.5 billion *yuan*, 1471 billion *yuan*, 1655.4 billion *yuan*, 2109.9 billion *yuan*, and 2857.1 billion *yuan*, respectively, accounting for 15%, 12.4%, 12.4%, 13.1%, and 14.1% of the total assets of all foreign investment enterprises in those years. From 2004 to 2007, the rate of increase was 16.9%, 12.5%, 27.5%, and 35.4%, respectively. In those four years, the assets of foreign investment in the real estate industry increased by 1.27.

According to results from a research report of the top 10 public real estate companies in China, jointly issued in 2008 by the Enterprises Institute of Developmental Research Center of the State Council, the Real Estate Research Institute of Tsinghua University, and others investigating the top 10 foreign investment real estate enterprises between 2005 to 2007, the total assets of the Chinese mainland expanded at an annual rate of 34.2%, among which, the increased rate of total assets in 2007 reached 35.8%. The average scale of total assets increased from 16.3 billion *yuan* in 2005 to 27.6 billion *yuan* in 2007. The rapidly-increasing statistics show that—even under the Chinese real estate policy of macro control and restrictions on foreign investment—foreign-invested real estate enterprises still have great results on the Chinese real estate market. Additionally, the value of the assets of foreign investment enterprises in the mining industry, the wholesale and retail industry, the accommodation and catering industry, the leasing and business service industry, public health, social security, and the social welfare industry also had steady increases. The value of the assets of foreign investment enterprises in education, agriculture, forestry, stock farming, the fishery industry, the construction industry, the financial industry, the production and supply industry of electric power, gas, fuel, and water, information transmission, computer services and the software industry, culture, sports and the entertainment industry, scientific research, technological services and the geological exploitation industry, water conservancy, the entertainment and public facilities management industry, and international services management had significant fluctuations between year 2003 to 2007.

The majority of foreign investment flowing into the Chinese manufacturing industry shows that it is still underdeveloped; competition is not fierce enough, so the level of profit is still high; the service industry is still not open enough; it is comparatively difficult to enter into and survive the service industry. Due to the comparatively few assets held by foreign investment enterprises in the service industry in China, China needs to open the service industry further, push foreign investment from the manufacturing industry into the service industry, and improve the overall proportion—not just the net number—of foreign investment being funneled into the service industry.

6.4.3. The Rate of Return on Investments and the Earnings Power of the Real Assets of Foreign Investment Enterprises in China is in Contrast to that of the World

The overall capital turnover rate of foreign investment enterprises in China has been accelerating yearly. From 2003 to 2007, the overall capital turnover rate of foreign investment enterprises in China was 0.69, 0.72, 0.8, 0.85, and 0.85. (See Table 6-9) However, the high speed of capital turnover of foreign investment enterprises in China has proven temporary. The overall capital turnover rate of global foreign direct investment enterprises showed an opposing trend to that found in China. In 1982, the capital turnover rate of global foreign direct investment enterprises was 1.24; it decreased to 1.01 in 1990; in 2006, it decreased greatly to 0.46; in 2007, it decreased to 0.43; in 2008, the capital turnover rate stayed almost the same as the previous year, at 0.43.

Table 6-9: The Earning Power of Foreign-Invested Real Estate Enterprises in China, the United States, and the World

	1982	1990	2000	2001	2002	2003	2004	2005	2006	2007	2008
World	1.24	1.01	-	-	-	-	-	-	0.46	0.43	0.43
U.S.	-	-	0.49	0.43	0.44	0.41	0.41	0.42	0.41	-	-
China	-	-	-	-	-	0.69	0.72	0.8	0.85	0.85	-

Data were calculated according to the statistics from UNCTAD and Ministry of Commerce of China and the United States.

The capital turnover rate of foreign investment enterprises in the United States shows a volatile and downward trend. In 2000, the capital turnover rate of foreign investment enterprises in the United States was 0.49; it slowed to 0.43 in 2001; in 2002, it increased slightly to 0.44; the capital turnover rate in2003, 2004, and 2006 stayed above 0.41; in 2005, the capital turnover rate was 0.01 higher than that of both previous and subsequent years, at 0.42. On the whole, the trend of the capital turnover rate of foreign investment enterprises in the United States was in accordance with that of the rest of the world. In 2006, the global capital turnover rate of foreign investment enterprises was 0.46, while in the United States, it was 0.41, so the capital turnover rate of foreign investment enterprises in the United States was somewhat lower than average. Conversely, however, the capital turnover rate of foreign investment enterprises in China increased yearly. The rates in 2006 and 2007 were almost the same, both 0.85. That rate was nearly twice of that of the world and the United States in 2007.

The average earnings power of real assets and the rate of return on investments by foreign investment enterprises in China are comparatively high. The average earnings power of the real assets of foreign investment enterprises serves as an index by which to reflect both investment profitability and the rate of return on investments. It is the proportion of profits in a normal year compared to total project investment after the enterprise has completed design and production. It is used to check the investment profitability of a given enterprise and the rate of return on investments. Real assets with high earnings power indicate strong profitability of an investment project and a high rate of return on an investment. Conversely, weak earnings power of real assets show weak profitability for an investment project and a low rate of return on an investment. Generally speaking, the earnings power of the real assets of an enterprise should not be lower than the basic social earnings power of real assets such as bank loan interest rates. According to statistics, from the years 2003 to 2007, the average earnings power of foreign investment enterprises' real assets in China were 5.3%, 4.7%, 5.7%, 7.6%, and 10.5%, respectively. Except for the year 2004, the average earnings power of real assets declined slightly, while the earnings power of real assets in other years maintained an upward trend, which means that—except in 2004—the profitability of foreign investment enterprises in China increased yearly and the rate of return on investments accelerated. The increasing trend of the earnings power of real assets is contrast to that of the rest of the world.

According to the statistics above, foreign investment enterprises in China show an increase in the earnings power of real assets and rate of return on investments, which contrasts with the United States and the rest of the world. The asset utilization ratio of foreign investment enterprises in China is higher than that of the world's average level, and is much higher than that of foreign investment enterprises in the United States. Therefore, large transnational corporations are enthusiastic about investing in China. The asset utilization ratio of foreign investment enterprises in China is almost twice that of the average global level. In other regions in the world, especially in developed economies like the United States, the scale of assets of transnational corporations increases only gradually and sales hardly increase at all, which leads to weak earnings power by real assets. As the level of economic development improves, the scale of assets of foreign investment enterprises will continue to expand; competition in market sales is becoming increasingly fierce, but sales are only expanding slowly. Therefore, when the earnings power of the real assets of foreign investment enterprises in China achieve a certain level, they must then subsequently decrease little by little. The overall trend of economic development leans towards a general decline in foreign investment enterprises. China is no exception to that rule.

6.5 Wholly Foreign-Owned Enterprises Develop Rapidly

Due to the influences of the policy in which China relaxed restrictions on the holdings of foreign investment and the requirements of joint ventures and cooperatives and expanded the range of access to market, cultural conflicts in Chinese-foreign joint ventures and cooperatives, inconsistent demands, and transnational corporations seeking more independence and an absolute advantage, all became more apparent. Furthermore, the growing dominance of wholly foreign-owned enterprises continued, which has influenced the Chinese economy to some degree. However, wholly foreign-owned enterprises are of comparatively high efficiency and have more advantages, including more freedom. The number of wholly foreign-owned enterprises, therefore, has been increasing recently.

6.5.1. Wholly Foreign-Owned Enterprises in China have Developed Rapidly

In recent years, while the assets of other foreign investment models have shrank, the assets of joint venture, wholly foreign-owned enterprises, joint stock, and cooperative foreign investment enterprises have, to different extents, expanded, of which the increase in assets of wholly foreign-owned enterprises and joint stock enterprises have been the greatest. According to related statistics, the proportion of the assets of wholly foreign-owned enterprises to the total assets of foreign investment enterprises increased from 36.2% in 2003 to 47.3% in 2007. The scale of assets of Chinese foreign joint ventures in 2003 was 3778.1 billion *yuan*, accounting for 44.9% of the total assets of foreign investment enterprises. When it came to 2007, the assets scale of joint ventures had doubled, reaching 7,537.3 billion *yuan*. The proportion of the assets scale of joint ventures to the total assets of foreign investment enterprises decreased to 37.1% of the total in that year. From 2004 to 2007, the rate of increase was 27.3%, 10.5%, 15.4%, and 22.9%, respectively. The assets scale of cooperative foreign investment enterprises in 2003 was 952.16 billion *yuan*, accounting for 11.3% of the total assets of foreign investment enterprises. The increase in the assets of cooperative foreign investment enterprises was slow, however. When it came to 2007, the scale of the assets of joint venture enterprises reached 1143.5 billion *yuan*. The share of the assets scale of cooperative foreign investment enterprises in the total assets of foreign investment enterprises decreased to 5.6% in that year. However, the assets scale of joint stock foreign investment enterprises in 2003 was 634.2 billion *yuan*, accounting for 7.5% of the total assets of foreign investment enterprises. From 2004 to 2007, the rate of increase was 19.3%, 72%, 14.7%, and 35.5%, respectively. When it came to 2007, the assets scale of joint stock foreign investment enterprises was 2023.17 billion *yuan*. The proportion of the assets scale of joint stock foreign investment enterprises to the total assets of foreign investment enterprises increased to 10% of the total. We can conclude based on the above statistics that wholly owned foreign enterprises and joint stock foreign investment enterprises will, comparatively, develop rapidly, while the development of Chinese foreign joint venture and cooperatives will be slower.

6.5.2. The Earnings Power of the Real Assets of Wholly owned foreign enterprises in China is highly Efficient

The number of investors in foreign investment enterprises in China is inversely proportional to the corresponding assets activity ratio. The operation of the assets of wholly foreign-owned enterprises in China is of the highest efficiency. The earnings power of the real assets of wholly foreign-owned enterprises in different years is generally higher than that of foreign investment enterprises based on other investment models. From 2003 to 2007, the earnings power of the real assets of wholly foreign-owned enterprises was 0.79, 0.79, 0.96, 0.95, and 0.91, respectively. The assets activity ratio of Chinese foreign joint ventures was slightly lower than that of wholly foreign-owned enterprises. The earnings power of the real assets of Chinese foreign joint ventures is comparatively high, however, and has maintained a steady increase. From 2003 to 2007, the earnings power of the real assets of wholly foreign-owned enterprises was 0.69, 0.74, 0.79, 0.86, and 0.88. The earnings power of the real assets of joint stock foreign investment enterprises is not high, and is just slightly higher than that of other cooperative foreign investment enterprises. From 2003 to 2007, the earnings power of the real assets of joint stock foreign investment enterprises was 0.53, 0.58, 0.5, 0.61, and 0.61, respectively, while the earnings power of the real assets of cooperative foreign investment enterprises was 0.46, 0.42, 0.46, 0.52, and 0.57. The earnings power of the real assets of foreign investment enterprises of other types fluctuated greatly. From 2003 to 2006, the earnings power of the real assets of foreign investment enterprises of other types was 0.39, 1.07, 2.47, and 0.16, respectively. The operational efficiency of foreign investment enterprises shows that the assets activity ratio of wholly foreign-owned enterprises was higher than that of joint ventures; the assets activity ratio of joint ventures was higher than that of joint stock foreign investment enterprises; and the assets activity ratio of joint stock foreign investment enterprises was higher than that of cooperative foreign investment enterprises. Therefore, we can primarily conclude that the more investors in foreign investment enterprises, the more complicated the property rights and the more difficult the internal governance; the weaker the control of investors, the lower the assets activity ratio; therefore, the fewer investors, the higher the assets activity ratio of foreign investment enterprises will ultimately be.

6.5.3. The Profitability of Foreign Investment Enterprises in China Increases Rapidly

In terms of the increased range of profits from 2003 to 2007, wholly foreign-owned enterprises have had the fastest rate of increased profits, joint stock foreign investment enterprises are second, and joint ventures are third. Cooperative foreign investment enterprises had the slowest rate of increase in profits. From 2003 to 2007, the total profits of all models of foreign investment enterprises in China maintained a steady and rapid increase, with the exception ofcertain years. According to related statistics, from 2003 to 2007, the total profits of wholly foreign-owned enterprises in China was 119,8 billion *yuan*, 229 billion *yuan*, 312.6 billion *yuan*, 457.6 billion *yuan*, and 623.4 billion *yuan*, respectively, accounting for 36.4%, 45.8%, 52.3%, 52.1%, and 48.8%, respectively, of the total profits of all foreign investment enterprises. From 2004 to 2007, the annual rate of increase of wholly foreign-owned enterprises was 91.3%, 36.5%, 46.4%, and 36.2%, respectively. The profits increased very quickly. Total profits in 2007 of wholly foreign-owned enterprises increased by 4.2 times compared to that of the previous year. From 2003 to 2007, the total profits of joint stock foreign investment enterprises was 41.3 billion *yuan*, 56 billion *yuan*,70.6 billion *yuan*, 92.1 billion *yuan*, and 141.6 billion *yuan*, respectively, accounting for 12.5%, 11.2%, 11.8%, 10.5%, and 11.1% of the total profits of foreign investment enterprises of all types. From 2004 to 2007, the annual increased rate of joint stock foreign investment enterprises was 35.5%, 26.1%, 30.5%, and 53.8%, respectively. The total profits of joint stock foreign investment enterprises in 2007 were 3.43 times those of the previous year. From 2003 to 2007, total profits of joint ventures was 146 billion *yuan*, 185.1 billion *yuan*,181.7 billion *yuan*, 282.2 billion *yuan*, and 457.6 billion *yuan*, accounting for 44.3%, 37%, 30.4%, 32.1%, and 35.8%, respectively, of the total profits of all types of foreign investment enterprises. From 2004 to 2007, the annual rate of increase for joint ventures was 26.8%, -1.8%, 55.3%, and 62.1%, respectively. The total profits of joint ventures in 2007 increased by 2.13 times compared to that of the previous year. The total profits of Chinese foreign cooperatives maintained a rapidly-increasing momentum. From 2003 to 2007, the total profits of cooperative foreign investment enterprises was 22.3 billion *yuan*, 29.9 billion *yuan*, 33 billion *yuan*, 47.1 billion *yuan*, and 55.4 billion *yuan*, respectively. The total profits of cooperative foreign investment enterprises in 2007 increased by 1.48 times compared to those of the previous year.

After being open to the outside of the world for more than thirty years, transnational corporations in China have made great progress. As China continues to absorb foreign investment, the number of wholly foreign-owned enterprises is increasing. Obtaining majority ownership by increasing investment and adopting wholly foreign-owned enterprises has been the main method of investment. (Xu Jie, 2003)15. As China gradually relaxes restrictions on stock rights for foreign investment enterprises, expanding shares has been one of the developmental trends for foreign investors actually investing in China. Transnational corporations have added their investment to joint ventures in China in succession, or put pressure on Chinese cooperation partners that require capital increases and the expansion of shares, which, in turn, stimulates a new trend among joint ventures to become wholly foreign-owned enterprises . More and more transnational corporations are therefore inclined to establish wholly foreign-owned enterprises and foreign-controlled enterprises. (Zhang Yu, 2006)16

The primary reasons for and the factors influencing the growing dominance of wholly foreign-owned enterprises among transnational corporations in China are not all the same. The internal reasons for greater preference for investing in wholly foreign-owned enterprises in recent years include the following five aspects: the economic changes of transnational corporations, the transformation of operational strategies, aggravating conflicts with Chinese foreign cooperation, the developmental stage of transnational corporations, and changes in the strategies of transnational corporations' intellectual property rights. The external reasons include the following

[15] Xu Jie, "Discussion on the Investment Methods Foreign Investors Choose in Making Investment in China,"*Journals of Wuhan University, Philosophy and Social Science Column*(2003): 56-60

[16] Zhang Yu, "Stock Rights Structure of Foreign Investment Enterprises and FDI Technology Spillovers Effects - Theory and Practice,"*World Economy Study No.11*(2006)

three aspects: changes in Chinese policies on foreign investment, changes in the investment environment, and the sustainable and steady development of the Chinese economy. (Dai Xiang and Wei Hao, 2004)17 The investment trend toward wholly foreign-owned enterprisesin China is the consequence of various aspects, including changes in the domestic investment environment and outlook after China entered the WTO, the strategy of globalization by transnational corporations, and internal conflicts inside Chinese-foreign joint ventures. (Zhao Zengyao, 2004)18. The most profound reasons for transnational corporations strengthening their inclination towards becoming wholly foreign-owned are the prospective earnings to be had from pursuing a strategic improvement of stock structures. (Li Wei'an and Li Baoquan, 2003)19From a different viewpoint, the reasons for the trend towards wholly foreign-owned enterprisesi in China include the desire for higher profits, intensifying market competition, strengthened technical controls, and the loosening of the policy environment. (Li Xiaohua and Sheng Ti, 2005)20

No matter which reason is true, in terms of the increased rate of assets, the assets activity ratio, and the increased rate of assets profitability, investors' preference for wholly foreign-owned enterprises in China has been gradually becoming more evident. Other investment methods are all less efficient and profitable than wholly foreign-owned enterprises.

6.6 The Tax Burden of Foreign Investment Enterprises

6.6.1. The Tax Burden of Foreign Investment Enterprises is generally lighter than that of Domestic Enterprises

The total tax levied on foreign investment enterprises in China increases year by year. Taxable income brought in from different items and economic sectors is an important component of state revenue. The scale of taxes reflects how much foreign economies contribute to state revenue. From 2003 to 2007, the total taxes collected from foreign investment enterprises was 319.5 billion *yuan*, 468.7 billion *yuan*, 536.7 billion *yuan*, 684 billion *yuan*, and 901.8 billion *yuan*, respectively. From 2004 to 2007, the increased rate of total taxes on foreign investment enterprises was 46.7%, 14.5%, 27.4%, and 31.8%, respectively. In terms of tax increase on foreign investment enterprises in China, the total tax of foreign investment enterprises increased greatly each year, demonstrating that the contributions made by tax-paying foreign investment enterprises continue to increase. Extending the scope of opening to the outside world and increasing the scale of utilizing foreign investment is realistically of important significance to the national economy and to an increase in national tax revenue.

The imports and exports of foreign investment enterprises in China account for more than half of those of the whole country, while their gross product and economic scale are around one third of that of the whole country. However, from 2003 to 2007, the proportion of the total tax of foreign investment enterprises to the total national tax revenue was only 15.6%, 18.2%, 17.4%, 18.2%, and 18.2%, respectively, with no significant increase. The proportion of the sales income

[17] Dai Xiang and Wei Hao,"Analysis of Clauses of the Trend of Sole Proprietorship of Enterprises of Transnational Corporations in China,"*Journal of Nanjing University of Finance No.2*(2004)

[18] Zhao Zengyao, "Evolutionary Mechanisms and Responses to the Trend of Sole Proprietorship of ForeignInvestment in China,"*World Economy Study No.4*(2004)

[19] Li Weian and Li Baoquan, "Analysis of Clauses on Sole Proprietorship of Transnational Corporations in China in the Perspective of Stock Rights Structural Strategy,"*Management World No.1*(2003)

[20] Li Xiaohua and Sheng Ti, "Analysis on the Trend of Sole Proprietorship of Joint Venture in China,"*Journal of Hebei University of Economic and Business*(2005): 26-1

of foreign investment enterprises in China as measured by gross domestic product in those years indicates an increasing gap between it and the proportion of tax paid by foreign investment enterprises in national tax revenue. Comparatively speaking, the tax burden of foreign investment enterprises becomes lighter every year. Therefore, the tax burden of foreign investment enterprises across the years being measured by this study is comparatively light, while domestic enterprises have a heavier liability, which is greatly unfair. That might be a big reason why some domestic enterprises not only enjoy the preferential tax policy, but also transfer profits and evade tax payments after becoming foreign investment enterprises by handling procedures outside of China.

6.6.2. Tariff Contributions Made by Foreign Investment Enterprises in China

Tariffs set for foreign investment enterprises in China fluctuate a great deal. The statistics show that from 2003 to 2007, the total tariffs on foreign investment enterprises in China was 35.8 billion *yuan*, 81.7 billion *yuan*, 49.6 billion *yuan*, 49.2 billion *yuan*, and 67.8 billion *yuan*, respectively. From 2004 to 2007, the increased rate of tariffs paid by foreign investment enterprises was 128.3%, -39.3%, -0.8%, and 37.8%, respectively. In the years from 2003 to 2007, the increase in tariffs on foreign investment enterprises in China was quite unsteady and fluctuated greatly. China's preferential import tariff policies on foreign investment enterprises had a positive effect in attracting foreign investment, but they also had some negative effects, as did other preferential tax policies. Abolishing preferential import tariff policies on foreign investment enterprises was therefore an inevitable choice, and has not negatively affected the country's ability to attract foreign investment. In the year when the import tariff was abolished, foreign direct investment flowing into China did not decrease, but instead, increased. An increasing amount of foreign investment has flown into the districts where there have never been preferential tax policies, which is beneficial to the equal distribution of foreign investment in various districts in China. (Li Zonghui and Cao Xiaochun, 2007)21

6.6.3. Adjustments and Improvements to Preferential Tax Policies on Foreign Investment Enterprises

At present, the preferential tax policy on foreign investment enterprises goes against the property tax for corporate policy as well as national standards, so it needs to be adjusted and improved. The tax burden of foreign investment enterprises is lighter than that levied against domestic enterprises, which is directly related to preferential tax policies for foreign investment enterprises. In the past, China's preferential tax policy on foreign investment enterprises had positive effects insofar as attracting foreign investment and economic construction, which, in turn, attracted a great deal of foreign investment, realized policy objectives, and promoted Chinese economic development. The preferential tax policy is the major factor leading to incoming foreign direct investment. Those policies have basically realized the national policy objectives, which were to lead foreign investment to certain regions within certain periods of time. (Li Zonghui and Lu Minghong, 2004)22

In the most recent version of The Law of the People's Republic of China on Enterprise Income Tax—which was passed in the fifth conference of the Tenth National People's Congress—it was stipulated that the flat tax rate of both domestic and foreign investment enterprises should be 25%; the double-track pricing system for enterprise income tax should be abolished.This was enacted

---

[21] Li Zonghui and Cao Xiaochun, "Influences Analysis on the Abolishment of Preferential Import Tariff Policy on Foreign Investment Enterprises,"*The Theory and Practice of Finance and Economics No.4*(2007)

[22] Li Zonghui and Lu Minghong, "Analysis of Effectiveness on the Preferential Tax Policy on Foreign Investment Enterprises in China,"*The Journal of World Economy*(2004): 27-10

with the intent to change the business environment, which must undergo significant changes in actual taxes due to preferential tax policies for foreign investment enterprises and differences of cost deduction, in order to provide a more transparent tax system that will be more stable and predictable for both domestic and foreign investment enterprises. It should be beneficial to improving the competitive power of enterprises and attracting foreign investment. Abolishing the preferential tax policy pushes foreign investment enterprises to pay more attention on local resources, talent, market environment, and also to adjust their business model, investment structure, financing strategy, and investment location.

Some people used to worry that variable income tax might lead foreign investors to countries with lower tax rates, which could possibly have a great influence on the total foreign direct investment in China. (Zhong Wei, 2005)23 An Tifu (2005) and other scholars think that the key factors in selecting a location for foreign direct investment are infrastructure, foreign investment conditions, the degree of industrialization, and market capacity at present; preferential tax policy has limited functionality in improving the competitive advantages of a host country in attracting foreign investment, so the income tax levied against joint venture enterprises would not influence incoming foreign investment24. However, Cao Xiaochun (2006) is of the opinion that the combination of differing income tax levels for domestic and foreign investment enterprises has a significant influence on the incoming amount of foreign investment as far as different originating sources, different investment purposes, different scales, and different directions of production flow, different departments, and different fields.25

China's preferential tax policy regarding foreign investment enterprises has historical significance, and has undergone appropriate adjustment and reforms as needed with the demand of national economic development. The promotional policies regarding the FDI of transnational corporations provided by the host country have generally gone through three generations. The first generation mainly focused on encouraging preferential measures. The second focused on liberalization and reform of the FDI regulation framework. The third puts emphasis on three proceedings in which local enterprises were linked to transnational corporations. At present, China has transitioned to the period between the second and third generation of investment absorption. Preferential policy is no longer the major factor in attracting foreign investment;it is instead the degree of regional openness and correlated effects brought about by industrial aggregation that primarily influences the location selected for and by foreign investment. A low level of local professionalization does not have any advantages in attracting FDI. (Liang Qi, 2003)26 According to the investigation on enterprises funded by the United States, Japan, the European Union, Hong Kong, Macao,and Chinese Taipei in Guangdong Province, preferential policies rank second to last in all the factors that may influence the investment decision of foreign investment enterprises. Enterprises instead shift their requirements to lowering and then gradually eliminating domestic trade barriers, improving the transparency of policy making, and opening the service

23 Zhong Wei, "Influence the Amalgamation Enterprises Income Tax Have on Absorbing Foreign Investment in China,"Modern Economic Research No.5(2005)

24 An Tifu and Wang Haiyong,"Discourse on the Combination of Domestic and Foreign Enterprises Income Tax Systems,"Taxation Research No.3(2005)

25 Cao Xiaochun, "Influences the Combination of Domestic and Foreign Investment Enterprises in China Has on Investment Inflow,"Finance and Trade Economics No.9(2006)

26 Liang Qi, "Oversea Investment and Industrial Aggregation of Transnational Corporation,"World Economy(2003): 26 -9

industry. (Xian Guoming and Ge Shunqi, 2002)27. On the basis of maintaining the steadiness and consistency of preferential tax policies, China needs to adopt various preferential tax methods, highlight industrial guidance qualities, adjust the location where regional preferential tax is implemented, and unify the preferential income tax of domestic and foreign investment enterprises to further improve the preferential tax policy of foreign direct investment in China (Liu Jianmin and Yin Hui, 2004)28. Foreign investment in China should meet the national industrial policy and strategies for developing the western and central regions, and make use of preferential tax policies in order to direct foreign investment into industries in need of development, as well as those western and central regions which need to be propped up by foreign investment.

6.7 The Profitability and Returns on Investment of Foreign Investment Enterprises

6.7.1. The Scale of Profit of Foreign Investment Enterprises in China is Increasing Rapidly and Keeping Pace with the World Economy

In the years 2003 to 2007, the total profit of foreign investment enterprises in China was 329.3 billion *yuan*, 500.2 billion *yuan*, 587.9 billion *yuan*, 879 billion *yuan*, and 1278 billion *yuan*, respectively. From 2004 to 2007, the increased rate of foreign investment enterprises' profit scales in China were 51.9%, 19.5%, 47%, and 45.4%, respectively, showing a steady increase. From 2003 to 2007, the total net profit of foreign investment enterprises in China was 429.2 billion *yuan*, 485.5 billion *yuan*, 465.4 billion *yuan*, 706.4 billion *yuan*, and 1049.1 billion *yuan*. In 2005, the scale of the net profit of foreign investment enterprises in China decreased slightly. From 2004 to 2007, the rate of increase of the net profit of foreign investment enterprises in China fluctuated greatly, ranging from 13.1%, -4.1%, 51.8%, to 48.5%.

According to the changes in the profit scale of global transnational corporations between 1997 and 2008(shown in Table6-1), the profit scale of transnational corporations between 1997 and 2008 increased yearly. After the profit peak of 2000, two consecutive years of a decrease in profit followed, bottoming out in 2002. From 2003 to 2007, the profit scale of global transnational corporations surged, which kept pace with the trend at which the profit scale of foreign direct investment enterprises increased.

---

27 Xian Guoming and Ge Shunqi, "The Evolution of the FDI of Transnational Corporation and Foreign Policies of Host Countries,"Nankai Economic Studies No.1(2002)

28 Liu Jianmin and Yin Hui, International Comparison and Lessons From Preferential Tax Policy on Foreign Direct Investment,"The Theory and Practice of Finance and Economics

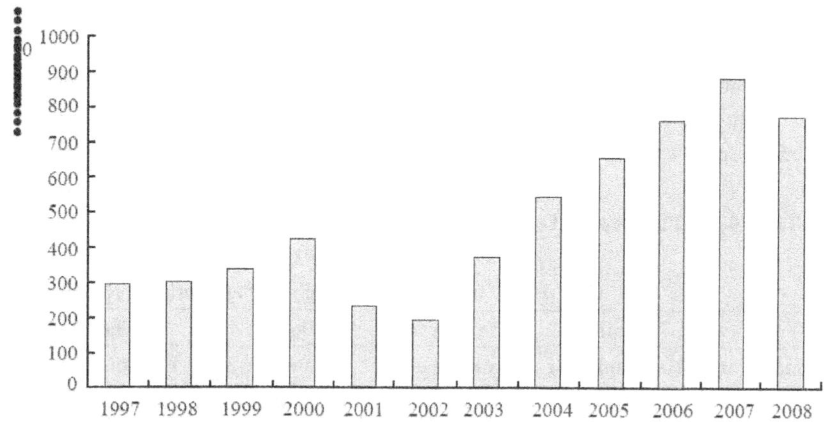

Figure 6-1: The Profit Scale of Foreign Investment Enterprises between1997 and 2008

Note: The profit rate is calculated as the proportion of net income in total sales. The calculation in the graph covers 987 companies.

Datum Resource: UNCTAD

Influenced by the global financial crisis of 2008, there was a slide in the profits scale of transnational corporations in the global economy. It was predicted that the profits scale of foreign direct investment enterprises in China would also be influenced by the financial crisis to some extent. Since the fourth quarter in 2008, according to the profits released by large transnational corporations in wide-ranging industrial fields in Europe, the United States, Japan, and more, many companies have performed poorly in gaining operating revenue, which has weakened their own financing capabilities. Transnational corporations have been trapped by daily increases in financial pressure. As the profits of transnational corporations have slumped from their peak in 2007, the cash liquidity of foreign direct investment also continues to decrease. At the same time, since January 2007, the global stock market has lost 50% of its market value, which has greatly weakened the financing capability of transnational corporations shifting onto the stock market, as well astheir ability to make use of stocks in conducting mergers and acquisitions operations.

6.7.2. Both Total Profitability and Areas of Deficit are increasing for Foreign Investment Enterprises

The scale of profit, the scale of deficit, and the number of foreign direct investment enterprises in China vary between different years. In general, the deficits posted by enterprises are increasing. According to related statistics, in 2003, among 143,000 foreign investment enterprises in China, 50,000 of them made profits, with total profits of 445.2 billion *yuan*. The profits scale was 35.2%. Eighty-eight thousand foreign investment enterprises gained zero net profits, accounting for 61.8%. Four thousand enterprises ran a deficit of 16 billion *yuan*. The deficits scale was 3% (Table 6-10). In 2004, among 172,000 foreign investment enterprises, 60,000 of them made profits, with total profits of 621.1 billion *yuan* at an increase of 39.5% compared to those of 2003. The profits scale was 34.6%. Seventy-six thousand foreign investment enterprises made zero net profit, accounting for 44.5%. Three thousand five hundred enterprises posted a collective deficit of 135.7 billion *yuan*, increasing 7.5 times that of 2003. The deficit scale was 20.6%. Additionally, 472 enterprises did not release their final gains and losses. In 2005, among 190,000 foreign investment enterprises, 68,000 of them made profits, with the total profits amounting to 687.7 billion *yuan*, increasing by 10.7% compared to that of the year 2004. The profits scale was 35.7%. Only 12,000 foreign investment enterprises gained zero profits, accounting for 6.5%, and 86,000 enterprises ran a deficit (with total deficits of 222.3 billion *yuan*, increasing by 63.9% compared to that of 2004). The deficits scale was 45.3%. Twenty-three thousand enterprises did not release their gains and losses.

Table 6-10: The Overall Gains and Losses of Foreign Investment Enterprises in China between Year 2003 and 2007

Unit: 100 million yuan; the number of enterprises *10,000

Year (by number of enterprises)	Profits (by number of enterprises)	Zero Profit (by number of enterprises)	Deficit (by number of enterprises)	The Number of Enterprises Withholding their Gains and Losses
2003	4452	0	-160	0
-14. 3	-5	-8. 8	-0. 4	
2004	6211	0	-1357	0.04
-17. 2	-6	-7. 6	-3. 5	
2005	6877	0	-2223	2.3
-19	-6. 8	-1. 2	-8. 6	
2006	9445	0	-2380	1.8
-20. 7	-8	-1. 6	-9. 3	
2007	13232	0	-2741	1.3
-22	-9	-1. 6	-10	

Data were drawn from the Chinese Academy of Social Sciences' Research Group on Foreign Investment and Trade Enterprises with Foreign Investment survey results. Similarly hereinafter.

In 2006, among 207,000 foreign investment enterprises, 80,000 of them made a profit, with total profits of 944.5 billion *yuan*, an increase of 37.3% compared to that of 2005. The profits scale was at 38.5%. Sixteen thousand foreign investment enterprises made zero profit, accounting for 7.6%, while 93,000 enterprises ran under deficit, with total deficits of 238 billion *yuan* increasing by 7% from 2005. The deficit scale was 45.1%. However, 18,000 enterprises did not release their gains and losses, so for 8.8% of total foreign investment enterprises in 2006 there is no data. In 2006, the total profits of foreign investment enterprises in Zhenjiang, Jiangsu Province was 3.534 billion *yuan*, increasing by 67.41% from the year before. The profits scale was 43.48%, which was close to the statistics of deficit areas of foreign investment enterprises for the country as a whole.

In 2007, among 220,000 foreign investment enterprises, 90,000 posted profits, with a collective total profit of 1323.2 billion *yuan*, an increase of 40.1% compared to that of 2006. The profits scale increased to 40.8%. Only 16,000 foreign investment enterprises gained zero profit, accounting for 7.5%. Ten thousand enterprises ran a deficit, with total deficits of 274.1 billion *yuan*, increasing by 15.2% compared to that of 2006. The deficits scale still was about 45.5%. Finally 13,000 enterprises did not release their gains and losses, so there is no data for 6.2% of the total foreign investment enterprises in 2007. In terms of the overall gains and losses of foreign investment enterprises from 2003 to 2007, both the scale of profit and the scale of deficits have increased. However, the profits scale of foreign investment enterprises calculated in this article is slightly lower than that of the statistics provided by Wang Jinmeng and Mao Ning (2008), which presented the average deficits scale of foreign investment enterprises in China as increasing by 51.06% from 2000 to 2005.

In the mainstream view, transferring pricing transfers profits abroad, leading to deficits. Although China has put many preferential policies particular to foreign investments in place, the tax duty level for foreign investment enterprises is not high.There still exist, however, foreign investment enterprises that transfer profits to regions where the tax duty level is very high. There are more and more foreign investment enterprises evading domestic tax payment (Chen Ruoxu, 2005).29 Taking advantage of transfer pricing, transnational corporations succeed in evading taxes in order to reach other financial goals, which leads to a great tax loss for host countries and other negative results (Wang Fengguo, 2006).30 However, by analyzing statistics of foreign investment enterprises in Nanjing, Wang Jinmeng and Mao Ning (2008) found that transfer pricing was not the reason for the deficits of foreign investment enterprises. The major reasons for the difference in deficits of foreign investment enterprises were attributable to poor efficiency of management, differences in transaction costs, policy influences, and insufficient investment.31 As for the gain and loss of foreign investment enterprises, experts disagree with each other. Further research, more scientific theories, and additional policies are needed.

6.7.3. The Overall Profitability of Foreign Investment Enterprises in China is High and Steadily Increasing

The net profit rate of the average social sales of foreign investment enterprises is different from that of the United States and the global economy. The net profit rate of sales by foreign investment enterprises is one of the important indexes indicating how a company operates and its profitability. The percentage of net profits is calculated by enterprises' profits minus the interest tax in sales income, which shows the scale of the overall net profits of enterprises brought in per every one-hundred-*yuan* sale and the profitability of new productions after being deducted the tax costs in new output values of enterprises.

According to related statistics, from the years 2003 to 2007, the average interest rates of social by foreign investment enterprises in China were 7.4%, 5.7%, 4.4%, 5.1%, and 6.1%, respectively, among which it reached the peak in 2003 and, in 2005, it bottomed out. According to statistics calculated by Li Yuanpeng (2009)32, from the year 2003 to 2006, average interest rates of social sales by foreign investment enterprises in China were only 1.1% , 0.1%, -3.4%, and 2.2%, respectively, which shows that average social sale interest rates of foreign investment enterprises are much higher than that of public companies in China. The trends of those two types of enterprises were almost the same. Both of them reached bottom in 2005—a bad year for business—yet average interest rates of social sales of foreign investment enterprises were much higher than that of public companies in China, from which we can conclude that the profitability of foreign investment enterprises is higher than that of public companies in China.

29Chen Ruoxu, "The Reasons, Manifestation and Countermeasures of Tax Evasion of Foreign Investment Enterprise in China,"Commercial Research No.2(2005)

30 Wang Fengguo, Analysis on Tax Avoidance and Anti Tax Avoidance in Transfer Pricing of Transnational Corporations No.2, 2006

31 Wang Jinmeng and Mao Ning, "Why Do Great Deficits Appear in Foreign Investment Enterprises in China?"World Economy No.1(2008)

32 Li Yuanpeng,"The Reasons Why the Economic Cycle Goes Against the Operating Performance of Public Companies,"Economic Research Journal No.3(2009)

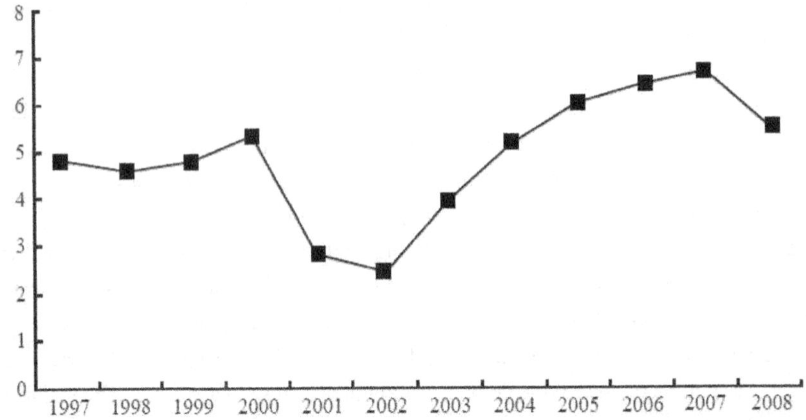

Figure 6-2: The Rate of Profit of Transnational Corporations from 1997 to 2008

Note: the profit rate is the percentage of net income in total sales. Those statistics cover 987 transnational corporations.

Data Resources: UNCTAD

According to the statistics found in Table 6-6, in the years from 2000 to 2006, the sales net profit rates were 1.2%, 2.5%, 2.7%, 1.4%, 3.1%, 3.9%, and 4.8%, respectively. The sales net profit rates of foreign investment enterprises in the United States in the years from 2003 to 2006 show an increasing upward trend, which is in accordance with the increasing trend of sales net profit rate of transnational corporations overall from the years between 2003 and 2007 (Table 6-2). However, the trend of sales net profit rates of foreign investment enterprises in China is different from that of the rest of the world. The poor business environment and effectiveness of2005 is more demonstrative of the individual case of China.

The return on the total assets of foreign investment enterprises is calculated from the ratio of enterprises' total profits to enterprises' average assets, which shows the comprehensive effects of the utilization of enterprises, while also reflecting the profitability level of those enterprises making use of the funds invested by creditors and investors. It is an index reflective of the overall operating management and profitability level. A high return on total assets indicates high efficiency in regards to assets utilization, high profitability, and a high operating and management level.

Based on related statistics, from the years 2003 to 2007, the average returns on the total assets of foreign investment enterprises in China were 3.9%, 4.2%, 4.5%, 5.5%, and 6.3%, respectively, which shows an increasing trend in the overall return on the total assets of foreign investment enterprises. The trend also shows that operating management level, technical investment skills, and industrial concentration have been improved. That trend is in accordance with the increasing trend of returns on the total assets of the Chinese industrial sector since 2000, as calculated by Chen Zhongchang and Wu Yongqiu (2005). According to their calculation results, the return on the total assets of the Chinese industrial sector from 2000 to 2003 was 19.5%, 20.9%, 23.9%, and 25.8%, respectively. They attribute such a trend to the improvement of Chinese industrial concentration.33The return on the total assets of the Chinese industrial sector since 2000 calculated by Chen and Wu is much higher than that in this article, perhaps because their calculation failed to include certain other elements as part of the total assets.

Still, the increasing trend of average returns on the total assets of foreign investment enterprises in China is in contrast to the decreasing trend of returns on the total assets of public companies in China as calculated by Li Yuanpeng. According to Li's calculation, from 1996 to 2006, the return on the total assets of public companies in China was 5.5%, 6.1%, 4. 8%, 4.3%, 3. 8%, 2.3%, 1.6%, 2.1%, 1. 8%, 0.7%, and 2.1%, respectively, demonstrating a fluctuating and downward trend. He attributed such a decrease to earnings manipulation by public companies when listed34. In order to get through the approval session, some companies in China may do some "earnings management" before being listed, while, generally speaking, foreign investment enterprises in China do not have such an inclination towards manipulating profits. Therefore, the level of profits reflected by foreign investment enterprises in China might be represented with more veracity. According to statistics (Table 6-6), from 2000 to 2006, the net profit rate of sales by foreign investment enterprises in the United States was 0.6%, -1.1%, -1.2%, 0.6%, 1.2%, 1.6%, and 2%, respectively. This trend is in accordance with that of the average social return on the total assets of foreign investment enterprises in China.

The increasing trend of returns on the total assets of foreign investment enterprises in China overall shows that the technology of products and services provided by those foreign investment enterprises haveimproved; both technical facilities and investment skills have become more advanced; the industrial concentration of foreign investment enterprises has also improved. Even though they may not at the top of the list in terms of scale, they must come to the forefront in terms of competitive market power in order to reach a high level of profits. In the meantime, it also indicates that the spillover and transfer of technology from foreign investment enterprises is becoming more prominent, and the effects and quality of utilizing foreign investment are correspondingly positively affected.

The return on assets of foreign investment enterprises is the ratio of after-tax net profits to paid-up capital, which is the index used by the owners of foreign investment enterprise to assess entrepreneurs' ability at operating and managing, utilizing debt capital, and making use of financial leverage to improve profitability; it is therefore an important index of profitability. A high return on total assets shows high profitability, while a low return on total assets shows low profitability.

In the years between 2005 and 2007, the average social returns on the assets of foreign investment enterprises in China were 10.4%, 13.3%, and 17.9 %, respectively, showing a yearly-increasing trend. That trend is in accordance with the similarly-increasing trend of the average social return on the total assets of foreign investment enterprises in China as a whole, which shows that the operating and management level of foreign investment enterprises in China, as well as their profitability, has gradually improved. In terms of a regional return on the assets of foreign investment enterprises in China, from the years 2005 to 2007, the returns on the assets of foreign investment enterprises in Qinghai, Tianjin, Hebei, Inner Mongolia, Beijing, and Anhui were comparatively high, while the returns on the assets of foreign investment enterprises in

33 Chen Zhongchang and Wu Yongqiu,"The Trend and Analysis of Causes of Return on Total Assets of the Chinese Industrial Sector,"Economic Research Journal No.5(2005)

34 Li Yuanpeng,"The Reasons Why Economic Cycle Goes Against the Operating Performance of Public Companies,"Economic Research Journal No.3(2009)

Guizhou, Yunnan, and Tibet autonomous regions were comparatively low. From 2005 to 2007, the return on the assets of foreign investment enterprises in Qinghai was 28.9%, 45%, and 31.5%, the highest in the country. From the years 2005 to 2007, the return on the assets of foreign investment enterprises in Guizhou was only 0.2%, 4.3%, and 9.9%, and from the years 2005 to 2007, the return on the assets of foreign investment enterprises in Yunnan was -0.3%, 7.1%, and 9.4%. In2006 and 2007, the return on the assets of foreign investment enterprises in Tibet was only 4.9% and 1.8%—the lowest level of return on assets for foreign investment enterprises in the whole country. The return on the assets of foreign investment enterprises in the eastern regions of the country were nearly distributed around a social return on assets. From 2005 to 2007, the return on the assets of foreign investment enterprises in Shanghai was 10.2%, 11.2%, and 18.2%, respectively, while in Guangdong Province it was 10.7%, 14.1%, and 19.2%. The return on assets in Shanghai and Guangdong are close to the average return on assets of foreign investment enterprises across the whole country. The return on assets of foreign investment enterprises in most of the provinces and cities indicates a steady yearly increase with fluctuations in individual provinces and cities.

The results of our analysis vary greatly from those results provided by Wang Dandan after analyzing the statistics of the national census, which is that the overall return on the assets of foreign investment enterprises was 4.26%; the return on the assets of foreign investment enterprises in eastern regions was 5.46%; the return on the assets of foreign investment enterprises in western regions was 1.72%; the operating performance of western regions was relatively poor compared with many other provinces—even when running a deficit35. As a matter of fact, this study found that not all returns on the assets of foreign investment enterprises in eastern regions were high, and not all returns on the assets of foreign investment enterprises in western regions were low. By our calculations, the social average returns on the assets of foreign investment enterprises are lower than that reported by the World Bank. After investigating 12,400 enterprises in 120 cities in China, the World Bank reported that the return on the investment of foreign investment enterprises in China was 22%36.

---

35 Wang Dandan,"Regional Distribution of Foreign Investment Economies in China,"Money China No.7(2007)

36 World Bank,"Return on Investment of Foreign Investment Enterprises in China Was 22%,"China Securities Journal (2006)

Chapter 7 The Employment Scale and Labor Remuneration of the Employees in Foreign-Invested Enterprises in China

Employment is of significant interest to China's economic development and social security, and under the current economic conditions, this issue becomes especially important. Foreign-capital enterprises play a large role in creating jobs for China. Analysis of the situation of the employees in those enterprises and the changing trend of this situation can provide us with a practical basis for making policies and effective measures for stimulating employment, and in this way help enlarge the number of workers and maintain the steady and rapid growth of China's economy.

7.1 Dynamic Changes in the Employment Scale and Labor Remuneration of the Employees of Foreign-Capital Enterprises in China

7.1.1. The Growth Rate of the Employment of Foreign-capital Enterprisesis Slowing Down

From 2003 to 2007, the employment volume of foreign-capital enterprises rose steadily—from 8.631 million to 15.83 million—for an increase of 0.83 times and an annual growth rate of 16.4%. But in 2008, impacted by the global financial crisis, this figure only increased by 2.5%, to 16.22 million.

7.1.2. The Contribution of Foreign-Capital Enterprises to China's Total Employment is increasing

Although the growth rate of the employment volume of foreign-capital enterprises is slowing down, its contribution to the total employment volume of China as a whole is increasing. From 2003 to 2008, the proportion of this employment volume to China's total employment volume grew from 1.2% of the total to 2.1%, an increase of 0.9%, and its proportion of China's urban employment volume rose from 2.9% to 2.5%, an increase of 2.5% (Figure 7-1 and Figure 7-2).

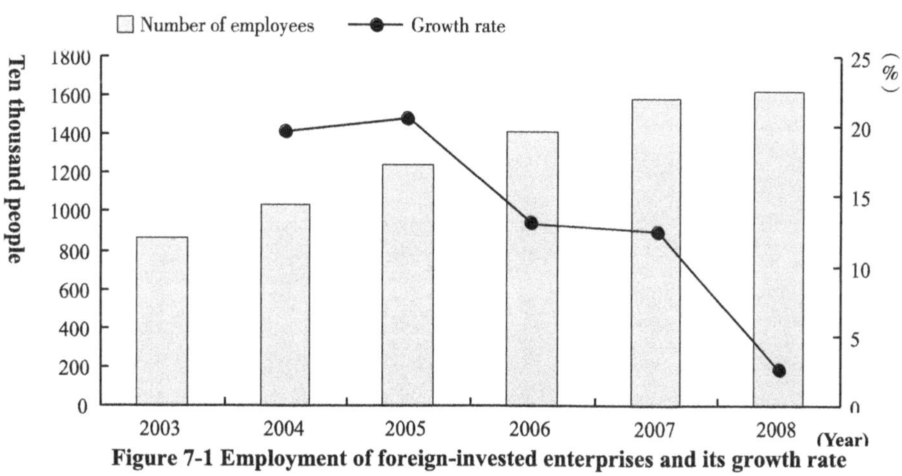

Figure 7-1 Employment of foreign-invested enterprises and its growth rate

Note: foreign-invested enterprises include enterprises invested by Hong Kong, Macao and Taiwan people. Number of employment refers to that counted at the end of a year. Same for charters below in this section.

Data source: calculated from China Statistical Yearbook over years. Same for figures below in this section.

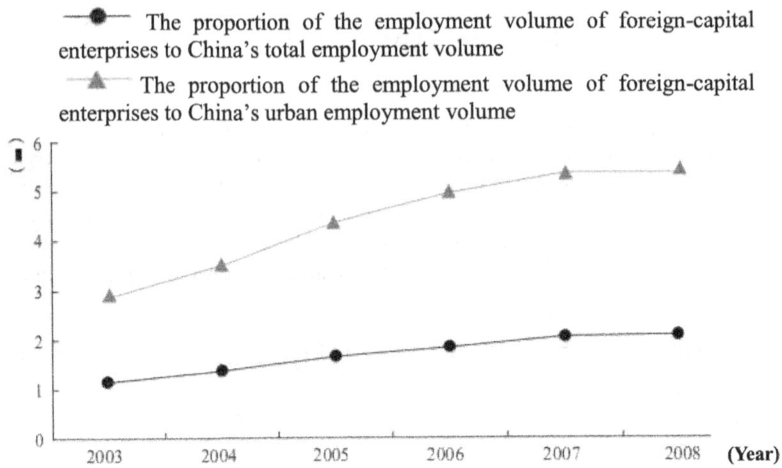

Figure 7-2 The Proportion of the Employment Volume of Foreign-capital Enterprises to China's Total Employment Volume and China's Urban Employment volume: 2003~2008

7.1.3. The Labor Remuneration of the Employees in Foreign-Capital Enterprises is relatively high and maintains a High Growth Rate

From 2003 to 2008, the average remuneration of the employees of foreign-capital enterprises was notably higher than that during the corresponding period of time for the employees in China's urban work units. In 2008, the average remuneration of the employees of foreign-capital enterprises reached 30,831.1 *yuan*, which was roughly 1,933.1 *yuan* higher than that of the employees in urban work units. From 2003 to 2008, the annual growth rate of the average remuneration of the employees of foreign-capital enterprises only increased 12.4%, somewhat less than the growth in wages of urban work units, which increased by 15.3%. In 2008, however, the former growth rate climbed 21.5%, higher than the rate of 15.9% for urban workers (see also Figure 7-3).

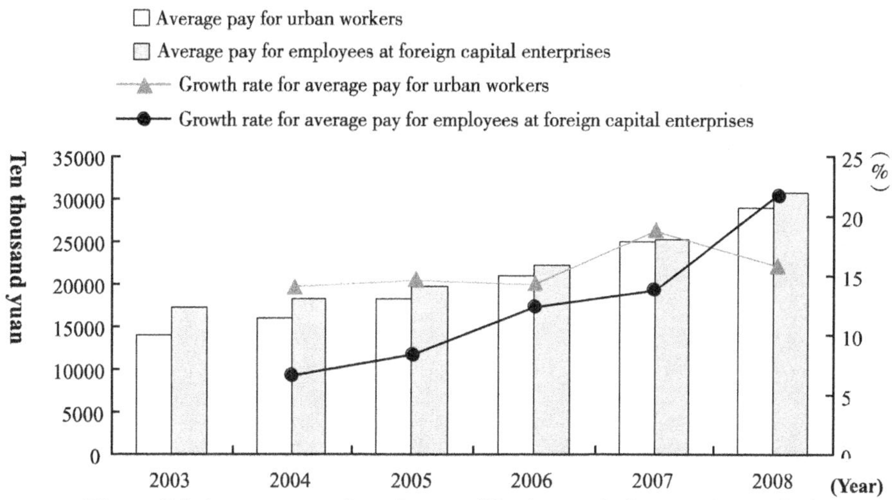

Figure 7-3: Average pay of employees of foreign capital enterprises and of urban workers and their respective growth rates: 2003~2008

7.2 The Employment Scale and Labor Remuneration of China's Manufacturing Industry

7.2.1. Leading Indicators are Consistently Stable and Beneficial to Employees

From 2003 to 2007, the gross output per capita of foreign-capital enterprises in China's manufacturing industry increased steadily, from 352,000 *yuan* to 542,000 *yuan*, an increase of 0.5 times with an annual growth rate of 11.4%. During those five years, the growth rate peaked in 2007, reaching 15.3% (see also Figure 7-4).

From 2003 to 2007, the value-added per capita of foreign-capital enterprises in China's manufacturing industry grew from 92,000 *yuan* to 137,000 *yuan*, an increase of 0.5 times with an annual growth rate of 10.3%. During those five years, the growth rate reached a peak in both 2005 and 2007, at 13.7% and 15.1%, respectively (see also Figure 7-5).

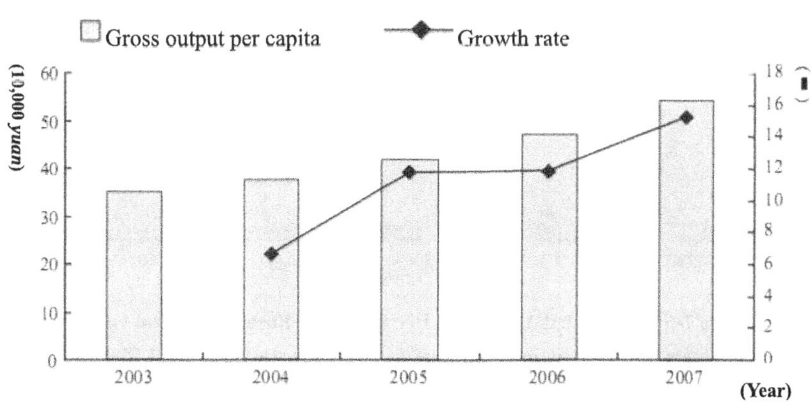

Figure 7-4: The Gross Output Per Capita of Foreign-Capital Enterprises in China's Manufacturing Industry and Its Growth Rate: 2003~2007

(Note: For purposes of this study, foreign-capital enterprises include enterprises funded by Taiwan, Macao, and Hong Kong, respectively or together. The employment volumes in this Figure are recorded at the end of every year. These notes are also applied to the other Figures as follow in this section.)
(Data source: Statistics in this Figure are weighted according to the statistics of all sectors in the annual database of China's manufacturing industry, which is provided by the Support System for China Statistical Application. This is also applied to the other figures as follow in this section.)

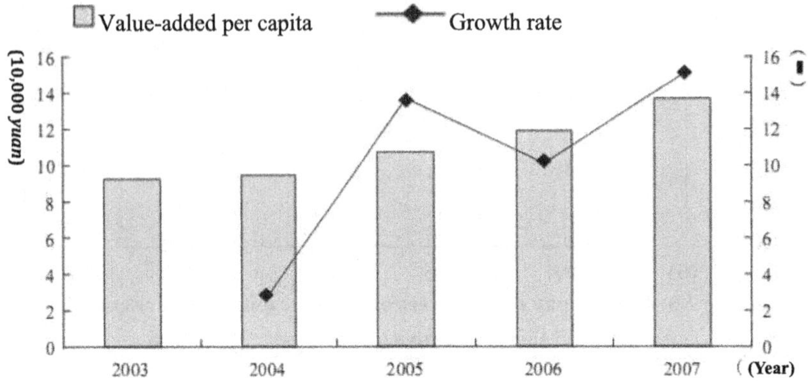

Figure 7-5: The Value-Added Per Capita of Foreign-Capital Enterprises in China's Manufacturing Industry and Its Growth Rate: 2003~2007

In 2004, the added-value tax per capita of foreign-capital enterprises in the manufacturing industry deceased from 9,228 *yuan* to 8,141 *yuan*. Over the next three years, however, its annual growth rate maintained steady around 15%. In 2007, this figure reached 12,348 *yuan* (see also Figure 7-6).

From 2003 to 2007, the average annual salary of the employees of foreign-capital enterprises in manufacturing industry increased from 14,877.3 *yuan* to 26,556.7 *yuan*, an increase of 0.8 times with an annual growth rate of 15.6%. During those five years, the growth rate in 2007 marked the highest rate of increase at 23.1% (see also Figure 7-7).

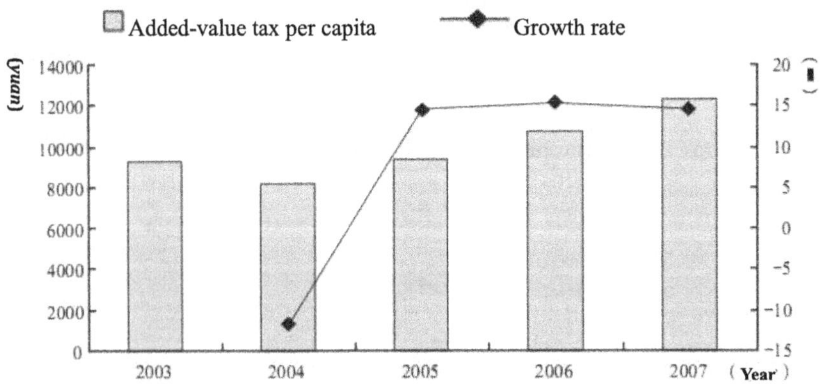

Figure 7-6: The Added-Value Tax Per Capita of Foreign-Capital Enterprises in China's Manufacturing Industry and Its Growth Rate: 2003-2007

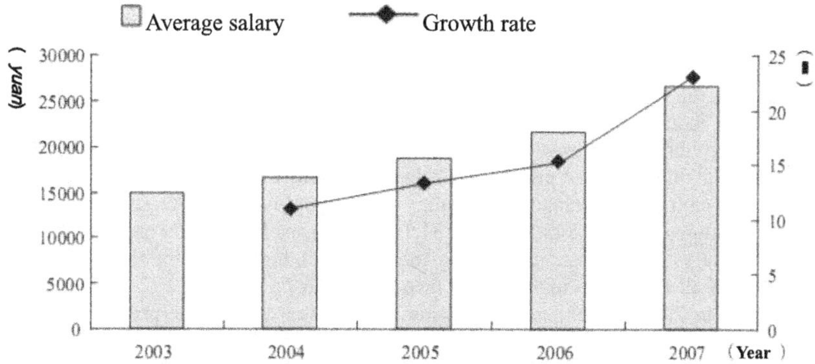

Figure 7-7: The Average Annual Salary of the Employees of Foreign-Capital Enterprises in China's Manufacturing Industry and Its Growth Rate: 2003-2007

7.2.2. The Conditions of Key Sectors in China' s Manufacturing Industry

China's manufacturing industry employs the majority of thoseworkers involved in foreign-capital enterprises, with those employees being mainly concentrated in the following sectors of the manufacturing industry: communication devices, computers, and other electronic devices (18.8%); clothing, shoes, and hats (9.3%); electric machinery and equipment (8.2%); textiles (6.7%); leather, fur, (down) feathers, and related products (6.7%); transportation and communication facilities (4.7%); and the manufacture of plastic products (4.2%). In 2007, the employees in those seven sectors accounted for 58.7% of all employees in foreign-capital enterprises in China's manufacturing industry (see also Figure 7-8).

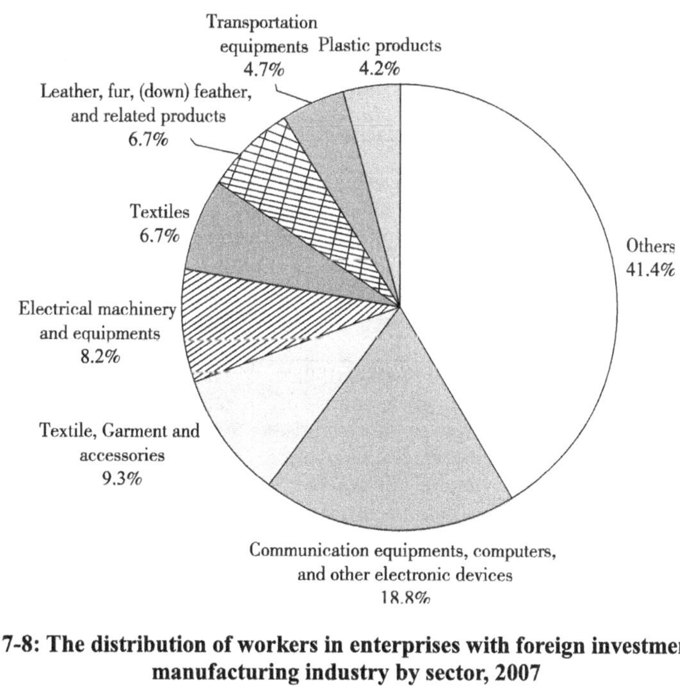

Figure 7-8: The distribution of workers in enterprises with foreign investment in the manufacturing industry by sector, 2007

The manufacture of communication devices, computers, and other electronic devices is the sector encompassing the majority of the jobs created by foreign-capital enterprises in China's manufacturing enterprises. From 2003 to 2007, the employment volume of foreign-capital enterprises in this sector expanded rapidly, from 1.776 million jobs to 4.427 million, an expansion of 1.5 times with an annual growth rate of 25.7%. This growth rate is significantly higher than that of the employment volume of foreign-capital enterprises in other sectors, and even that of the total employment volume of other foreign-capital enterprises in the manufacturing industry during the same period. At the same time, foreign-capital enterprises absorbed nearly three quarters of the employees in this sector, which demonstrates that those enterprises—not domestic enterprises—provide the majority of employment.

During this period, the average annualsalary of the employees of foreign-capital enterprises in this sector surged from 18,842.3 *yuan* to 31,117.5 *yuan*, with an annual growth rate of 13.4%, which was 13.0% higher than that during the corresponding period of time of the average annualsalary of all employees in this sector (see also Table 7-1).

From 2003 to 2007, the employment volume of foreign-capital enterprises involved in the manufacture of clothing, shoes, and hats increased by 50.9% from 1.448 million to 2.186 million, with an annual growth rate of 10.8%. During this period, the proportion of this volume to the employment volume of the manufacturing sector as a whole remained above 50%, which demonstrates that foreign-capital enterprises also provide the majority of employmentin this sector (see also Table 7-2).

Table 7-1: Conditions of the Employees of Foreign-Capital Enterprises in the Manufacture of Communication Devices, Computers, and Other Electronic Devices: 2003~2007

Year	The employment volume of foreign-capital enterprises (unit: 10,000 people)	The proportion of the employment volume of foreign-capital enterprises to the whole employment volume of this sector (unit: percent)	The average salary of the employees in this sector (unit: *yuan*)	The average salary of the employees of foreign-capital enterprises in this sector (unit: *yuan*)
2003	177.6	64.9	18635.3	18842.3
2004	269.0	71.0	19387.8	19856.2
2005	318.5	72.4	21644.4	21664.3
2006	374.7	74.2	25321.6	25442.5
2007	442.7	75.3	30415.0	31117.5

The average annual salary of the employees of foreign-capital enterprises in this sector rose from 11,282.6 *yuan* to 19,268.2 *yuan*, with an annual growth rate of 14.3%—slightly lower than 14.8%, the growth rate of the corresponding period of the average annual salary of all employees in this sector as a whole.

Table 7-2: The Conditions of the Employees of Foreign-Capital Enterprises in the Manufacture of Clothing, Shoes, and Hats: 2003~2007

Year	The employment volume of foreign-capital enterprises (unit: 10,000 people)	The proportion of the employment volume of foreign-capital enterprises in the whole employment volume of this sector (unit: percent)	The average salary of the employees in this sector (unit: *yuan*)	The average salary of the employees of foreign-capital enterprises in this sector (unit: *yuan*)
2003	144.8	50.1	10486.2	11282.6
2004	173.7	52.3	11729.9	12731.0
2005	178.7	51.7	12948.5	13810.9
2006	194.4	51.5	14844.2	15788.5
2007	218.6	52.8	18221.3	19269.2

From 2003 to 2007, the employment volume of foreign-capital enterprises in the manufacture of electrical machinery and equipment expanded from 0.903 million to 1.928 million, an expansion of 1.1 times, with an annual growth rate of 20.9%. Since 2004, the proportion of this volume to the whole employment volume of this sector remained above 40%, indicating that foreign-capital enterprises create the majority of this type of employment.

The average annualsalary of the employees of foreign-capital enterprises in this sector grew from 14,777.7 *yuan* to 27,010.4 *yuan* with an annual growth rate of 16.3%, which was a little bit lower than the 16.6% growth rate for the corresponding period of time of the average annualsalary of all employees in this sector (Table 7-3).

Table 7-3: The Conditions of the Employees of Foreign-Capital Enterprises in the Manufacture of Electrical Machinery and Equipment: 2003~2007

Year	The employment volume of foreign-capital enterprises (unit: 10,000 people)	The proportion of the employment volume of foreign-capital enterprises in the whole employment volume of this sector (unit: percent)	The average salary of the employees in this sector (unit: *yuan*)	The average salary of the employees of foreign-capital enterprises in this sector (unit: *yuan*)
2003	90.3	34.1	12926.8	14777.7
2004	139.8	40.1	14609.6	16287.2
2005	148.1	41.7	16200.2	17730.0
2006	155.3	42.6	19229.6	21858.3
2007	157.6	42.9	23887.6	27010.4

From 2003 to 2007, the employment volume of foreign-capital enterprises in the manufacture of textiles increased from 0.934 million to 1.576 million, an increase of 0.7 times with an annual growth rate of 14.0%. During this period, the proportion of this volume to the employment volume of the entire manufacturing sector maintained a nearly 25% share.

The average annualsalary of the employees of foreign-capital enterprises in the textile manufacturing sector rose from 11,302.9 *yuan* to 19,408.4 *yuan*at an annual growth rate of 14.5%, which was somewhat lower than 16.2%, the growth rate for the corresponding period of time of the average annualsalary of all employees in this sector (Table 7-4).

Table 7-4: The Conditions of the Employees of Foreign-Capital Enterprises in the Manufacture of Textiles: 2003~2007

Year	The employment volume of foreign-capital enterprises (unit: 10,000 people)	The proportion of the employment volume of foreign-capital enterprises in the whole employment volume of this sector (unit: percent)	The average salary of the employees in this sector (unit: *yuan*)	The average salary of the employees of foreign-capital enterprises in this sector (unit: *yuan*)
2003	93.4	18.7	8745.3	11302.9
2004	147.2	25.0	10194.1	12399.4
2005	148.1	25.1	11766.5	13899.6
2006	155.3	25.2	13392.5	16376.7
2007	157.6	25.2	15947.1	19408.4

From 2003 to 2007, the employment volume of foreign-capital enterprises in the manufacture of leather, fur, (down) feathers, and related products increased steadily by nearly 50%, from 1.02 million to 1.569 million with an annual growth rate of 11.4%. During this period, foreign-capital enterprises absorbed over 60% of the employees in this sector, demonstrating that those enterprises provide the majority of employment in this sector as well.

The average annual salary of the employees of foreign-capital enterprises in this sector swelled from 10,495.5 *yuan* to 18,876.5 *yuan* with an annual growth rate of 15.8%, slightly lower than the 16.1% growth rate for the corresponding period of time of the average annual salary of all employees in this sector (Table 7-5).

Table 7-5: The Conditions of the Employees of Foreign-Capital Enterprises in the Manufacture of Leather, Fur, (Down) Feathers, and related Products: 2003~2007

Year	The employment volume of foreign-capital enterprises (unit: 10,000 people)	The proportion of the employment volume of foreign-capital enterprises in the whole employment volume of this sector (unit: percent)	The average salary of the employees in this sector (unit: *yuan*)	The average salary of the employees of foreign-capital enterprises in this sector (unit: *yuan*)
2003	102.0	61.7	9950.2	10495.5
2004	132.8	62.9	11104.9	11536.3
2005	146.0	63.8	12808.9	13135.9
2006	153.6	62.5	14513.0	15173.9
2007	156.9	61.1	18089.0	18876.5

From 2003 to 2007, the employment volume of foreign-capital enterprises in the manufacture of transportation and communication facilities increased rapidly from 0.504 million to 1.115 million, achieving an increase of 1.2 times with an annual growth rate of 21.9%. The proportion of this volume to the whole employment volume of this sector concurrently rose from 16.2% to 27.3%.

The average annual salary of the employees of foreign-capital enterprises in this sector rose from 23,050.5 *yuan* to 35,251.8 *yuan*, with an annual growth rate of 11.2% that was lower than 14.6%, the growth rate for the corresponding period of time of the average annualsalary of all employees in this sector.

Table 7-6: The Conditions of the Employees of Foreign-Capital Enterprises in the Manufacture of Transportation and Communication Facilities: 2003~2007

Year	The employment volume of foreign-capital enterprises (unit: 10,000 people)	The proportion of the employment volume of foreign-capital enterprises in the whole employment volume of this sector (unit: percent)	The average salary of the employees in this sector (unit: *yuan*)	The average salary of the employees of foreign-capital enterprises in this sector (unit: *yuan*)
2003	50.4	16.2	15817.2	23050.5
2004	68.6	20.1	17706.3	25582.1
2005	78.1	22.2	19457.9	27460.7
2006	95.0	25.4	22705.0	30445.0
2007	111.5	27.3	27326.5	35251.8

From 2003 to 2007, the employment volume of foreign-capital enterprises in the manufacture of plastic products expanded by only 24.2%, from 0.588 million to 0.731 million, with an annual growth rate of 5.6%. This was significantly lower than the growth rate for the whole employment volume in this sector during the corresponding period. The proportion of this employment figure to the whole employment volume of this sector, however, stayed at or around 45.0%, which demonstrates that foreign-capital enterprises still provide the majority of employment in this field.

The average annual salary of the employees of foreign-capital enterprises in this sector rose from 13,069.0 *yuan* to 23,536.8 *yuan*, with an annual growth rate of 15.8%. Thiswas very close to the 15.7%growth rate during the same period of the average annualsalary of all employees in this sector (see also in Table 7-7).

Table 7-7: The Conditions of the Employees of Foreign-Capital Enterprises in the Manufacture of Plastic Products: 2003~2007

Year	The employment volume of foreign-capital enterprises (unit: 10,000 people)	The proportion of the employment volume of foreign-capital enterprises in the whole employment volume of this sector (unit: percent)	The average salary of the employees in this sector (unit: *yuan*)	The average salary of the employees of foreign-capital enterprises in this sector (unit: *yuan*)
2003	58.8	41.8	11066.7	13069.0
2004	79.1	45.1	12681.7	14698.1
2005	82.1	44.8	14228.6	16211.2
2006	88.8	44.1	16306.9	18891.9
2007	73.1	44.0	19829.8	23526.8

7.3 The Scale of Employmentof Different Regions in China and the Characteristics of Labor Remuneration

7.3.1. The Unbalanced Distribution of the Scale of Employment across Different Regions

The eastern region, the central region, the western region, and the northeastern region of China are the four major economic regions of China, but the distribution of employment by foreign-capital enterprises in those regions is not balanced. From a static perspective, the eastern region enjoys the majority of foreign-capital enterprises' employment. In 2008, total foreign-invested employment figures were distributed across the eastern region, the central region, the western region, and the northeastern region at 13.790 million, 1.080 million, 0.614 million and 0.728 million, accounting for 85.0%, 6.7%, 3.8%, and 4.5%, respectively,of the entire employment volume of foreign-capital enterprises in China. From a dynamic perspective, from 2003 to 2008, the proportion of the employment volume of foreign-capital enterprises in the eastern region to the whole employment volume of foreign-capital enterprises in China witnessed an increase from 83.2% to 85.0%, while the same proportion of the central region also rose from 5.7% to 6.7%. The same figure for the western region, however,actually decreased slightly, from 4.7% to 3.8%, as did the one for the northeastern region, from 6.3% to 4.5% (Figure 7-9).

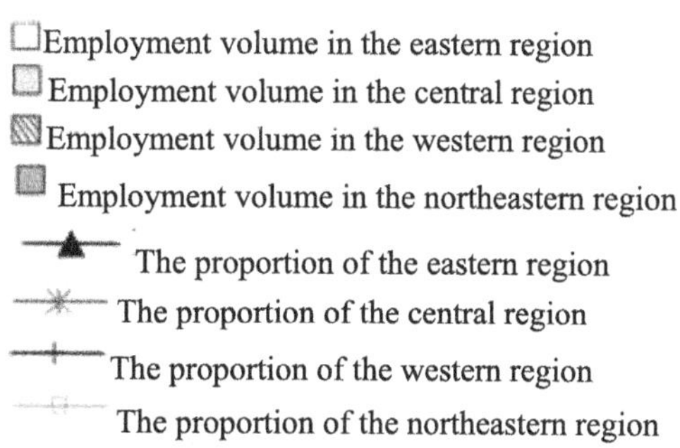

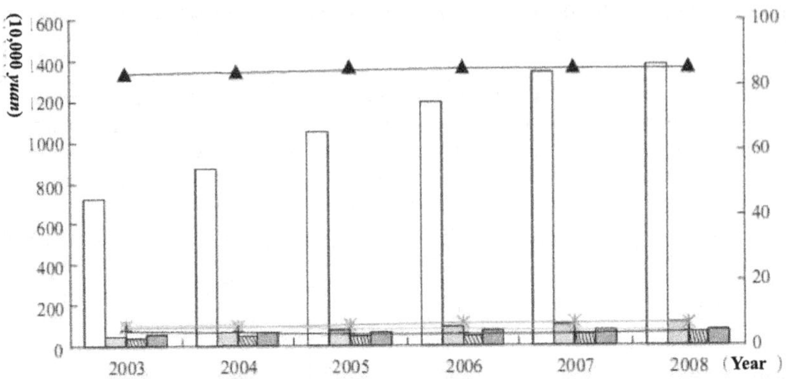

Figure 7-9: The Distribution of the Employees of Foreign-Capital Enterprises across the Four Major Economic Regions: 2003~2008

(Note: For purposes of this study, foreign-capital enterprises include enterprises funded by Taiwan, Macao, and Hong Kong, respectively or together. The employment volumes in this figure are recorded at the end of every year. These notes are also applied to the other figures as follow in this section.)

(Data source: Statistics in this figure are calculated according to data from the *China Statistical Yearbook* for each relevant year. This is also applied to the other figures as follow in this section.)

It's obvious that the average annual remuneration of the employees of foreign-capital enterprises in the eastern region is much higher than that of other economic regions. From a static perspective, in 2008, the annualaverage of this remuneration in the eastern region was 32,080.6 *yuan*, which surpassed the same figures in the central region (21,432.7 *yuan*), the western region (23,848.1 *yuan*), and the northeastern region (28,110.8 *yuan*) by 49.7%, 34.5%, and 14.1% respectively. From a dynamic perspective, however, from 2003 to 2008, the growth rate of this remuneration in the eastern region was only 11.8%, lower than the same figure in the central region (13.3%), the western region (13.2%) and northeastern region (14.2%) (Figure 7-10).

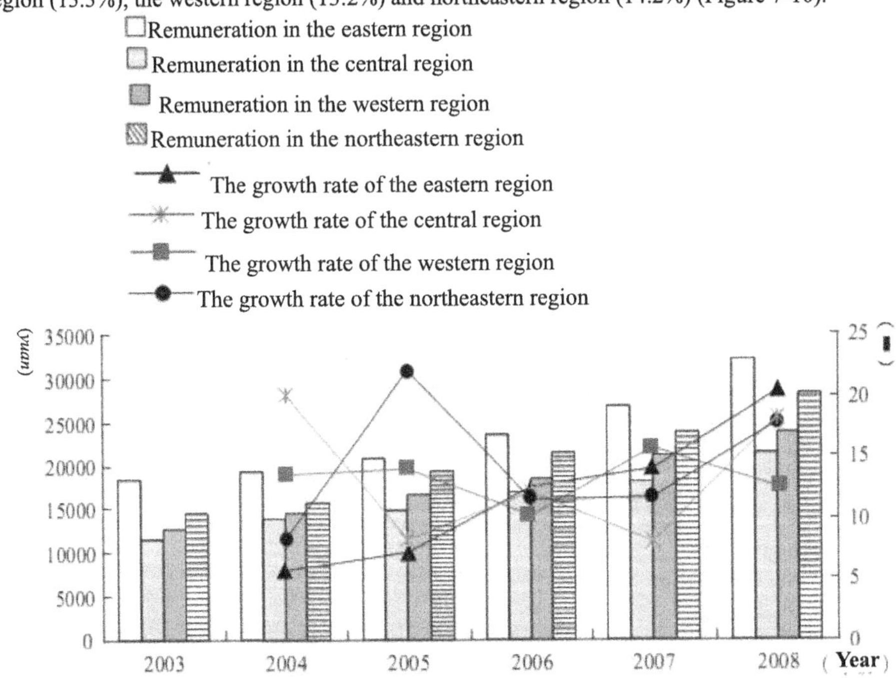

Figure 7-10: The Average Annual remuneration of the Employees of Foreign-capital Enterprises in the Four Major Economic Regions and its Growth Rate: 2003~2008

7.3.2. The Distribution of the Scale of Employment across Different Provinces, Municipalities, and Autonomous Regions

In 2008, there were certain areas among China's 31 provinces, municipalities, and autonomous regions thatemployed the majority of workers of foreign-capital enterprises, including Guangdong province (22.4%), Jiangsu province (11.6%), Zhejiang province (11.4%), Fujian province (11.2%), Shandong province (8.3%), Shanghai Municipality (8.2%), Beijing Municipality (6.5%), and Tianjin Municipality (3.5%). The employees of foreign-capital enterprises in those eight provinces and municipalities accounted for 83.2% in the total employees of foreign-capital enterprises working in China as a whole (Figure 7-11).

From 2003 to 2008, Guangdong Province consistently retained the most employees of all foreign-capital enterprises among the 31 provinces, municipalities, and autonomous regions in China—nearly 25% of all employees of foreign-capital enterprises in China. In 2003, there were 2.068 million employees of foreign-capital enterprises in Guangdong, and,by 2008, this figure had surged to 3.636 million with an annual growth rate of 12.0%. Foreign-capital enterprises made an increasing-significant contribution to the local employment volume during those years. The proportion of their employment volume to Guangdong's entire employment volume in general and urban employment volume specifically rose from 5.0% and 9.6% in 2003 to 7.0% and 18.0% in 2007, though it fell to 6.6% and 16.9%, respectively, in 2008.

Compared with the employees of local urban work units, however, the employees of foreign-capital enterprises in Guangdong received lower average annual remunerations. In 2008, the average annual labor remuneration of the employees of foreign-capital enterprises in Guangdong was 26,907.1 *yuan*, 60% higher than that of 2003, which was 16,996.6 *yuan*. The annual growth rate of this figure, 9.6%, was not only lower than the 12.4% growth rate of the average annual labor remuneration of the employees of all foreign-capital enterprises in China from 2003 to 2008, but also the 10.7% growth rate of the average annual labor remuneration of the employees of urban work units in Guangdong during the same period (Table 7-8).

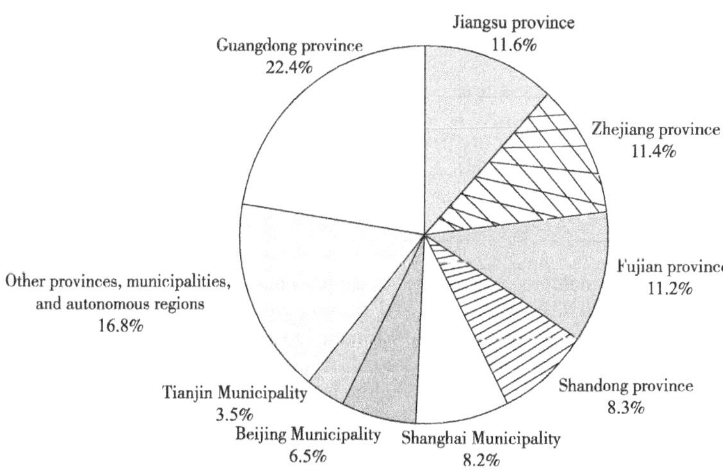

Figure 7-11: Regional distribution of workers in enterprises with foreign investment: 2003 – 2008

Table 7-8: The Conditions of the Employees of Foreign-Capital Enterprises in Guangdong Province: 2003~2008

Year	2003	2004	2005	2006	2007	2008
The employment volume of foreign-capital enterprises (unit: 10,000 people)	206.8	249.7	302.2	333.0	369.8	363.6
The proportion of the employment volume of foreign-capital enterprises in local employment volume (unit: percent)	5.0	5.8	6.4	6.3	7.0	6.6
The proportion of the employment volume of foreign-capital enterprises in the employment volume of local urban work units (unit: percent)	9.6	12.1	16.3	18.0	18.0	16.9
The proportion of the employment volume of local foreign-capital enterprises in the employment volume of all foreign-capital enterprises in China (unit: percent)	24.0	24.2	24.3	23.7	23.4	22.4
The average labor remuneration of the employees of local urban work units (unit: *yuan*)	19986.0	22116.0	23959.0	26186.0	29443.0	33282.0
The average labor remuneration of the employees of local foreign-capital enterprises (unit: *yuan*)	16996.6	17946.7	19009.5	20822.9	22959.2	26907.1

From 2003 to 2008, the employment volume of foreign-capital enterprises in Jiangsu Province achieved a rapid net growth from 0.821 million to 1.881 million with an annual growth rate of 18.0%. The proportion of this employment figure to the total employment volume of foreign-capital enterprises in China rose from 9.5% to 11.6% during that period, while its proportion to the entire employment system and the employment volume of urban work units in Jiangsu grew from 2.3% and 4.9% to 4.3% and 11.2%, respectively.

The employees of foreign-capital enterprises in Jiangsu received a lower average annual remuneration thanthe employees of local urban work units. From 2003 to 2008, the average annual labor remuneration of the employees of foreign-capital enterprises in Jiangsu increased from 16,641.0 *yuan* to 27,511.1 *yuan*, a one-time increase. The annual growth rate of this average was 10.6%, which was lower than that of the average annual remuneration of the employees of urban work units in Jiangsu during the same period, 14.8% (Table 7-9).

Table 7-9: The Conditions of the Employees of Foreign-Capital Enterprises in Jiangsu Province: 2003~2008

Year	2003	2004	2005	2006	2007	2008
The employment volume of foreign-capital enterprises (unit: 10,000 people)	82.1	102.1	130.1	158.4	181.6	188.1
The proportion of the employment volume of foreign-capital enterprises in local employment volume (unit: percent)	2.3	2.7	3.4	3.5	4.3	4.3
The proportion of the employment volume of foreign-capital enterprises in the employment volume of local urban work units (unit: percent)	4.9	6.7	9.3	11.3	11.9	11.2
The proportion of the employment volume of local foreign-capital enterprises in the employment volume of all foreign-capital enterprises in China (unit: percent)	9.5	9.9	10.4	11.3	11.5	11.6
The average labor remuneration of the employees of local urban work units (unit: *yuan*)	15712.0	18202.0	20957.0	23782.0	27374.0	31297.0
The average labor remuneration of the employees of local foreign-capital enterprises (unit: *yuan*)	16641.0	17436.7	18597.6	20793.8	23488.1	27511.1

From 2003 to 2008, Zhejiang province boasted the most rapid employment growth in foreign-capital enterprises among all provinces, municipalities, and autonomous regions in China. During this period, employment figures surged from 0.43 million to 1.85 million, an increase of 3.3 times with an annual growth rate of 33.9%. The proportion of this to the whole employment volume of foreign-capital enterprises in China rose from 5.0% to 11.4% from 2003 to 2008, while its proportion to the entire employment volume as a whole and the employment volume of urban work units in Zhejiang grew from 1.5% and 3.1% to 5.0% and 13.4%, respectively, during this same period.

From 2003 to 2008, the average annual labor remuneration of the employees of foreign-capital enterprises in Zhejiang increased from 15,903.3 *yuan* to 25,551.7 *yuan*, for an annual growth rate of 9.9% that was higher than that of the average annual remuneration of the employees of urban work units in Zhejiang during the same period, 9.5%. In terms of absolute values, however, the average annual remuneration of the employees of local foreign-capital enterprises was still lower than that of the employees of urban work units in this province (Table 7-10).

Table 7-10: The Conditions of the Employees of Foreign-capital Enterprises in Zhejiang Province: 2003~2008

Year	2003	2004	2005	2006	2007	2008
The employment volume of foreign-capital enterprises (unit: 10,000 people)	43.0	64.5	99.9	135.6	166.2	185.0
The proportion of the employment volume of foreign-capital enterprises in local employment volume (unit: percent)	1.5	2.1	3.1	4.3	4.6	5.0
The proportion of the employment volume of foreign-capital enterprises in the employment volume of local urban work units (unit: percent)	3.1	5.0	9.3	12.6	12.8	13.4
The proportion of the employment volume of local foreign-capital enterprises in the employment volume of all foreign-capital enterprises in China (unit: percent)	5.0	6.2	8.0	9.6	10.5	11.4
The average labor remuneration of the employees of local urban work units (unit: *yuan*)	21367.0	23506.0	25896.0	27820.0	31086.0	33622.0
The average labor remuneration of the employees of local foreign-capital enterprises (unit: *yuan*)	15903.3	15915.2	17597.9	19728.2	22495.1	25551.7

From 2003 to 2008, the employment volume of foreign-capital enterprises in Fujian province increased steadily, from 1.218 million to 1.818 million, with an annual growth rate of 8.3%. The proportion of this figure to the total employment volume of foreign-capital enterprises in China as a whole decreased from 14.1% to 11.2%, while its proportion to the entire employment volume and the employment volume of urban work units in Zhejiang grew from 6.9% and 17.2% to 8.7% and 25.6%, respectively, during the same period.

The employees of foreign-capital enterprises in Fujian received lower average annual remunerations than the employees of local urban work units. From 2003 to 2008, the average annual labor remuneration of the employees of foreign-capital enterprises in Fujian increased from 12,375.7 *yuan* to 21,192.3 *yuan*, an increase of 0.7 times. The annual growth rate averaged11.4%, which was lower than that of the average annual remuneration of the employees of urban work units in Fujian during the same period, 12.3% (Table 7-11).

Table 7-11: The Conditions of the Employees of Foreign-Capital Enterprises in Fujian Province: 2003~2008

Year	2003	2004	2005	2006	2007	2008
The employment volume of foreign-capital enterprises (unit: 10,000 people)	121.8	149.0	163.5	163.5	185.9	181.8
The proportion of the employment volume of foreign-capital enterprises in local employment volume (unit: percent)	6.9	8.2	8.8	8.8	9.3	8.7
The proportion of the employment volume of foreign-capital enterprises in the employment volume of local urban work units (unit: percent)	17.2	22.1	26.8	26.8	27.6	25.6
The proportion of the employment volume of local foreign-capital enterprises in the employment volume of all foreign-capital enterprises in China (unit: percent)	14.1	14.4	13.1	13.1	11.7	11.2
The average labor remuneration of the employees of local urban work units (unit: *yuan*)	14310.0	15603.0	17146.0	17146.0	22283.0	25555.0
The average labor remuneration of the employees of local foreign-capital enterprises (unit: *yuan*)	12375.7	13406.5	14357.8	18389.7	18389.7	21192.3

From 2003 to 2008, the employment volume of foreign-capital enterprises in Shandong Province increased at a rapid rate, from 0.69 million to 1.353 million. This almost doubled the total employment volume, for an annual growth rate of 14.4%. The proportion of this employment figure outnumbered the whole employment volume of foreign-capital enterprises in China by 8%, while its proportion to the total employment volume and the employment volume of urban work units in Shandong grew from 1.4% and 5.0% to 2.5% and 9.7%, respectively.

From 2003 to 2008, the average annual remuneration of the employees of foreign-capital enterprises in Shandong rose from 11,168.6 *yuan* to 23,411.2 *yuan* with an annual growth rate of 16.0%. This growth rate was basically the same as the growth rate of the average annual remuneration of the employees of urban work units in Shandong Province during the same period, 15.9%. In terms of absolute values, however, this average was still lower than the same measurement for local urban work units (Table 7-12).

Table 7-12: The Conditions of the Employees of Foreign-Capital Enterprises in Shandong Province: 2003~2008

Year	2003	2004	2005	2006	2007	2008
The employment volume of foreign-capital enterprises (unit: 10,000 people)	69.0	82.0	124.1	134.4	135.7	135.3
The proportion of the employment volume of foreign-capital enterprises in local employment volume (unit: percent)	1.4	1.7	2.4	2.3	2.6	2.5
The proportion of the employment volume of foreign-capital enterprises in the employment volume of local urban work units (unit: percent)	5.0	5.8	9.0	9.8	9.7	9.7
The proportion of the employment volume of local foreign-capital enterprises in the employment volume of all foreign-capital enterprises in China (unit: percent)	8.0	7.9	10.0	9.5	8.6	9.7
The average labor remuneration of the employees of local urban work units (unit: *yuan*)	12567.0	14332.0	16614.0	19228.0	22844.0	26234.0
The average labor remuneration of the employees of local foreign-capital enterprises (unit: *yuan*)	11168.6	12406.9	14070.4	16944.6	19867.2	23411.2

From 2003 to 2008, the employment figures for foreign-capital enterprises in Shanghai Municipality grew stably, from 0.816 million to 1.328 million, with an annual growth rate of 10.2%. The proportion of this volume to the entire employment volume of foreign-capital enterprises in China, however,declined from 9.5% in 2003 to 8.2% in 2008, while at the same time, its proportion to the whole employment volume of Shanghai and the employment volume of local urban work units increased from 10.6% and 12.0%, respectively, to 14.8% and 19.5%.

In 2003, the average annual remuneration of the employees of foreign-capital enterprises in Shanghai was 7.0% higher than that of the employees of local urban work units. For the next five years, however, the annual growth rate of the average annual remuneration of foreign-capital enterprise employees, 9.5%, was far lower than the annual growth rate of local urban work unit employees, 13.8%. As a result, the first average was lower than the second one from 2004 to 2008, when the average annual remuneration of the employees of foreign-capital enterprises in Shanghai was 46,025.2 *yuan*, 13.2% lower than that of the employees of local urban work units, which was 52,122.0 *yuan* (Table 7-13).

Table 7-13: The Conditions of the Employees of Foreign-Capital Enterprises in Shanghai Municipality: 2003~2008

Year	2003	2004	2005	2006	2007	2008
The employment volume of foreign-capital enterprises (unit: 10,000 people)	81.6	84.4	89.8	92.4	123.7	132.8
The proportion of the employment volume of foreign-capital enterprises in local employment volume (unit: percent)	10.6	10.4	10.5	10.4	14.1	14.8
The proportion of the employment volume of foreign-capital enterprises in the employment volume of local urban work units (unit: percent)	12.0	12.8	14.6	15.0	18.8	19.5
The proportion of the employment volume of local foreign-capital enterprises in the employment volume of all foreign-capital enterprises in China (unit: percent)	9.5	8.2	7.2	6.6	7.8	8.2
The average labor remuneration of the employees of local urban work units (unit: *yuan*)	27304.0	30085.0	34345.0	41188.0	49310.0	52122.0
The average labor remuneration of the employees of local foreign-capital enterprises (unit: *yuan*)	29207.3	29538.4	31682.3	37866.6	40942.9	46025.2

From 2003 to 2008, the employment volume of foreign-capital enterprises in Beijing Municipality increased rapidly, from 0.487 million to 1.061 million, an increase of 1.2 times with an annual growth rate of 16.8%. Its proportion to the employment volume of foreign-capital enterprises in China as a whole stepped up from 5.6% to 8.2% during this period, while its proportion of the entire employment of Beijing and the employment volume of local urban work units increased from 5.7% and 5.8% to 9.0% and 12.5%, respectively.

Differently from the provinces and municipalities discussed above, in recent years, the average annual remuneration of the employees of foreign-capital enterprises in Beijing was generally higher than that of the employees of local work units. In 2003, the average income of foreign-capital enterprises was 50% higher than that of local work units, and in 2008, though the overall figures experienced a slight decrease, the income of workers at foreign-invested enterprises in Beijing was still nearly 40% higher than that of local urban work units. The annual growth rate of the first average, 15.7%, was lower than that of the second average, 17.1%, however (Table 7-14).

Table 7-14: The Conditions of the Employees of Foreign-Capital Enterprises in Beijing Municipality: 2003~2008

Year	2003	2004	2005	2006	2007	2008
The employment volume of foreign-capital enterprises (unit: 10,000 people)	48.7	63.3	71.3	80.9	98.1	106.1
The proportion of the employment volume of foreign-capital enterprises in local employment volume (unit: percent)	5.7	7.1	7.7	8.8	8.8	9.0
The proportion of the employment volume of foreign-capital enterprises in the employment volume of local urban work units (unit: percent)	5.8	7.9	9.1	10.3	12.3	12.5
The proportion of the employment volume of local foreign-capital enterprises in the employment volume of all foreign-capital enterprises in China (unit: percent)	5.6	6.1	5.7	5.7	6.2	6.5
The average labor remuneration of the employees of local urban work units (unit: *yuan*)	25312.0	29674.0	34191.0	40117.0	46507.0	55844.0
The average labor remuneration of the employees of local foreign-capital enterprises (unit: *yuan*)	38939.8	42942.7	48941.2	55493.0	59639.4	80601.7

From 2003 to 2008, the employment volume of foreign-capital enterprises in Tianjin Municipality rose from 0.456 million to 0.565 million with an annual growth rate of 3.5%. Its proportion to the whole employment volume of foreign-capital enterprises in China fell from 5.3% to 3.5% during this period, while its proportion of the entire employment volume of Tianjin and the of local urban work units increased from 10.9% and 14.7% in 2003 to 13.4% and 23.2% in 2007, then falling to 11.2% and 18.3% in 2008.

From 2003 to 2008, the average annual remuneration of the employees of foreign-capital enterprises in Tianjin Municipality increased from 18,551.8 *yuan* to 38,193.6 *yuan* with an annual growth rate of 15.5%, slightly lower than the growth rate of the average annual remuneration of the employees of local urban work units during the same period, which was 16.5%. In terms of absolute values, however, this average was still lower than the same figure for local urban work units, though the gap between those two figures remained relatively small (Table 7-15).

Table 7-15: The Conditions of the Employees of Foreign-Capital Enterprises in Tianjin Municipality: 2003~2008

Year	2003	2004	2005	2006	2007	2008
The employment volume of foreign-capital enterprises (unit: 10,000 people)	45.6	48.3	51.1	55.0	57.8	56.5
The proportion of the employment volume of foreign-capital enterprises in local employment volume (unit: percent)	10.9	11.4	12.0	9.8	13.4	11.2
The proportion of the employment volume of foreign-capital enterprises in the employment volume of local urban work units (unit: percent)	14.7	19.4	20.2	21.8	23.2	18.3
The proportion of the employment volume of local foreign-capital enterprises in the employment volume of all foreign-capital enterprises in China (unit: percent)	5.3	4.7	4.1	3.9	3.7	3.5
The average labor remuneration of the employees of local urban work units (unit: *yuan*)	18648.0	21754.0	25271.0	28682.0	34938.0	39990.0
The average labor remuneration of the employees of local foreign-capital enterprises (unit: *yuan*)	38939.8	42942.7	48941.2	55493.4	59639.4	80601.7

Chapter 8 New Growth Points for Foreign Investment: Theoretical & Practical Basis

Since the adoption of the reform and opening-up policy 30 years before, China has become a major country in trade and investment. China occupies an important place in the world in terms of the utilization of foreign investment and Chinese enterprises' overseas investment. As a basic policy of opening-up, utilizing foreign capital will undoubtedly be persisted in a long period of time and must be improved in practices. So we should proceed from latest practices in China, draw from western theories about the international investment, explore and recognize the regularity of utilizing foreign capital in China and innovate our theory and policies in utilizing foreign capital, with a view to improving the quality and level of utilizing foreign capital. This chapter, based on the analysis of important features of the foreign investment in recent years, intends to interpret the theoretical and policy meaning of those features and clarify the practical demands.

8.1 Important Features of the Foreign Investment Absorption in China

Since the start of the 21st century, great progress has been made in absorbing foreign investment in China. Since the late 10th Five-Year Plan period, some important features of the foreign investment in China have emerged and meanwhile, they have important meanings. Analyzing these features is a fundamental way for us to recognize and understand the theoretical and policy meanings and practical needs of utilizing the foreign capital in this new stage of an open economy. These features are as follows.

8.1.1. Significant Increase of the Proportion of Foreign Investments in the Tertiary Industry and Insufficient Investments in the Secondary Industry

With a subtitle of *"The Shift towards Services"*, the *World Investment Report in 2004* summarizes the new trend since the 1990s that the international direct investment is shifting towards the service sector, which has drawn the attention from the Chinese government and scholars. Since then, appealing China to attract more foreign investments in the service sector has become a concern for scholars' studies and the Chinese government in making decisions.

Table 8-1 Foreign Investment Inflow Structure of Three Industries in China (2001-2008)

Unit: Billion USD, %

Year	2001	2002	2003	2004	2005	2006	2007	2008
Actual Amount of FDI Inflow	46.878	52.743	53.505	60.63	72.406	72.715	83.521	108.3
Growth Rate	15.1	12.5	1.4	13.3	19.4	0.4	14.9	29.7
Amount in the Primary Industry	0.9	1.03	1	1.11	0.72	0.6	0.92	1.19
Growth Rate	33.3	14.4	−0.3	11	−35	−16.7	53.3	29.3
Proportion	1.9	2	1.9	1.8	1	0.8	1.1	1.1
Amount in the Secondary Industry	34.8	39.46	39.18	45.47	44.68	42.51	42.85	49.9
Growth Rate	17.6	13.5	−0.8	16.1	−0.2	−4.9	0.9	16.3
Proportion	74.2	74.9	73.3	75	61.7	58.4	51.3	46.1
Amount in the Tertiary Industry	11.178	12.253	13.325	14.05	27.006	29.605	41.93	57.21
Growth Rate	6.8	9.6	8.7	5.4	92.2	9.6	41.6	36.4
Proportion	23.9	23.1	24.8	23.2	37.3	40.8	47.6	42.8

Notes: The actual amount of FDI inflow is a full-scale number.

Source: The data of 2008 is from January issues of *Trends of Foreign Investment* in 2009 by the Department of Foreign Investment Administration, Ministry of Commerce, China; Other data comes from statistics in the *China Statistical Yearbook.*

From the table 8-1, we can see that the growth of foreign investment inflow in manufacturing from 2001 to 2008 is not a significant one, and we have witnessed negative growth or feeble growth in 4 years while 3 out of the another 4 years with the high growth rate are in the 10th Five-Year Plan period, leaving only one year with the high growth rate in the 11th Five-Year Plan period and it's just a growth accumulated after 3 consecutive years of negative and feeble growth. The highlight of the foreign investment absorption in the 11th Five-Year Plan period is the rapid growth of the foreign investment in service industry in 2007 and 2008, which has increased the proportion of the foreign investment in service industry in the total foreign investment in China in the 11th Five-Year Plan period. Then, two questions have emerged. First, why is there a stagnation of the foreign investment in the secondary industry? Second, why is there a breakthrough growth of the foreign investment in service industry?

8.1.2. Increasing Dominance of "Wholly Foreign-owned Enterprises

Among all forms of foreign capital utilization, the wholly foreign-owned enterprises has become a favorite for foreign-funded businesses. According to the annual survey statistics of foreign-funded enterprises collected by the Department of Foreign Investment Administration of the Ministry of Commerce in 2008, by 2003, the proportion of wholly foreign-owned enterprises in foreign-funded enterprises has reached 52.21%, and the number continued to increase, reaching 64.44% at the end of 2007. The proportion of Sino-foreign cooperative joint ventures and Sino-foreign equity joint ventures in foreign-funded enterprises keeps decreasing; the number of foreign-invested joint-equity enterprises increases rapidly but the total number remains a small one; other forms of foreign-funded enterprises are gradually vanishing. By the end of 2007, among the 221,000 foreign-funded enterprises, the majority shareholders of 173,000 enterprises are foreign investors, accounting for 78% of the total number of these enterprises.

Along with their growing preference for investing in wholly foreign-owned enterprises, foreign investors attach more importance to their control of equities. The majority shareholders of most Sino-foreign cooperative joint ventures are foreign investors. However, Chinese side is the majority shareholder of more than half of Sino-foreign equity joint ventures and over 70% of foreign-invested joint-equity enterprises.

With their growing dominance, wholly foreign-owned enterprises have gradually become the main form of foreign investment utilization, and its share in total foreign investment keeps increasing. Since 2000 when the amount of foreign investment utilized by wholly foreign-owned enterprises exceeded that by Sino-foreign cooperative joint ventures for the first time, its proportion has been on the rise, reaching 68.57% at the end of 2007. In recent years, in terms of the actual utilization of foreign investments, the proportion of Sino-foreign equity joint ventures is about 25% and the proportion of Sino-foreign cooperative joint ventures has started to decrease, while the amount of foreign investments utilized by foreign-invested joint-equity enterprises has increased significantly, but its proportion remains a relatively small one.

Table 8-2 Proportion Changes of Different Forms of Foreign-Invested Businesses from 2005 to 2007 in Terms of the Actual Utilization of Foreign Investments

Unit: billion USD, %

Type of Enterprises	2005		2006		2007	
	Amount	Proportion	Amount	Proportion	Amount	Proportion
Wholly foreign-owned enterprises	261.544	65.84	335.159	62.34	448.049	68.57
Sino-foreign equity joint ventures	116.162	25.39	129.242	27.69	154.963	23.72
Sino-foreign cooperative joint ventures	31.315	6.29	32.019	7.46	32.569	4.98
Foreign-invested joint-equity enterprises	10.53	0.248	12.622	2.51	17.837	2.73
Others	0.008	0	0.007	0		

Source: compiled on the basis of survey data from Foreign Invested Enterprise Operation Research Group of Finance and Trade Economics Research Institute of Chinese Academy of Social Sciences

With regard to this phenomenon, one of its interpretations (by Luo Yuduo, etc. 2008) is that foreign investors make use of their advantages in capital, technologies and management to exclude and control Chinese industries with a view to expanding their business. More discussion is needed to confirm whether this interpretation is comprehensive and right. If this is a bad thing, then why can it be allowed to happen? We can see that it is not that simple.

8.1.3. Free Port Becomes the Main Source of Foreign Investments

Since 1992, the investment growth speed of Virgin Islands, Cayman Islands, Western Samoa and Mauritius has been on the rise in China. Especially in the late 1990s, the foreign investment from the four free ports leaps to a new level, which becomes the main source of foreign investment of China. According to statistics, by the end of 1994, the main sources of foreign capital inflow are: Chinese Hong Kong and Macau (59.3 billion USD), Chinese Taiwan (8.45 billion USD), US (7.73 billion USD), Japan (7.28 billion USD), Singapore (2.07 billion USD), Korea (1.273 billion USD), UK (1.268 billion USD), France (0.80 billion USD), German (0.786 billion USD) and Thailand (0.626 billion USD). At that time, the total foreign capital inflow volume was 0.18 billion USD from the four free ports. Among the 11 years from 1995 to 2005, the foreign capital inflow of free ports has been on the rise rapidly, surpassing US, Japan and EU including UK, France and German (Table 8-3).

Table 8-3 Ratio Rise of Foreign Capital Inflow of Free Ports between 1995 and 2005

Unit: billion USD, %

Year	Total	Hong Kong	Taiwan	Free Ports	US	Japan	Korea	Singapore	EU
1995	37.52	5.35	0.843	0.101	0.822	0.828	8.278	0.493	0.568
1996	41.73	4.96	0.833	0.157	0.825	0.882	0.325	0.538	0.656
1997	45.26	4.56	0.727	0.455	0.716	0.956	0.473	0.576	0.922
1998	45.46	4.07	0.641	0.986	0.858	0.748	0.397	0.749	0.875
1999	40.32	4.06	0.646	0.803	1.046	0.737	0.316	0.655	1.111
2000	40.71	3.81	0.564	1.161	1.077	0.716	0.366	0.534	1.1
2001	46.88	3.57	0.638	1.411	0.946	0.928	0.459	0.457	0.892
2002	52.74	3.39	0.753	1.55	1.028	0.794	0.516	0.443	0.703
2003	53.5	3.31	0.735	1.426	0.785	0.945	0.839	0.385	0.735
2004	60.63	3.13	0.514	1.633	0.65	0.899	1.031	0.331	0.699
2005	60.32	2.98	0.357	1.718	0.507	0.902	0.714	0.304	0.717

Source: Institute of Finance and Trade Economics, Chinese Academy of Social Sciences: *China Foreign Investment Report in 2007*

Since the beginning of 2000, free ports have become the second main foreign capital inflow source inferior to Hong Kong. Besides, because of the up ratio of foreign capital inflow of Taiwan and Singapore and down ratio of Korea, the order[37] of ten foreign capital inflow sites of China have been changed as followed: Hong Kong (259.522 billion USD), Japan (53.375 billion USD), US (51.09 billion USD), Virgin Island (45.916 billion USD), Taiwan (41.757 billion USD), Korea (31.104 billion USD), Singapore (27.744 billion USD), UK (13.196 billion USD), German (11.439 billion USD) and Cayman Islands (8.66 billion USD). This order is on the basis of separating four free ports from each other. If taking the statistics of four free ports, such as Virgin Islands, Cayman Islands, Western Samoa and Mauritius together, its order ranks the second. Between 2006 and 2008, the foreign capital inflow from free ports has been increased to the new level from 13 billion USD to 22.6 billion USD and 23.1 billion USD successively, which makes free ports become the most active foreign capital inflow sources. Based on these three years'

[37] The foreign capital inflow excludes financial investment.

statistics, the order of ten foreign capital inflow sources is as followed: Hong Kong (88.972 billion USD), Virgin Islands (43.754 billion USD), Japan (11.839 billion USD), US (8.421 billion USD), Taiwan (5.809 billion USD), Korea (10.708 billion USD), Singapore (8.629billion USD), Cayman Islands (7.811billion USD), Western Samoa (6.258Western Samoa) and German (3.613 billion USD). Since 2007, the foreign investment in China of Mauritius has enjoyed leap to be the eleventh source with 2.8 billion USD in three years after UK (2.47 billion USD). What's the meaning of free ports becoming the main source of foreign capital? The popular explanation is the hot money inflow. But it is only an assumption without investigation and statistics. What can we learn from this status?

8.1.4. Foreign Capital Inflow Ratio of China Declines Globally

Since the 1990s, with the international industrial structure adjustment and rapid growth of industrial transfer, FDI has been on the rise with the peak value in 2000. Then after three years' decline, FDI rebounded in 2003 and reached the new peak value in 2007. With the global FDI growth, the total volume of foreign capital inflow in China is growing constantly. On the contrary, the share of Chinese foreign capital in the world goes down successively. In other words, our foreign capital growth speed is lower than that of global FDI (Table 8-4).

Table 8-4 Chinese FDI Attraction Ratio and Ratio of FDI in Total Domestic Investment between 1991 and 2008

Year	Chinese FDI Attraction (billion USD)	Global FDI (billion USD)	Ratio (%)	Exchange Rate Annual Average Price	Chinese FAI (billion RMB)	Ratio (%)
1991	4.366	198.1	2.2	532.23		
1992	11.008	201.5	5.5	551.46	808.01	7.51
1993	27.515	239.1	11.9	576.2	1,307.23	12.13
1994	33.767	251.1	13.4	861.87	1,704.23	17.08
1995	37.621	338.7	11.1	835.1	2,001.93	15.65
1996	41.726	359.0	11.6	831.42	2,297.4	15.1
1997	45.257	464.0	9.8	828.98	2,530.0	14.79
1998	45.483	644.0	7.1	827.91	2,845.7	13.23
1999	40.319	865.0	4.7	827.83	2,987.6	11.17
2000	40.715	1,270.8	3.2	827.84	3,261.9	10.32
2001	46.878	735.0	6.4	827.7	3,689.8	10.51
2002	52.743	625.2	8.4	827.7	4,320.2	10.1
2003	53.505	561.1	9.5	827.7	5,511.8	8.03
2004	60.63	717.7	8.4	827.68	7,007.3	7.16
2005	72.406	958.7	7.6	819.17	8,860.4	6.69
2006	72.715	1,411.0	5.2	797.18	10,987.0	5.28
2007	83.521	1,833.0	4.6	760.4	13,723.9	4.63
2008	108.3	1466.0	7.4	684.6	17,229.1	4.3

Note: Chinese and global FDI unit is billion USD. Chinese FAI unit is billion RMB. Exchange rate annual average price is very 100 USD to RMB.

Sources: Chinese FDI attraction statistics come from China's Ministry of Commerce. Since 2005, the statistics include financial FDI. Global FDI comes from new version of *World Investment Report* published by UNCTAD with the statistics estimation by author in 2008. Exchange rate annual average price comes from *China Statistical Yearbook* with the statistics estimation by author in 2008. Chinese FAI comes from *China Statistical Yearbook* and State Statistics Bureau.

Since 2002, USD has depreciated to other western prime currencies. The global FDI has been lifted on the basis of USD calculation. Since the second half year of 2008, USD has appreciated to Europe currencies, which results in undervaluation of global FDI. With the RMB exchange rate reform since July, 2005, RMB exchange rate to USD has appreciated by 21%. Taking the appreciation of RMB into consideration, the practical ratio of FDI in total domestic investment needs to be revised. The decline trend is clear with ratio of 6.8%, 5.5%, 5.0% and 5.2% between 2005 and 2008 respectively by taking the exchange rate annual average price of 2004 as the basis.

China has made great efforts to attracting FDI since 1990s with investment of over ten billion USD in 1992. During the "8th Five-year Plan" period between 1991 and 1995, foreign capital attraction of China accounted for 8.8% of global FDI flow. But the ratio declined to 7.3%, 6.7% and 5.7% respectively in the "Ninth Five-year Plan" between 1996 and 2000, "Tenth Five-year Plan" between 2001 and 2005 and the first three years between 2006 and 2008 of the "Eleventh Five-year Plan". The popular and simple explanation to the decline is that China does not need foreign investment with the economic and people's savings growth and less demand for foreign investment. Indeed, China does not depend on foreign capital so much, but it does not mean that China will not introduce foreign investment. In the world, developed countries like US and UK are big countries to absorb global FDI. Even the small but rich Belgium has attracted more global FDI than China in 2006. But this does not reflect that rich countries desire for foreign capital. So, how to explain it in theory? In practice, local governments of China don't decrease their passion on attracting foreign investment but desire to attract more, which shows their expectation on foreign investors to develop local economy. In conclusion, both theory and practice need economics study to give convincing answer to foreign investment attraction of China.

8.2 Theoretical Basis of Important Features of the Foreign Investment

8.2.1. From the Two-Gap Theory to the Global Value Chain Theory

Development economics explain that the reason why developing countries want to bridge the two gaps of capital and foreign exchange so as to realize economic take-off is that they wish to introduce FDI. This is the famous "two-gap model" theory, raised by US economists in the 1960s. It provided theoretical basis for developed countries such as US and UK to justify their capital export. It also drew the attention and became the guiding principle of the newly born developing nations which need to develop their economies eagerly. With the rapid growth of foreign direct investment, western economists have formed a relatively complete theory for FDI and multinationals. Important theoretical contributions include the Monopolistic Advantage theory by

S.H.Hymer (1976) and Charles P. Kindleberger (1969), the Internalization theory by Peter J. Buckley (1970) and Mark Casson (1970), the Eclectic Paradigm of International Production by John H. Dunning as well as the Marginal Industrial Expansion theory by Kiyoshi Kojima(1978). Having provided new theoretical bases for western multinationals for their global production and expansion, these theories were quite popular with international monopolistic capital and western economic circle. However, as one great pitfall, these theories did not explain the reason why host countries of FDI, especially the developing countries need to attract foreign investment, thus can not provide policy information for those countries. Therefore, they are less practicable than the two-gap model theory. With the rise of newly emerging markets and the FDI flow from developing countries, global multinational investment has displayed such new patterns as South-South mutual investment, investment from South to North, North-North mutual investment and capital flow to developed nations. As a result, the two-gap theory has shown more limitations in explaining international direct investments.

Since the 1980s, US economy has accelerated its transformation to the service economy with decreased competitiveness of industrial products. Industrial products from Japan and Europe have occupied the US market. The deficit in goods market in current account has been increasing all the time. This has drawn close attention of US government and with it a heated discussion over the competitiveness of US industry. Pessimistic economists argue that government intervene and formulate industrial policies to raise the competitiveness of US industrial products. While optimistic economists argue that changes in the US industrial structure should be determined by free market forces and government has no need for intervention. They believe the decrease in competitiveness of US industrial products is only a strategy to give up temporary interest for competitive advantage in the next stage. Professor Michael E. Porter (1990) of Harvard Business School summarized this debate and set up a new research analysis framework of international industrial competitiveness. Porter judged the two views not from the perspective of values, but of corporate strategic management where multinationals could win international competition. Through analysis of new practices in international industrial competition, Porter raised the new concept of international competition in industrial "global value chain", introduced the new standards of international competitiveness and explained how developed countries, especially US can maintain its international competitiveness in a context of transnational production. By learning Porter's theory, Chinese scholars have raised that in the process of international increment of values, the value chain of multinationals is globalized in nature and under the management of multinationals. (Wang Linsheng,1994)

Porter's global value chain theory does not intend to explain international direct investment directly, but to offer advice to US multinationals on firmly grip "strategic links" of the value chain. Nevertheless, it offered a subject analysis of the new forms of international competition in the context of growing international direct investment and transnational production. It also shed some light on the inevitable trend of global mobility and relocation of production factors and resources. Relocation of production factors and resources is achieved through international capital movement. Existing value chains are constantly changed and new global value chains formed. Mobility and relocation of production factors are rational and necessary as long as it can maintain or strengthen the position as "strategic link" of the parent company. In this regard, these theories explain why developed nations need to introduce foreign capital in large amounts. Meanwhile, for developing countries, only by introducing large amounts of FDIs, can they enter the "global value chain" system, and only by entering this system, can they have the opportunity to attract advantageous production factors across the world, strengthen their comparative advantages and foster their own competitiveness. And only by this, can they gradually raise their level of division of labor in the world. Being not involved in the value chain means being marginalized in the global economy and less benefits in the international division of labor. Therefore, the global value chain theory explains why developing countries need to constantly attract foreign investment, and why the scale and capability of attracting foreign investment has become an important index for evaluating developing countries in terms of resources integration and overall international competitiveness. Of course, the global value chain theory has, to some extent, blurred the boundaries of countries and national interests, which is a limitation of western capitalist theories. Nevertheless, it has much to offer to us in guiding our modernization drive and using foreign capital in the future.

8.2.2. Capital and risk control theory and the structure of capital inflow

In practice, multinational investment is the market behavior of microcosmic bodies, so corporate investment strategy is also an important theory in explaining international direct investment. US economists have analyzed the impacts of these factors on international direct investment from capital and currency imperfections, interest rate and foreign exchange rate fluctuations, international capital market structure and efficiency, etc. In particular, Robert I. Aliber(1970) regards foreign direct investment as a kind of flow of capital in different regions. So it is less a production behavior than a currency behavior. He believes that currency premium exists due to the fluctuation of interest rates and foreign exchange rates, which is the reason of high yield of multinational corporations and multinational direct investment. Currency premium theory assume that in times of weak currency in investing countries and strong currency in investment receiving countries, investors can gain the assets calculated by the currency of investing countries, which leads to actual or paper gains. We can see here that this theory is based on the failure of capital market and foreign currency market, which gives edge to enterprises pricing their assets with a certain currency. Domestic investment risk control theory can also be used to explain multinational investment. For example, modern asset portfolio theory believes that for a certain asset, risks and returns are symmetrical, and it would be hard to seek expected returns under certain risks and seek minimum risks under certain returns. However, if we combine different asset portfolios, we could dramatically reduce risks and achieve relatively high returns. This is because asset risks generally fall into two categories, systematic risks which are determined by external factors and non-systematic risks which can be basically eliminated through appropriate asset portfolios. These two theories can explain the reason why China's service industries have shown a higher speed in attracting foreign investment.

Since China's accession into the WTO, China has made a huge step in opening up its financial sectors. In particular, the joint stock reforms of large state-owned commercial banks such as Bank of Communications, Industrial and Commercial Bank of China, Construction Bank of China and Bank of China, etc and the introduction of strategic investors have accelerated the pace of China's banking sector in utilizing foreign capital. Since 2005, as China's banking sector introduced more and more foreign capital, China's Ministry of Commerce has added two types of data "non-financial" and "full aperture" in its statistics of foreign capital. In fact, the "non-financial" statistics also include data about the establishment of foreign financial institutions and capital inflow. The figure in "full aperture" financial statistics about foreign capital during 2005 to 2008 is respectively 12.3 billion dollars, 9.988 billion dollars, 9.010 billion dollars and 16.478 billion dollars.

Table 8-5 Proportion of foreign investment in financial and housing property sector in total foreign capital in the tertiary industry

Year	2005	2006	2007	2008
Total foreign investment in tertiary industry (billion dollars)	27.006	29.605	41.93	57.21
Proportion of financing sector (%)	45.5	33.74	21.5	28.8
Foreign investment in housing property (billion dollars)	5.418	8.23	17.089	18.59
Proportion of housing property (%)	20.1	27.8	40.76	32.5
Proportion of other industries (%)	34.4	38.46	37.74	38.7

Source: the Department of Foreign Investment Administration, Ministry of Commerce, China: *China Foreign Statistics 2007, 2008*; *Foreign Capital Dynamics* Jan. 2009.

Table 9-5 shows that 60% of the foreign capital inflow in tertiary industry in recent years falls into financing sector and housing property sector. Except for the financial sectors has further opened to the outside world, the appreciation of RMB to US dollars (which peaked in 2008, coupled with the largest foreign capital inflow the same year) and depreciation of US dollars to major western currency are important reasons, which changed the structure and efficiency of international capital market and gave Chinese RMB what Aliber calls "currency premium". As a result, multinationals gained monopolistic advantages to invest in China's financing and housing property sectors, which played a major role in international capital flow. The increase of foreign capital in financing and housing property sector can help introduce market competition mechanism and improve corporate governance. However, there also exists a problem of speculative hot money, which is hard to be eliminated. The key for the host country is to choose the right currency premium to offer and better regulate the conditions to seek the best outcome. This kind of risk is non-systematic risk for financing and housing property sectors are capital intensive sectors with high risks and high returns. Though international capital has a craze for this kind of assets, but we have to combine this kind of assets with other portfolios out of concerns for risk control. Whether it is investment in financing and housing property sectors, or portfolio investment in assets with systematic risks, the operating capital is expected to have high liquidity. Therefore, such investment is driven by financial capital in nature rather than industrial capital. With little regulations, high liquidity and maximum efficiency, free port has become the paradise for financial capital, which has become important sources for foreign investment in China.After 30 years of reform and opening up, China has gained a better understanding of the outside world. Meanwhile, foreign investors have gained more knowledge of the Chinese market. It is only natural and wise for overseas investors to adopt risk control strategies in their investment. With the development of multinational merger, especially merger in service sectors in international direct investment, the direct investment and securities investment have shown trends of overlapping and integration. Therefore, there will be more overseas investment in free port in the future, so we cannot indiscriminately regard them as hot money or "fake foreign capital". On the contrary, we should allow foreign capital flow into our financing and housing property sectors, encourage them to engage in portfolio investment and encourage them to invest in other service or manufacturing sectors which need foreign capital eagerly. Only by this, can we reach the purpose of mutual benefit and win-win result.

8.2.3. Internalization theory and Wholly Foreign-owned Enterprises

The growing dominance of wholly foreign-owned enterprises can be explained by the internationalization theory, represented by UK scholar Buckley and Casson. They believe that in the context of dominance of research-based and technology intensive products, intermediate goods transaction are facing greater difficulties. Faced with such market conditions, enterprises should try to realize the internal transfer of intermediate goods within their own system. Here, market failure is represented by represented by the lack of guarantee for the interest of intermediate goods. And because intermediate goods such as technology, knowledge and information are always treated as a whole, exclusive in nature, available to be shared, hard to divided or transferred to others, and must be kept in secret, they cannot be easily priced in market. Even after transaction, they can be leaked to be shared by all the society. Market failure drives sales person to engage in purchase operations, and when they cross national borders, multinational enterprises are born.Another reason for internalization is that the high costs prevents the market to be formed and drives enterprises to seek internal transfer, which may include costs of setting prices for intermediate goods, determining rights and responsibilities for contract parties, accepting relevant risks, paying fees and taxes for market transactions as well as fees paid to government for intervention of foreign exchange rates and customs.

The reason why foreign investors have become more inclined toward investing in wholly foreign-owned enterprises is, according to popular explanations, that Chinese socialist market economic system is already relatively sound and foreign investors no longer need the help of Chinese partners in entering the Chinese market. This, though right, tells just a small part of the story. In fact, the Chinese employees in foreign enterprises can also serve as consultants and market guides for the company in terms of production, management and PR, which frees the enterprises from being equity joint ventures. The real reason is that foreign investment in early times is mostly restricted to small scale ventures, which do not possess advanced technologies and can be transferred to joint ventures with no fear of technology leakage. As the time goes on, more and more multinationals have come to China, with larger and larger scales. According to the 2008 annual survey statistics of foreign ventures, enterprises with registered foreign capital over 100 million US dollars accounts for a larger and larger proportion in all foreign invested enterprises, with proportions of 0.14%, 0.17%, 0.17%, 0.2%, and 0.29% respectively from 2003 to 2007. Enterprises with foreign investment of over 50 million and below 100 million US dollars account for 0.22%, 0.26%, 0.34%, 0.42% and 0.57% respectively in foreign invested enterprises from 2003 to 2007, with an increasing trend. Capital intensive enterprises nowadays possess more and more advanced technologies, leading to difficulties in market transactions. By taking the form of wholly foreign-owned enterprises, multinationals in China can not only overcome difficulties in market transactions, achieve internal transaction and transfer, but also protect their technologies and intellectual property rights. Therefore, the rise of wholly foreign-owned enterprises sends an important message, and that is multinationals are raising their technology and knowledge intensity. This, on the other hand, reflects a necessity for China to improve technology market building and intellectual property rights protection.

Moreover, compared with joint ventures, wholly foreign-owned enterprises can enjoy relatively low costs for internal transactions and relatively high efficiency, which are the benefits of internalization.

Table 8-6 Asset turnovers of different types

Year / Type of enterprise	2003	2004	2005	2006	2007
Wholly Foreign-owned	0.79	0.79	0.96	0.95	0.91
Stock-holding enterprise	0.53	0.58	0.5	0.61	0.61
Joint venture	0.69	0.74	0.79	0.86	0.88
Partnership	0.46	0.42	0.46	0.52	0.57
Others	0.39	1.07	2.47	0.16	—
Total	0.69	0.72	0.8	0.85	0.85

Source: compiled on the basis of survey data from Foreign Invested Enterprise Operation Research Group of Finance and Trade Economics Research Institute of Chinese Academy of Social Sciences

From table 9-6 we can draw conclusions similar to the internalization theory, which is the less contributors there are, the simpler the property right is, the easier internal governance will be, the stronger the contributor's control will be, and the higher the asset utilization rate will become. This reflects the requirements of foreign capital in raising operation efficiency of investment in China. This has nothing to do with equity control and squeezing out living space of private enterprises. We should not view the growing dominance of wholly foreign-owned enterprises in a negative light or see it as some kind of a conspiracy. As long as capital intensive foreign investors increase in the future, the preference for wholly foreign-owned enterprises will inevitably continue. And as long as foreign investors have plans to engage in long-term investment, the rise of asset operation efficiency would also be inevitable. Investing in wholly foreign-owned enterprises is just a natural choice. Since we allow for the existence of wholly foreign-owned enterprises, we should have no reason to fear them. We should think about what we can gain from them. The good side is obvious, for wholly foreign-owned enterprises, especially those large ones have advanced technologies and managerial experience. Although internal transfer is possible in a certain period of time, technology overflow is unavoidable. Multinational corporate theories tell us that the forward and backward association industries are both important channels to gain technology overflows, which are unavoidable for foreign invested enterprises. As long as domestic enterprises can play into full their comparative advantages and utilize the favorable conditions of production factors, market and some intermediate products in host country, we can gain benefits by getting technology overflows from forward and backward industries associated with these enterprises.

8.2.4. Evolution of National Economy Security Theory

This is a big issue in theory and practice that bothers us in actively attracting foreign capital, and also an important reason of slow growth in attracting FDI in the second industry in recent years. In the early years of capitalist industrial revolution, debate of free trade and protectionism had already happened during struggle for domestic and international markets. Those with advantages would argue for free trade, and those with disadvantages would argue for protectionism. In fact, the protection of domestic market is also an issue of economic security, and in essence a protection of different nations and their capitalist classes. Today as we develop the socialist market economy, we should also bear economic security in mind. But what's different is that we are talking about economic security in our participation of economic globalization and opening up to the outside world, instead of talking about protectionism like some monopolistic capitalist class. To sum up, our economic security should include the following aspects: first, safeguard the security of the basic system of socialist market economy; second, strengthen our overall national strength and withstand the impacts of foreign economic risks while we make good use of the strategic opportunities of trade and investment liberalization; third, maintain a rational order of openness and competition in domestic market. And safeguard the interests of various economic participants; finally, make sure of the state control of sectors involved in state security, important infrastructure and of overall importance to national economy.

Whether the inflow of large quantities of foreign investment will threaten our basic economic system? Deng Xiaoping had already answered this question. Deng remarked that the economic foundation of socialism is already big enough, so the inflow of tens of, or hundreds of billion dollars is just not strong enough to threaten it. He also said that compared with the positive effects of foreign capital, the negative sides are far too small and far less dangerous. Today, the socialist economic system has grown much stronger than Deng's age, so we do not have to worry that basic socialist economy system should be overthrown by foreign investment.

We should also see that with the dramatic changes in the world, some western countries pursuing free trade in the past have turned to protectionism. In 2008, the Pew Research Center made a survey and found the supporters of free trade among the Americans dropped from 78% of the population in 2003 to 59% in 2007. In UK, the proportion dropped from 87% to 78%, and this figure also experienced dramatic drop in France, Italy and Germany. However, developing countries have seen this figure rise in recent years, such as China, India, Pakistan, Bangladesh, Argentina and Jordan. This shows that in current economic globalization, some developing nations has won the opportunities of growth offered by free trade and welcomes that. The more developed the economy becomes, the higher the security of the system would be. For China, the boundaries of economic security have extended to a large extent, and the extension of overseas market and resources has become the major issue in China's economic security. China's strategic interest of economic security has shifted from domestic market to overseas market, leading to the "China Threat Theory" and the shift of western public opinion from trade freedom to trade protectionism. So in this point, westerners are more a sober mind than us. Of course, we still have to be vigilant against external economic risks, which mainly refer to the financial risks. Therefore, China should take a prudent, progressive and controlled way in opening up domestic capital market and capital account of international BOP, and draw the lessons of US financial crisis so as to better regulate the market.

In terms of the real economy, our national economy has already gained strong controlling force over China's economy. The state owns the most important resources and infrastructure, with SOEs and state holding enterprises the most powerful economic entities. So, we should not hesitate to open up the economy to attract more foreign investment and introduce competition mechanism with it. The dominance of investment proves the advantage of foreign capital in terms of capital and technology, which are also what we need. When national economy has developed, the situations will change, just as what has happened in our home appliance industry. As long as the government passes the Anti-monopoly Law and the rational market structure and orderly competition forms, it would be a natural thing. While we observe what we can get in these sectors, we should not only obsess ourselves with the proportion of investors, we should also take into consideration what most people can get from it. According to the research of some scholars, in 2004, half of the national income exists in the form of salaries, while foreign invested enterprises pay their employees 30% and 80%% higher than SOEs and collectively owned enterprises respectively. Besides, a proportion of the profits of foreign investors will go back to re-investment. In 2007, the foreign exchange outflow under the item of investment income only reached 76.2 billion US dollars, which include payment of foreign debt interests, accounting for just 2.3% of GDP. And the proportion will be lower if we just count the profits of foreign invested enterprises. With the rising expectation of RMB appreciation in 2008, the proportion of profits of foreign invested enterprises in GDP will continue to drop.

In terms of the economic security, multinationals are both our competitors and our partners. We compete with each other and depend on each other. In 2000, OECD put forward the "Code of Conduct for Multinational Corporations" in which it stressed the global responsibility of multinationals. This concept is not only a moral issue, but reflects the interest and appeal of multinationals. By global responsibility, we mean all multinationals are obliged to maintain global business order and avoid global risks. Multinationals have become global companies, and they cannot avoid damage if the host country suffers. In this regard, the significance of economic security caused by conflicting interests between foreign capital in conventional sense and national economy has been weakened by multinationals in their global risk management.

8.3 New Growth Points to Attract Foreign Investments

8.3.1. Essential Export-oriented and Import Substitution Manufacturing Industry

Industry has absorbed the most foreign investment. But during these years the growth has been slowing down apparently with the only recovery in 2008. In 2007, the total output value of foreign capital industry accounted for 30.91% of the national industries above the scale with 24% of industrial added value, 24.9% of immobilizations and 31.4% of prime operating revenue. But the industry especially manufacturing is an important driver to attract foreign investment, which means a lot to industrial modernization escalation and industrialization improvement. Taking advantage of 30 years' successful foreign investment experience, one rule can be found that is strategic trade policy including favorable exchange rate and tax rebate policy to improve export, favorable tax on processing trade, different tax rates in the import tariff, order of trade liberalization measures as well as efforts to attract more foreign investment. The foreign capital manufacturing has become two structures of labor-oriented and capital and technique import substitution. However, in practice, capital and technique import substitution enterprises are also export-oriented. These two structures mix together sometimes, which does not influence the division and analysis.

The labor-intensive and export-oriented foreign capital manufacturing mainly appears in the processing trade, which is the important national area to absorb labors and to keep international competitiveness in industrial products in the long term. In recent years, the employment figure has been on the rise in foreign-invested enterprises. Between the year 2004 and 2007, this figure has increased by 4.57 folds from 0.81 million to 4.53 million with average annual growth rate of 77.2%. The foreign-invested enterprises contribute a lot to providing the positions around china.

In 2004, the newly increased positions in foreign-invested enterprises accounted for 8.29% of the national newly increased positions in urban. And between 2005 and 2007, the figure was 39.01%, 31.66% and 37.60% respectively, higher than the ratio of foreign-invested enterprises employees to national urban employees (Table 8-7).

Table 8-7 Distribution of Foreign-Invested Enterprise Employees in Three Industries

Industry	Year / Index	2003	2004	2005	2006	2007
Primary Industry	Population(Million)	0.199	0.188	0.170	0.152	0.145
	Ratio (%)	1.1	0.7	0.6	0.5	0.4
Secondary Industry	Population(Million)	16.763	22.813	24.853	29.823	30.305
	Ratio (%)	89.1	88.8	89.9	89.3	86.4
Tertiary Industry	Population(Million)	1.852	2.680	2.631	3.429	4.628
	Ratio (%)	9.8	10.4	9.5	10.3	13.2

Sources: Department of Foreign Investment Administration in Ministry of Commerce of the People's Republic of China; Foreign Investment Research Materials from Institute of Finance and Trade Economics, Chinese Academy of Social Sciences.

Cai Fang (2008) does researches on the Chinese labor growth future. He believes that large-scale employment needs with high ratio will keep in a long time. Developing labor-intensive manufacturing industry is critical to the interests of Chinese. Besides, China has its comparative advantage in labor-intensive manufacturing industry, which pushes us not to give up this advantage in the short term to sustain the economic growth. Because the products of labor-intensive manufacturing industry have great share in overseas market, we need to absorb more foreign investment in this area besides the consideration of improving international competitiveness. We should make full use of the advantages of foreign investment in capital, technique and especially international market and sales channels to enlarge the export and to safeguard the interests of employment positions and salary for Chinese.

Due to the arrangements of trade liberalization, the tariff structures show protection to certain products and industries in different times although the Chinese trade tariff is narrowing down. This becomes a motivation for foreign investment in capital and technique-intensive industries, such as transportation equipments manufacturing, communication and computer equipments manufacturing and chemicals manufacturing, which become foreign capital import substitution businesses. But a great deal of export also remains in these businesses with many enterprises in processing trade. It is an inevitable channel for Chinese manufacturing industry to import, absorb technique and renovate, upgrade industry and optimize structure. Schott (2006) found that the export products structure of China was similar to that of OECD members in 2001. Among the most similar economies, China ranked 3. The similarity factors were 0.80 of Mexico, 0.78 of Korea, 0.75 of China, 0.64 of Taiwan, 0.60 of Brazil, 0.54 of India, 0.51 of Israel, 0.46 of Hong Kong, 0.45 of Thailand and 0.44[38] of Singapore. This was related to the foreign investments in capital and technique-intensive businesses. In 2008, the export of high-technology products of China accounted for 29% of the total export volume. The products were mainly manufactured by foreign-invested assembling lines. Of course, in the global value chain production system, China

[38]Schott, 2006.

possesses the low-end technology, which is the foundation of China to increase the status of international division by enlarging business in high-end manufacturing and service industry. During this movement, constant growth of foreign-invested import substitution manufacturing industry plays a great role.

8.3.2. Large Space for Second Industry to Absorb Foreign Investment

In manufacturing sector, the foreign investment mainly lies in communication equipments, computer and other electrical equipments, transportation equipments, electric apparatus and equipments, chemical raw materials and products. So there is a great space for foreign investment to drive forward the process of developing new industries. In the second industry, only manufacturing sector attracts most of the foreign investment. The rest three sectors have little foreign investments (Table 8-8).

Table 8-8 Distribution of Registered Foreign Investment Volume in Second Industry between 2003 and 2007

Unit: Billion USD

Year	2003	2004	2005	2006	2007
Mining	4.181	2.887	4.457	5.419	6.442
Manufacturing	205.448	326.687	350.505	400.909	464.462
Electricity, Gas and Water production and supply	9.390	13.261	14.481	18.603	21.243
Construction	4.716	4.929	3.435	5.800	6.382
Total	223.736	347.763	372.877	430.732	498.529

Sources: Foreign Investment Research Materials from Institute of Finance and Trade Economics, Chinese Academy of Social Sciences.

At the beginning of middle and late 1980s, China attracted foreign investments to build and operate infrastructure by franchising of BOT and TOT. With the development of urbanization and lack of municipal building funds, we need more and more investments in infrastructure and municipal engineering. So how to take advantage of foreign capital becomes an urgent and important issue. First of all, in the fiscal expenditure of China, there are still gaps and contradiction in the social undertakings and fundamental construction, which show the needs of the society. In 2007, all the social undertakings fiscal expenditure accounted only for 8.6% of GDP. But the figure of developed countries was 16%-30% at the end of 1900s. And the average figure of East Asian Economies was 15%. China has still a large gap in social undertaking fiscal expenditure to catch up with the average level of East Asian Economies. If we improve the social undertaking expenditure, the fiscal expenditure of fundamental construction shall be narrowed, which is very difficult. Although the fiscal expenditure of fundamental construction was declined to 12%[39], the fact was not that easy. More nongovernmental capitals including foreign capitals are in need to drive forward the infrastructure building. Besides, over the past years, the debt is still very heavy in city infrastructure building. According to the standards of NUDP, the infrastructure investment of developing countries should be 3%-5% of GDP or 9%-15% of FAI. The heavy debt left in infrastructure in the last half centuryhas not been paid although its status has been improved

39 *China Statistical Yearbook* (2008)

in this century. On the basis of estimation at the low level, every 1% growth of urbanization needs 260 billion RMB[40] in infrastructure. In 2003, 40.5% of urbanization demanded 320 billion RMB. By 2020, the urbanization rate will be 50%, which will need 2.8 trillion RMB. With total fiscal investment and heavy debt, the contradiction will be resulted between different expenditures, which will worsen the fiscal status and increase the inflation pressure. Therefore, nongovernmental capital especially foreign capital shall be involved to build infrastructure. Against the background of financial crisis, new paths and experiences shall be explored to attract more foreign capital to involve in the infrastructure building and other livelihood need. With the involvement of foreign capital, introduction of competitiveness and marketization, welfare changes of infrastructure supply and social undertaking development, management system and operation mechanism reform of infrastructure and social undertaking as well as increase of supply, the need of people can be satisfied.

8.3.3. Larger Space for the Tertiary Industry to Attract Foreign Capital

In recent years, the financial sector and real estate have accounted for above 60% of the total foreign investment in tertiary industry with unbalanced development because of the less foreign capital involvement in other sectors. So there is still a large space for foreign capital to get in. From the perspective of returns, the return rate of service sector is not worse than that of financial sector and real estate, which means there is attraction to the foreign investment.

In table 8-9, we can see the return level of foreign investment in manufacturing sector is lower than the average level of total foreign investment returns according to the status of 2007. But the service sector with higher return level includes transportation, storage and postal business, information transmit, computer service and software, whole sale and retail sector, financial sector, lease sector and commercial service. On the contrary, the real estate has lower returns level than average. In the service sector of science and technology and social undertakings, the foreign capital can be attracted if new breakthroughs can be made in market access and structure reform.

Table 8-9 Investment Returns Ratio of Foreign-invested Enterprises in Different Sectors between 2003 and 2007

Year / Sector	2003	2004	2005	2006	2007
Agriculture, Forestry, Animal Husbandry and Fishery	0.014	-0.08	0.011	0.001	0.032
Mining	0.172	0.422	0.53	0.471	0.562
Manufacturing	0.055	0.053	0.051	0.066	0.095
Electricity, Gas and Water Production and Supply	0.096	0.012	0.044	0.061	0.073
Construction	0.049	0.049	0.061	0.083	0.108
Transportation, Storage and Postal Business	0.069	0.092	0.05	0.096	0.131
Information Transmit, Computer Service and Software	0.286	0.289	0.282	0.244	0.406
Wholesale and Retail	-0.1	0.088	0.08	0.092	0.138

[40] Chen Jinliang, 2009

Accommodation and Restaurant	-0.01	0	0	0.009	0.015
Financial Sector	-0.04	0.018	0.08	0.042	0.114
Real Estate	0.005	0.018	0.026	0.037	0.057
Lease and Commercial Service	0.056	0.089	0.146	0.147	0.178
Science Research, Technical Service and Geological Exploration	0.03	0.047	0.036	0.039	0.074
Water, Environment and Infrastructure Management	0.038	0.04	0.027	0.022	0.033
Neighborhood Service and other Services	0.205	-0.02	0.015	0.021	0.028
Education	0	0.06	0	-0.03	0.017
Sanitation, Social Security and Welfare	-0.01	-0.01	-0.01	-0.01	-0.01
Culture, Sports and Entertainment	-0.02	-0.01	-0.02	-0.01	0
Public Management and Social Organization	0.019	0.062	0	-0.04	-0.36
International Organization	0.02	0.341	0.029	0.095	-0.08
Total	0.053	0.047	0.057	0.076	0.105

Sources: Foreign Investment Research Materials from Institute of Finance and Trade Economics, Chinese Academy of Social Sciences.

8.4 Conclusions and Policy Significance

The global value chain theory explains why developing countries need to attract foreign investment constantly and why the scale and ability of attracting foreign investment has been the important index to access the level of developing countries to use the external resources and to enhance the international competitiveness. In recent years, the foreign capital flows into the financial sector and real estate, that is useful to introducing competitiveness and to improving enterprise management. But there is also the "hot money" problem, which should be forbidden in introducing foreign capital. The key is in which way that the host country should provide and control the currency premium to give full play to the foreign investment. Out of rational consideration and normal business behavior, the foreign investors from free port take risk-control strategy when they enter the Chinese market. We should not resist this kind of investment. On the contrary, we should encourage them to become portfolio investment. Thus, the foreign capital can not only flow into the financial sector and real estate, but also gains position in other service sectors or manufacturing sector, which is a win-win situation. By analyzing the "solo-ownership" trend of foreign investment with "internalization" theory, the important information is found that the growth of technique and knowledge intensity of multinational investment in China, who shall improve the technical market building and IPR. Against the new background, the economic security of China has been greatly changed with focus on enlarging overseas market, safeguarding external resources supply and defending international financial crisis. In the real economy sector, we can increase accesses to domestic market and give more efforts to attract foreign investment. Right now and in future, our second and tertiary industry have the potential and demand to absorb foreign investment. Therefore, we should be more open-minded by eliminating the theory of foreign investment surplus, the theory of foreign investment squeezing domestic investment, the theory of foreign investment threat to improve the mechanism and policy of utilizing foreign capital. To fight against the impact of international financial crisis on Chinese economy, the keys to polish the foreign investment policy are as followed.

8.4.1. Keeping Preferential Policy on Encouraging Processing Trade

Foreign investors are sensitive to processing trade policy. It has been right for China to take preferential policy in the past. But the policy during these two to three years are too far, which need to be improved. We should do researches on preferential policies of providing different tariffs on products according to various domestic supporting rates. The measures of mixing external and domestic business together to invigorate the processing trade business and of encouraging both investments to get involved in production and service area of processing trade should be taken.

8.4.2. Relaxing Merger and Acquisition Policy and Encouraging Foreign-invested Enterprises with High-tech to Merge and Purchase Domestic Enterprises

The investment of merger and acquisition is the main way of FDI. If we can't make breakthroughs in merger and acquisition, the sayings "innovating foreign investment ways" in the Report of the 17th National Congress of CPC are hollow words. In civil industry, we need to give up stock rights and to be not afraid of the foreign investment controlling. Of course, as a professional commercial activity, merger and acquisition needs the service of high qualified experts and agencies.

8.4.3. Keeping Competitive RMB Exchange Rate

Since July, 2005, the exchange rate of RMB to US dollars has been growing, which weakens the competitiveness of export commodities and makes overmuch "currency premium" interests. This leads to more foreign investment including "hot money" in financial sector and real estate. This is not good for settling normal "currency premium" expectation and guiding foreign investment in service sector. Therefore, the RMB exchange rate should be adjusted to keep competitiveness of export commodities and to guide foreign investment rationally.

8.4.4. Enlarging Infrastructure and Service Market to Attract Foreign Investment

The market access is made according to different categories in infrastructure market with price settlement by inviting bids and bidding. Especially in economic and technical development zones, more foreign-invested enterprises move to the new regions of a city. The management system and citizens' ideas of the new city zones are new, which can more easily attract foreign investors to involve in infrastructure and social services. Even the new zones of old cities, costal SEZ and cities are also equipped with conditions to attract foreign investors to involve in infrastructure and social services. So these cities need to be opened. By taking BOT or stocks rights, large-scale infrastructures, such as branch airport, branch railway, partial high-way and ports can also attract foreign investment, which results in the win-win achievement in cooperation.

References

Aliber, R. Z. 1970."A Theory of Direct Foreign Investment,"*Kindleberger* (ed.) The International Corporation. Cambridge, MA: MIT Press.

An Tifu and Wang Haiyong. 2005. "Lun neiwai liangtao qiye suode shuizhi de hebing [On the Combination of Domestic and Foreign Corporate Income Tax]."*Shuiwu yanjiu*: vol. 3.

Buckley, Peter J. and Mark Casson. 1976.*The Future of the Multinational Enterprise*. New York: Holmes and Meiers.

Buettner, Thiess; Michael Overesch, Ulrich Schreiber, and Georg Wamser. 2006. "The Impact of Thin-Capitalization Rules on Multinationals Financing and Investment Decisions." ZEW Discussion Paper No. 06-068.

Cai Fang. 2008. *Liuyisi zhuanzhe dian—Zhongguo jingji fazhan xin jieduan* [*Louis Turning Point—New Stage of Development of China's Economy*]. Beijing: Social Sciences Academic Press.

Cao Xiaochun. 2009. "Zhongguo neiwai shang touzi qiye suodeshui hebing dui waizi liuru de yingxiang [Influence of China's Combination of Domestic and Foreign Corporate Income Tax on Foreign Capital Inflow]."*Caimao jingji*: vol. 9.

Cai Yufeng. 2009. "Jingji weiji xia waizi qiye caiwu fengxian yingdui [Response to financial risks of foreign-invested enterprises in the context of financial crisis]."*Zhejiang jingji*: vol. 11.

Chen Jinliang. 2009."Chongfen liyong minjian ziben he waizi fazhan jichu sheshi [Developing Infrastructure by Fully Utilizing Private Capital and Foreign Capital]."*China Economic Times*: 2009, pg 7.

Chen Ruoxu. 2005. "Woguo waishang touzi qiye taobi shuishou de yuanyin [The Reason Why Foreign-invested Enterprises in China Evade Tax]."*Shangye yanjiu*: vol. 2.

Chen Zhongchang and Wu Yongqiu. 2005. "Zhongguo gongye bumen ziben lirunlv biandong qushi ji yuanyin fenxi [Analysis on the Trend and Reason of Changes of Capital Profitability in China's Industrial Departments]."*Jingji yanjiu*: vol.5.

Chenery, Hollis B. 1984. "Foreign Assistance and Economic Development."*Selected Papers of Contemporary Foreign Theses on Economics*. Beijing: Commercial Press.

Dai Jinping. 2003. "Waiguo zhijie touzi yu zhongguo de chukou jingzhengli [Foreign Direct Investment and China's Export Competiveness]."*Nankai jingji yanjiu*: vol. 5.

Dai Xiang and Wei Hao. 2004. "Kuaguo gongsi zaihua qiye duzihua qushi yuanyin fenxi [Analysis on the reason behind the growing dominance of wholly foreign-owned enterprises among multinational corporations]."*Nanjing caijing daxue xuebao*: vol. 2.

Deng Qifeng. 2007. "Waishang zhijie touzi dui zhongguo jiuye yingxiang de shizheng fenxi [An empirical study on the influence of Foreign Direct Investment on China's employment]."*Beifang jingji:* vol. 22.

Deng Xiaoping. 1993. *Deng Xiaoping wenxuan, Volume III* [*Selected Works of Deng Xiaoping*]. Beijing: People's Publishing House.

Ding Bing, etc. 2006. *Woguo liyong waizi he duiwai maoyi wenti yanjiu* [*Study on China's Untilization of Foreign Capital and Problems Confronting Foreign Trade*]. Beijing: China Economy Press.

Dunning, John H. 1981.*International Production and the Multinational Enterprise*, London:

George and Unwin.

Fu Jianshe and Fan Yi. 2006. "Kuaguo gongsi ziben jiegou jueding jizhi tanxi [Analysis on the determining mechanism of asset structure of multinationals]."*Hubei minzu xueyuan xuebao (zhexue shehui kexue ban)*: vol. 6.

Gong Xiaoying. 2006. *Guoji maoyi yu guoji zhijie touzi de guanxi ji zhengce xuanze* [*Relationship between International Trade and International Direct Investment as well the Policy Options*]. Beijing: Economic Management Press.

Hu Yi. 2006. *Guoji touzi lilun chuangxin yu yingyong yanjiu—jiyu zhongjian ceng zuzhi de fenxi* [*Study on the Theoretical Innovation and Practice of International Investment—An Analysis Based on Organizations in the Middle*]. Beijing: People's Publishing House.

Hymer, Stephen. H. 1976.*The International Operations of National Firms: A Study of Direct Foreign Investment*, Cambridge, MA: MIT Press.

Jiang Hexin. 2007. "Woguo duiwai maoyi jiuye xiaoying de shizheng yanjiu—yi waizi qiye weili [An empirical study on the employment effect of China's foreign trade—taking foreign-invested enterprises as an example]."*Guoji maoyi wenti*: vol. 10.

Jiang Ning and Hu Yigong. 2000. "Woguo qiye zichan jiegou bianhua jiqi fenxi [Analysis on the changes of China's Assets Structure]."*Guanli shijie*: vol. 6.

Jiang Xiaojuan, etc. 2004. *Quanqiu hua zhongde keji ziyuan chongzu yu Zhongguo chanye jishu jingzheng li tisheng* [*Restructuring of Scientific and Technological Resources in the Context of Globalization as well as the Promotion of Competitiveness of China's Industrial Technology*]. Beijing: China Social Sciences Press.

Jiang Xiaojuan, etc. 2007. *Zhongguo jingji de kaifang yu zengzhang 1980-2005* [*The Opening-up and Growth of China's Economy between 1980 and 2005*]. Beijing: People's Publishing House.

Jiang Xiaojuan. 2002. "Zhongguo waiji jingji: dui zengzhang, jiegou shengji he jingzhengli de gongxian [China's Foreign Economy: the Contribution to Growth, Structure Upgrading and Competiveness]."*Zhongguo shehui kexue*: vol. 6.

Jiang Xiaojuan. 2002. "Zhongguo chukou zengzhang yu jiegou bianhua: waishang touzi qiye de gongxian [The Growth and Structural Changes of China's Export]."*Nankai jingji yanjiu*: vol. 2.

Jiang Xiaojuan. 2002. *Zhongguo de waizi jingji: dui zengzhang, jiegou shengji he jingzhengli de gongxian* [*China's Foreign Economy: the Contribution to Growth, Structure Upgrading and Competiveness*]. Beijing: China Renmin University Press.

Jiang Xiaojuan, Yang Shengming and Feng Lei edited. 2001. *Zhongguo duiwai jingmao lilun qianyan (2)* [*Leading Theories on China's Foreign Economy and Trade Vol II*]. Beijing: Social Sciences Academic Press.

Jiang Xiaojuan, Yang Shengming and Feng Lei edited. 2003. *Zhongguo duiwai jingmao lilun qianyan (3)* [*Leading Theories on China's Foreign Economy and Trade Vol III*]. Beijing: Social Sciences Academic Press.

Kan Xuan. 2007. "Woguo kuaguo gongsi rongzi wenti fenxi [Analysis on the financing of multinationals in China]."*Shidai jingmao (xueshu ban)*: vol. 5.

Kindleberger, Charles P. 1969.*American Business Abroad*. New Haven: Yale University Press.

Kojima, Kiyoshi. 1978.*Direct Foreign Investment*. New York: Praeger.

Liang Qi. 2003. "Kuaguo gongsi haiwai touzi yu chanye jiju [Overseas Investment and Industrial

Agglomeration of Multinational Corporations]."*Shijie jingji*: vol. 9.
Li Wei'an and Li Baoquan. 2003. "Kuaguo gongsi zaihua duzi qingxiang chengyin fenxi [Analysis on the reason behind the growing dominance of wholly foreign-owned enterprises among multinational corporations in China]."*Guanli shijie*: vol.1.
Li Xiao. 2006. "Yindu jingji nenggou ganshang zhongguo ma?—jianlun 'zhongyin bijiao' de yiyi [Can the Indian economy catch up with China's?—also on the meaning of 'comparison between China and India']."*Guoji jingji pinglun*: vol. 11 and vol. 12.
Li Xiaohua and Sheng Ti. 2005. "Zaihua hezi qiye de 'duzihua' qushi jiexi [Analysis on the Reason behind the growing dominance of wholly foreign-owned enterprises among foreign capital-invested enterprises in China]."*Hebei jingmao daxue xuebao*: vol. 1.
Li Yangdan. 2008. "Yu wucheng gongsi zichan fuzhailv xiajiang [Over 50% enterprises have their asset-liability ratio down]."*Zhongguo zhengquan bao/zhongzheng wang*. April 17th, 2008.
Li Yuanpeng. 2009. "Jingji zhouqi yu shangshi gongsi jingying jixiao beili zhimi [The Mystery of Deviation of Economic Cycle from Operating Performances of Listed Companies]."*Jingji yanjiu*: vol. 3.
Li Zonghui and Cao Xiaochun. 2007. "Waishang touzi qiye jinkou guanshui youhui zhengce de quxiao dui waizi liuru de yingxiang fenxi [Analysis on the Influence of Cancelling Tax Preferential Policies for FDI Export on Foreign Capital Inflow]."*Caijing lilun yu shijian*: vol. 4.
Li Zonghui and Lu Minghong. 2004. "Zhongguo waishang touzi qiye shuishou youhui zhengce de youxiaoxing fenxi [Analysis on the Efficiency of Tax Preferential Policies for Foreign-invested Enterprises in China]."*Shijie jingji*: vol.10.
Lin Guijun. 2008. *Dangqian woguo waijingmao suo mianlin de jige wenti [A Few Problems Facing Our Foreign Economy and Trade]*. Theses of Foreign Economic and Trade University.
Liu Yongjun and Wang Jinmeng. 2009. "Neiwaizi qiye ziben jiegou chayi bijiao yanjiu [A comparative study on the asset structures of domestic and foreign-invested enterprises]."*Dongbei caijing daxue xuebao*: vol. 4.
Liu Jianmin and Yin Hui. 2004. "Waishang zhijie touzi shuishou youhui zhengce guoji bijiao yu jiejian [International Comparison and Lessons Drawn from the Tax Preferential Policies of Foreign Direct Investment]."*Caijing lilun yu shijian*: vol. 6.
Lu Feng and Huang Xiaobo. 2004. "Guoyou qiye zichan fuzhai jiegou de wenti he duice [The problem of the asset-liability of state-owned companies and the countermeasures]."*Hubei jingji xueyuan xuebao: renxue shehui kexue ban*: vol. 1.
Lu Yuduo. 2008. "FDI dui woguo minzu gongye de qinshi xiaoying fenxi [An Analysis on the Erosion Effects of FDI on Our National Industries]." China International Trade Society Proceedings.
Markowitz, H. M. 1959.*Portfolio Selection: Efficient Diversification of Investments*. New York: Wiley.
Mei Xinyu. 2008. "Zhuqi fangfan waiqi qichang taoyi falv changcheng [Bulding a Law Great Wall to prevent foreign-invested enterprises to abandon factories and run away]."*Shanghai shangbao*.December 31, 2008.
Mei Xinyu. 2009. "Fangfan waiqi de 'weiji chuanran xiaoying' [Preventing the 'contagious effect of risks' of foreign-invested enterprises]."*21 shiji jingji baodao*. March 11, 2009.

Pan Zhen. 2006. *Tansuo zhongde shou—Zhongguo waishang zhijie touzi zhengce jiqi youxiao yanjiu [The Hand in Searching—Study on the Policies of China's Foreign Direct Investment and the Efficiency]*. Beijing: Economic Management Press.

Pei Changhong. 1998. *Liyong waizi yu chanye jingzhengli* [*Utilizing Foreign Capital and Industrial Competiveness*]. Beijing: Social Sciences Academic Press.

Pei Changhong and Feng Lei edited. 2008. *Zhongguo guoji shangwu lilun yu qianyan (5) [Leading Theories on China's International Business Vol V]*. Beijing: Social Sciences Academic Press.

Peng Changhong edited. 2006. *Zhongguo duiwai jingmao lilun qianyan (4)* [*Leading Theories on China's Foreign Economy and Trade Vol IV*]. Beijing: Social Sciences Academic Press.

Ross, S. A. 1976b."The Arbitrage Theory of Capital Asset Pricing."*Journal of Economic Theory:*vol.13 (3), pg. 341-360

Sang Baichuan. 2006. "Zai duiwai kaifang zhong weihu guojia jingji anquan [Maintaining National Economic Security during the Opening-up]."*Zhongguo liutong jingji,*: vol. 12.

Schott, Peter K. 2006: *The relative Sophistication of Chinese Exports*, NBER, Working Paper 12173.

Sha Wenbing and Tao Aiping. 2007. "waishang zhijie touzi de jiuye xiaoying fenxi—jiyu xiezheng lilun de shizheng fenxi [A study on the employment effect of foreign direct investment—an empirical analysis based on the Cointegration Theory]."*Caijing kexue*: vol. 4.

Shi Guangsheng edited. 2001. *Zhongguo jiaru shijie maoyi zuzhi zhishi duben* (3) [*Knowledge Book on China's Entry of World Trade Organization: vol. III*]. Beijing: People's Publishing House.

State-owned Assets Supervision and Administration Commission of the State Council. 2006. *Zhonguo guoyou zichan jiandu guanli nianjian 2006* [*China State-owned Assets Supervision and Administration Yearbook 2006*]. Beijing: China Economy Publishing House.

Wang Dandan. 2007. "Zhongguo waizi jingji quyu fenbu zhuangkuang [Regional Distribution of Foreign-invested Enterprises in China]."*Caijing jie*: vol. 7.

Wang Fengguo. 2006. "Kuaguo gongsi zhuanyi dingjiazhong de bishui yu fan bishui fenxi [Tax evasion and anti-tax evasion during the transfer pricing of multinationals]."*Shangye yanjiu*: vol. 2.

Wang Jinmeng and Mao Ning. 2008. "Zaihua waishang touzi qiye weishenme damianji kuisun [Why foreign-invested enterprises in China suffer large losses]."*Shijie jingji*: vol. 1.

Wang Linsheng. 1994. *Kuaguo jingying lilun yu shiwu* [*Theory and Practice on Cross-border Business*]. Beijing: Foreign Trade and Education Press.

World Bank. 2006. "Waishang touzi qiye zai Zhongguo touzi huibaolv da 22% [The return rate of investment in China by foreign-invested enterprises reach 22%]."*Zhongguo zhengquan bao*, November 13, 2006.

Xi Junyang and Liu Weijiang. 2001. "Waishang zhijie touzi de maoyi xiaoying shizheng fenxi [Empirical analysis on trade effects of foreign direct investment]."*Shanghai caijing daxue xuebao*: vol. 6.

Xian Guoming and Ge Shunqi. 2002. "Kuaguo gongsi FDI yu dongdaoguo waizi zhengce yanbian [Evolution of multinationals' FDI and host countries' polices on foreign investment]."*Nankai jingji*: vol. 1.

Xian Guoming. 2001. "Cujin guanlian—dongdaoguo waizi jingzheng zhengce de xin qushi [Promoting relevance—the new trend in policies of competing for foreign capital by host countries]."*Guoji jingji hezuo*: vol. 1.

Xu Jie. 2003. "Lun waishang dui Zhongguo touzi fangshi de xuanze [On the options of foreign investors for investment ways in China]."*Wuhan daxue xuebao: zhexue shehui kexue ban*: vol. 6.

Yan Bing. 2006. "FDI yu Zhongguo chukou jingzhengli [FDI and the competiveness of China's export]."*Caijing maoyi*: vol. 8.

Yang Shengming, Chen Jiaqin and Feng Lei edited. 1999. *Zhongguo duiwai jingmao lilun qianyan (1)* [*Leading Theories on China's Foreign Economy and Trade Vol I*]. Beijing: Social Sciences Academic Press.

Yang Xianming. 2000. *Fazhan jieduan yu guoji zhijie touzi* [*Development Stages and International Direct Investment*]. Beijing: Commercial Press.

Yin Xiaoyu and Fan Jiuhong."Guanyu ziben ruohua de diaocha he sikao [On the investigation and considerations of capital dilution]."*Jiangsu Tax Investigation*: vol. 30.

Zhan Xiaoning and Chen Jianguo. 2002. "Chukou jingzhengli yu kuaguo gongsi FDI de zuoyong [Competiveness of export and the effect of multinationals' FDI]."*Shijie jingji*: vol. 11.

Zhang Erzhen, etc. 2004. *Maoyi touzi yitihua yu Zhongguo de zhanlue [Integration of Trade and Investment as well as China's Strategies]*. Beijing: People's Publishing House.

Zhang Yu. 2006. "Waishang touzi qiye guquan jiegou yu FDI jishu waiyi xiaoying—lilun yu shizheng [Shareholding structure of foreign-invested enterprises and technology spillover effect of FDI—theory and demonstration]."*Shijie jingji yanjiu*: vol. 11.

Zhang Zhihong. 2002. "Woguo guoyou qiye ziben jiegou zhli de xianshi sikao [A practical pondering over the governing of asset structure of state-owned enterprises in China]."*Kuaiji luntan*: vol. 2.

Zhao Zengyao. 2004. "Waishang zaihua touzi duzihua qushi de yanhua jili ji yingdui celue [Evolution of the trend towards greater dominance of wholly foreign-owned enterprises in China and policies]."*Shijie jingji yu zhengzhi*: vol. 4.

Zhong Wei. 2005. "Qiye suodeshui binggui dui woguo yinjin waizi de yingxiang [The impact of corporate income tax on China's introduction of foreign capital]."*Xiandai jingji tantao*: vol. 5.

Zhongguo duiwai jingji maoyi baipishu [*White Paper of China's Foreign Economy and Trade*]. 1991, 2001. Beijing: China Foreign Economy and Trade Press, Commercial Press.

Zhongguo disan chanye tongji nianjian (2006, 2007 and 2008) [*StatisticalYearbook of China's Tertiary Industry (2006, 2007 and 2008)*]. 2007, 2008, and 2009. Beijing: State Statistical Bureau.

Zuo Jianlong. 1995. "Woguo neiwai shang touzi qiye jingying tiaojian de bijiao fenxi [A comparative study on the operation conditions of domestic and foreign-invested enterprises in China]."*Zhongguo gongye jingji*: vol. 12.

Postscript

This study was launched as a key research subject set up by the Finance, Trade and Economic Institute under the Chinese Academy of Social Sciences. It was originally aimed at collecting the broadest possible resources and data on foreign-invested enterprises over the past 30 years, especially after entering the 21st century, so as to objectively describe the situation of the operation of foreign-invested enterprises and provide necessary basic research for further enhancing our ability to utilize foreign capital.

The global financial crisis, triggered by the U.S. subprime mortgage crisis in 2008, has not only heavily damaged the world economy, but has also had a hugely adverse impact on China's economic structure. Foreign-invested enterprises in China, impacted as they are by domestic and foreign economies and markets, have suffered unprecedented difficulties. In particularly, our commodity export trade in the first six months of 2009 endured a substantial decline compared to the same period during the previous year. In response to the impact of the global financial crisis, governments at different levels have formulated proactive and effective policies, especially various trade bailout measures, not only alleviating the difficulties of domestic enterprises but also benefiting foreign-invested ones. Thus, in the second half of 2009, enterprises in China began to enjoy renewed, steady, and positive operations. The export trade of foreign-invested enterprises rebounded better than other domestic enterprises, while processing trade exports dominated by foreign-invested enterprises rebounded significantly better than enterprises of any other kind. This demonstrates the vigor and vitality of foreign-invested enterprises in China's market economy. Meanwhile, when global foreign direct investment declined by 39% in 2009, China attracted foreign direct investment up to $90 billion at a decrease of only 2.6% from the previous year, demonstrating the continued attraction of the Chinese economy to foreign capital.

China's practices in responding to the impact of the international financial crisis showed that many foreign-invested enterprises had the capability to withstand external economic fluctuations, which was favorable to China flexibly tackling the various changes and risks posed by the global economy. Meanwhile, it also showed that it was necessary for China to strengthen its research on foreign-invested enterprises in the expanded context of its opening-up policies.

I would like to extend my heartfelt thanks to relevant functional departments under the Ministry of Commerce for their strong support and assistance. Meanwhile, my thanks also go to other departments and local governments for their support and assistance.

The task of writing this book was divided as follows: Pei Changhong was in charge of writing the preface, chapter 8 and the postscript as well as revising the whole book; Feng Lei was in charge of writing chapters 1 and 5 as well editing the whole book; Li Feng was in charge of writing chapter 2; Peng Lei was charge of writing chapters 3 and 4; Xia Xianliang was in charge of writing chapters 6; and Dong Minjie was in charge of writing chapter 7.

Due to the limitation of the authors' academic level and deficiency in data collection, shallowness in this book is inevitable, and is open to the criticism and correction of readers.

Written in Beijing, February 15, 2010

This book is the result of a co-publication agreement between Social Sciences Academic Press (China) and Paths International Ltd (UK).

This book is published with the financial support of the Chinese Fund for the Humanities and Social Sciences.

Foreign Enterprises in China (Volume 1)
Chief Editors: Pei Changhong, Feng Lei
Translators: Chen Ling, Zhao Wenxuan
Polisher: Virginia L. Conn
ISBN: 978-1-84464-300-4

Paths International Ltd

Published in the United Kingdom
www.pathsinternational.com

CPSIA information can be obtained at www.ICGtesting.com
Printed in the USA
LVOW03*0430160115

422877LV00012B/61/P

9 781844 643004